POPULAR FICTION
BEFORE RICHARDSON

POPULAR
FICTION BEFORE
RICHARDSON

NARRATIVE PATTERNS
1700–1739

BY

JOHN J. RICHETTI

CLARENDON PRESS · OXFORD

Oxford University Press, Walton Street, Oxford OX2 6DP
Oxford New York Toronto
Delhi Bombay Calcutta Madras Karachi
Petaling Jaya Singapore Hong Kong Tokyo
Nairobi Dar es Salaam Cape Town
Melbourne Auckland
and associated companies in
Berlin Ibadan

Oxford is a trade mark of Oxford University Press

Published in the United States
by Oxford University Press, New York

© Oxford University Press 1969
Introduction © John J. Richetti 1992
First published 1969
First published in paperback 1992

British Library Cataloguing in Publication Data
Data available

Library of Congress Cataloging in Publication Data
Richetti, John J.
Popular fiction before Richardson: narrative patterns,
1700–1739 / by John J. Richetti.
Includes index.
1. English fiction—18th century—History and criticism.
2. Popular literature—Great Britain—History and criticism.
3. Narration (Rhetoric). 4. Rhetoric—1500–1800. I. Title.
PR851.R5 1992 823.509–dc20 92–9979
ISBN 0–19–811263–7

Printed and bound in
Great Britain by Biddles Ltd.,
Guildford and King's Lynn

TO

FRAN, DION, AND NOEL

ACKNOWLEDGEMENTS

MY greatest tangible debt is to the United States–United Kingdom educational commission for sending me to England to study and to the Danforth Foundation of St. Louis, whose generosity made my stay in London pleasant as well as productive. I am thankful as well to the staff of the British Museum for their gentle efficiency and to the Modern Language Association of America for allowing me to reprint, as part of Chapter VI, an essay on Elizabeth Rowe which appeared in the December 1967 issue of *PMLA*. Less evident but equally substantial is my debt to those who read the manuscript at various stages and offered advice and encouragement: Professor James R. Sutherland of University College, London, and Professors Alice G. Fredman, J. A. Martin, John H. Middendorf, John D. Rosenberg, and R. K. Webb of Columbia University. But my greatest obligation is to Professor James L. Clifford of Columbia University, whose incredible patience and enthusiasm made this book possible.

CONTENTS

INTRODUCTION:
TWENTY YEARS ON

READING a book I wrote more than twenty years ago is instructive, if a bit depressing, like looking at photographs of yourself turned out in once-fashionable clothing. To reflect on one's intellectual past from this distance is to discover just how much one is inevitably caught, unaware, in history, and to see clearly how individual and indeed rather lonely effort is inevitably guided by the steady force of deep historical currents. Looking back, I realize that in writing this book I was giving voice to something more than those notions I had worked out about the meaning of fiction in the early eighteenth century. From the vantage point of twenty-five years since I started working on the early eighteenth-century novel, I am now in a fairly good position to understand those prevailing academic and intellectual trends that intersected with my own efforts and shaped the book and were a part of its limitations. I can also appreciate how those same historically determined blinkers encouraged the book's ambitions and its scope, and contribute to its continuing usefulness. Chiefly, I am amazed now that I thought I could encompass in one book such an extensive body of diverse fiction.[1] What impelled this

---

[1] In the last ten or fifteen years more specialized studies of the early eighteenth-century novel have been published. Some of these, like Lincoln Faller's *Turned to Account: The Forms and Functions of Criminal Biography in Late Seventeenth- and Early Eighteenth-Century England* (Cambridge, 1987), are much more comprehensive in particular areas than I could have been. Others, like J. Paul Hunter's *Before Novels: The Cultural Contexts of Eighteenth-Century Fiction* (New York, 1990) go back into the seventeenth century and survey different sorts of material than the strictly fictional to which I restricted myself. Finally, individual studies of particular authors, notably Mary Delariviere Manley and Eliza Haywood, have only recently begun to appear. See, for example, Mary Anne Schofield, *Quiet Rebellion: The Fictional Heroines of Eliza Haywood* (Washington, DC, 1982), and her *Eliza Haywood* (Boston, 1985); Patricia Koster's edition of Manley's novels: *The Novels of Mary Delariviere Manley* (Gainesville, Fla., 1971). See as well some of the essays in the valuable collection *Fetter'd or Free? British Women Novelists, 1670–1815*, ed. Mary Anne Schofield and Cecilia Macheski

ambition was my strong sense, as I embarked on the project, that the cultural meanings and ideological functions of this mass of eighteenth-century narrative were crucially neglected topics, missing links in the study of the emergence of the novel. Although I still feel that this is an important part of the story of the novel in England, I would now hesitate to take on such a daunting task. My caution is partly the hardening of intellectual arteries that passes for maturity, but it is also the result of my much more complicated understanding of the relationships among concepts such as literature, culture, and society.

All this is to say that the book looks its age. The title, for example, has an old-fashioned academic ring to it, forthright, modest, and circumscribed but actually fairly imperious in its definitive claims and in its assumptions about fiction and the literary canon summed up in its opening word, *popular*. The book itself was an abridged version of my doctoral dissertation, a thesis written in London from 1965 to 1967 and defended at Columbia University in New York City at the end of 1968, just before the student revolutions erupted there and all over the world. My dissertation had grown out of rather less dramatic developments, slow shifts 'of scholarly and critical attention in the study of early eighteenth-century English fiction. In 1960, W. H. McBurney had published *A Check List of English Prose Fiction 1700–1730*,[2] and in 1963 he edited a paperback edition of four of those novels, *Four Before Richardson: Selected English Novels 1720–1727*. In 1966, as I was beginning to write my dissertation, Robert Adams Day published *Told in Letters: Epistolary Fiction Before Richardson*. Students of George Sherburn at Harvard, McBurney and Day were well-trained literary historians, and

---

(Athens, Ohio, 1986). Among the best and most recent reassessments of Manley is a powerful essay by Catherine Gallager which re-examines the political and literary implications of her works: 'Political Crimes and Fictional Alibis: The Case of Delarivier Manley', *Eighteenth-Century Studies*, xxiii (Summer 1990), 502–21.

   [2] Cambridge, Mass., 1960.

both of them remarked at the outset of their studies that they hoped to fill in what they felt had become an embarrassingly blank space in literary history, especially after the great success of Ian Watt's *The Rise of the Novel* (1957). McBurney, for example, in the Introduction to his anthology praised Professor Watt's 'valuable study', but called its radical selectiveness a symptom of a general tendency to treat the great novelists of the period as if they had somehow developed 'autonomously'.[3] Novels like the four short ones he had exhumed must have formed, McBurney says, a significant backdrop for Defoe, Fielding, and Richardson; they had to have something, in this case a debased sub-literary genre, to despise and to revolutionize. None the less, McBurney looked for signs of progress in the great ones' predecessors; here he argues that these four novels illustrate in varying small ways improvements of the state of the art and anticipations of the novels to come. His collection selects for reprinting four novels that feature a few modest technical innovations in narrative technique, and the book culminates with an amusing novella, *The Accomplished Rake: Or Modern Fine Gentleman* (1727) by Mary Davys, a 'forerunner of Fielding', as McBurney called her in another essay.[4]

For his part, Day, in his much more elaborate and sophisticated work, also set out to make distinctions that Watt had ignored and in the process to substitute more strictly literary history for *The Rise of the Novel*'s socio-cultural emphasis. Day proposed to trace developments in epistolary technique in what he calls sub-literary fiction so that 'Richardson's work may be viewed historically as the culmination of a process of development rather than as a literary eruption', his clear implication being that Watt treats Richardson as just that sort of volcano.[5] Like McBurney, Day searches for small advances and minor refinements buried in long-forgotten epistolary

[3] *Four Before Richardson: Selected English Novels, 1720-1727* (Lincoln, Nebr., 1963), p. xi.
[4] 'Mrs Mary Davys, Forerunner of Fielding', *PMLA*, lxxiv (1959), 348-55.
[5] *Told in Letters: Epistolary Fiction Before Richardson* (Ann Arbor, Mich., 1966), p. 9.

fiction. Both of their investigations are Darwinian tracings of whatever small adaptations and evolutionary turnings can be found that help to explain the appearance of a new and triumphant narrative species. For them, we may say, the emergence of the novel is an unresolved problem in an ideal literary history in which everything is linked, in which there cannot be leaps or ruptures of continuity. Their assumption is that there must have been development or evolution in fictional technique in order for the novel to emerge as a distinct or perhaps a unique narrative entity in the middle of the eighteenth century.

My book's title echoes the work of both of these scholars, and indeed my thesis topic had been provoked by a seminar report I did in 1963 for Professor James L. Clifford at Columbia on McBurney's *Checklist*, which I eventually used as a working bibliography as I struggled, during many long and dark afternoons of the fall and winter of 1965, in the British Museum to read every title he had listed. But in due course, as I sat down to write the thesis, I found that in spite of myself I was doing something rather different from either of my immediate predecessors, from whom I had learned a great deal. Like them, I thought of myself as a literary historian (there was nothing else that I could in those days imagine myself to be), but unlike Day and McBurney I was not looking for the buried trail that led to the technical breakthroughs and social-artistic fullness of the major novelists. Or at least I knew pretty soon, as I began slogging through all those fading and yellowing pages, that there was no such trail. So, just about from the start, I was not out to fill in lost influences or incomplete literary genealogies. Because of the nature of the material, my attempt went necessarily in another direction that led me to try to account for these narratives in terms of what it seemed to me they manifestly were, rather than to attempt to redeem some of them as part of the buried teleology of the novel. What, I wondered, was the significance of their nearly absolute neglect of elementary narrative values, summed up in the critical terms that encompass realism of various sorts, such as depth and variety of characterization, psychological complexity, socio-historical particularity and accuracy, spatio-temporal control, moral complexity, and rhetorical and thematic variety? Although I can't claim that I possessed much theoretical self-consciousness then, what evolved for me as working assumptions turned out to be distinct from those of the traditional literary history such as McBurney and Day exemplified. Instead of trying to recover the past to find current literary values in it, I was led to historicize it as I wondered why on earth anyone with the least intelligence or taste would want to read these narratives. Since they no longer served our purposes and pleasures, what was their attraction for the readers who bought them in pretty large quantities? Some of the material, for example the cruder sorts of criminal and travel narrative, was clearly meant for naïve or socially and intellectually underprivileged readers, and I found in even the more pretentious narratives of amatory tragedy and pious exaltation an implicit appeal to readers pathetically eager for new knowledge and experience. The existence of all this fiction testified, at the least, to an audience hungry for narrative's basic and vulgar pleasures, for vicarious excitements and imaginative extensions of daily life.

So the eventual title of the thesis was 'The Uses of Fiction', an echo of Richard Hoggart's study of twentieth-century English working-class culture, *The Uses of Literacy*.[6] Books like the ones I was struggling with clearly served the purposes and pleasures of many eager but long-dead readers, but in those days before the development of 'reader response' criticism very few scholars talked about the actual audience for literature. When they did speak of readers, they wrote about an audience in formalist terms to evoke an internal or ideal reader that a complicated text projected. Actual readers were beyond the ken of formalist analysis and were properly left to sociology,

[6] *The Uses of Literacy: Aspects of Working-Class Life, with Special References to Publications and Entertainments* (London, 1957).

but in this case there is almost nothing left in the historical record about the consumers of this fiction. Material like early eighteenth-century fiction clearly implied an internal reader with a rather different ideological profile from that of the high Augustan literary mode contemporary with it, which demanded a connoisseur of irony, of subtle verbal and cultural echoes and effects.

I could not hope to identify with any precision the actual audience for these narratives, but I did find in Raymond Williams's work a way of talking about what their implied readers might have shared. It seemed to me then that I was after something resembling what Williams had articulated in *The Long Revolution* as a 'structure of feeling'. Williams meant by that quasi-anthropological term something elusive but positive: that which is communicated by the arts of a period and a place in their 'characteristic approaches and tones in argument', and 'in the actual living sense, the deep community' that makes communication possible.[7] Pre-Richardsonian narrative seemed to offer fields of implicit meanings that resembled these structures of feeling in their lost immediacy and, especially, in their mysterious remoteness from my latter-day understanding. Instead of the communal unity and vitality that 'structure of feeling' implied for Raymond Williams, however, I heard in these narratives the confused and contradictory buzz of imperfect ideological communication, messages received by individuals who were only in a temporary sense, as readers, members of a group. This fiction seemed to point to their authors' attempts to offer narrative satisfactions and pleasures that had become garbled with the passage of a few hundred years.

It wasn't called that in those days, but I now suppose I was practising an untheoretical version of cultural studies, although one that was firmly grounded in, and of course limited by, the prevailing values of literary history and critical evaluation. Still, I knew that I wasn't doing the usual sort of formalist analysis of one of the canonical masters or historical-

[7] *The Long Revolution* (Harmondsworth, Penguin edition, 1965), p. 65.

biographical investigation of minor background figures such as my supervisors at Columbia at first expected of me. I was both depressed and encouraged, when I thought about it, by one of them wondering aloud if I couldn't include a bit more biography about the writers I was dealing with. I got up the courage to reply that I wasn't interested in the actual biographies of the hacks who had turned out the stuff but rather in the product itself, not books by particular authors but entertainment machines, as I came to call them. Ultimately there was a certain brash originality in my declaring, rather too grandly I would now say, that in order to write the literary history of this early eighteenth-century fiction it was 'necessary to discard the customary pious gestures that "literature" extracts and to treat fiction as a set of emotional and ideological stimuli, machines for producing pleasurable fantasies'.[8]

As I look back now I can see a tension in my book between the practical, day-to-day, apprentice scholar's job of work of reading non-canonical narrative and making sense of it, and literary history's grander project of finding coherence and continuity, of tracing the triumphant evolution of a new literary form called the novel. Even though I resisted the latter and announced at various times in the book that these narratives were not 'literature', my approach was limited by expectations fostered by literary or aesthetic values, and my irritation with the lack of coherence and formal shapeliness in what I was writing about shows through on occasion. There is, I freely admit, a condescension in my attitude to early fiction, and I confess that I often wished at the time that I had chosen better material to work with. The word 'popular' on which the book eventually turned was thus very much a defensive and élitist reaction, since I was wedded to the notion that 'popular' equals anything except those works that we have since canonized. Indeed, the word 'popular' itself as a term of analysis always has a controlling distance built into it. The

---

[8] *Popular Fiction Before Richardson: Narrative Patterns 1700–1739* (Oxford, 1969), p. 8.

popular is that which is 'other' for the dominant and legitimate culture to examine and perhaps to value, but always from
a position of superiority.[9]

And yet much of the material I wrote about hardly, in one
sense, deserves that designation, since no matter how devoid
they may be of what some critics would still call literary value,
a good many of these books (especially scandal chronicles and
amatory and/or didactic fiction) were probably the reading
matter, primarily, of a small (by modern standards) élite
group, privileged and leisured for the most part, but not
deeply cultivated or sophisticated. Or perhaps, if we judge
from current reading habits of similar groups in our own day,
many such readers may have been slumming, relaxing with
pleasant or trashy material. 'Popular', clearly, is a rather misleading term for some of the material I dealt with, since the
mass audience now implied by the notion just did not exist. In
so far as there was a mass audience, it fed on even more primitive reading, the chapbook versions of fairy tales and chivalric
legends consumed by ordinary and nearly unlettered folk and
sold, for the most part, by itinerant pedlars since at least
Elizabethan times.[10] In addition, 'popular' perpetuates the
opposition between the canonical and the non-canonical that
was the ruling assumption of literary history when I came of
intellectual age in the early 1960s. One does well to remember
that this opposition was not then being hotly contested.
Literature was, in those innocent days, an unambiguous term
that could still be used without apology in academic circles.
The word 'canon' itself was, in those years, in so far as I can
remember it being used, a term of art, the exclusive property
of Catholic theologians. What is now called the non-canonical
was not then perceived as the culturally excluded, but rather
as that which had, for excellent reasons, failed to survive.

[9] A useful recent book on popular culture that makes this point is Morag
Shiach, *Discourse on Popular Culture: Class, Gender and History in Cultural
Analysis, 1730 to the Present* (Stanford, Calif., 1989), p. 31.

[10] See Margaret Spufford, *Small Books and Pleasant Histories: Popular Fiction
and its Readership in Seventeenth-Century England* (Athens, Ga., 1982).

Nowadays we have developed a less deterministic and impersonal view of how literary value is decided, but the issue of value itself is far from settled.

None the less, for my book, then and now, 'popular' turns out to be a very useful if not entirely appropriate designation, and the issue of literary value remains central, precisely in its radical absence from most of this material. Properly considered, all narrative from this period, whether we see it as bad or good, readable or unreadable, has similar historical resonance and ideological purpose or at least some effect in that direction. Most of the substantial mass of narrative from the first forty years of the eighteenth century which McBurney and Day complained Ian Watt had ignored and which I seized upon for my dissertation is still, to put it mildly, of little immediate interest to a modern reader. Who, except the most thorough of specialists or most dedicated of graduate students, has read this stuff even now? I remember my own struggle, during those long afternoons I spent reading these novels, to sustain my wandering attention and overcome a longing for hot coffee and adult reading-matter. My difficulties in concentrating grew, however, only in part from a preference for the sort of coherence and narrative control that we have learned to value from the established tradition of canonical writers, especially novelists from the nineteenth and early twentieth centuries. Taken each on its own, the 'popular' or non-canonical narrative that I was attempting to account for lacked as well just that cultural density, that mixture Watt had identified of proto-realistic technique and ideological intensity, to be found in the three eighteenth-century novelists he singled out for attention, Defoe, Richardson, and Fielding.

That is to say that Manley, Haywood, Aubin, Barker, and other women writers of novellas both scandalous and pious, the anonymous producers of religious autobiographies, the writers of travel narratives, real and imaginary, and the compilers of criminal and rogue stories constitute a body of work that we can say was more or less secreted by its cultural moment, giving voice to various sorts of pressing concerns and ideologies and responding to commercial publishing opportunities, but lacking, with only rare exceptions, the complexity, density, and authorial singularity of particular novels by Defoe, Fielding, or Richardson. That complexity is no doubt mysteriously caused by some imponderable that deserves to be called genius, but aesthetic achievement is also undoubtedly the result of certain male authors having full access to the means of cultural production as in the case of the Eton-educated Fielding, or in the case of Richardson to special leisure for protracted creative work, or in the case of Defoe to intense involvement in literary production for commercial purposes. Genius requires privilege and opportunity. But, more to the point, what distinguishes the major eighteenth-century novelists from the decidedly minor ones is the rich interplay in their texts between ideological fullness and aesthetic achievement. Or to put it another way, what I think I had learned from Watt's *The Rise of the Novel*, or simply absorbed from the critical climate of the early 1960s, was that the formal and technical achievements of those writers we label the major eighteenth-century novelists are inseparable from their ability to render their unique and strenuous situation in the midst of cultural complexity, as opposed to the ideological simplicities and formulae of what I then called popular fiction. The canonical works of the new genre, then, are defined by their bringing to something like full expression what other contemporary narratives by themselves, for whatever reasons, could only sketch out clumsily and partially. By omitting them Ian Watt clearly implied that these predecessors and forgotten coevals were the origins of the novel only in that, by their incompleteness and lack of distinctive authorial signature and control of language, they provoked the full achievements of the writers who used to be called the early masters. But was the relation between the masters of the emerging genre and their long-forgotten contemporaries simply one of contemptuous superiority? Did they provide nothing but a negative example, provoking by their ineptitude and incoherence the controlled and intensely meaningful fictions of the eighteenth-century novelists we still read or are told to read by the cultural and educational establishment?

In his recent massive reconsideration of this problem, *The Origins of the English Novel 1600–1740* (1987), Michael McKeon has sought to answer these questions by proposing, with arresting theoretical brilliance, that when Fielding and Richardson burst on the scene in the 1740s the body of narrative that had preceded them in the late seventeenth and early eighteenth century stood in a complicated, essentially enabling relationship to their powerful originality. Fielding's and Richardson's novels and the theory of the new genre that supports them depend, says McKeon, on their participating in a 'quasi-objective category . . . which both preexists and is precipitated by its own conceptual formulation'.[11] At that moment in the early 1740s when Richardson's and Fielding's novels initiated a debate about the proper form of the novel, the question could only be posed about their works because the novel existed as what McKeon calls a 'simple abstraction', a difficult notion whereby Marx in the *Grundrisse* sought to explain how an abstracting consciousness operates on experience, recognizing in its general formulations the result of a dialectical interplay with a host of pre-existing concrete particulars and seeing the 'complex determinacy of its own abstraction' (p. 17). McKeon's thesis is that the new genre recognized in the 1740s as the novel could only appear as such when this prehistory of the novelistic was in place next to another 'simple abstraction', the romance, which had emerged as such in the previous two centuries. In the decades preceding the emergence of the realistic novel these simple abstractions interact dialectically, and McKeon finds in the early eighteenth-century novel evidence for the productive lingering of romance alongside an emerging novelistic realism (p. 424).

[11] *The Origins of the English Novel 1600–1740* (Baltimore and London, 1987), p. 15. All further references are in parenthesis in the text.

And yet McKeon, in the final analysis, has little to say about the early narratives themselves except to make them (as a fairly undifferentiated corpus) part of his elaborate scheme of the novel's development and complex mediation of moral and social crises peculiar to the early modern period in England. He writes briefly about criminal biography, comments on one of Mary Davys's and one of Eliza Haywood's novellas (the ones in McBurney's *Four Before Richardson*), and discusses Haywood's and Delariviere Manley's scandal chronicles in the same few pages. The bulk of his analysis of particular eighteenth-century texts deals with the major novelists, whose works arrive in order to perform just that task which their immediate eighteenth-century predecessors were incapable of—the work of cultural mediation that he sees as the distinctive and defining mission of the novel. Surprisingly enough, the final and most brilliant critical turn in *The Origins of the Novel* is McKeon's argument that the genre emerges in its fullness in the work of Fielding and Richardson precisely because their perfecting of narrative techniques represents a negation by aesthetic means of their predecessors' confused examination of those special novelistic issues that he calls questions of truth and virtue. In the novel as Fielding and Richardson establish it, the category of history separates from 'literature', and the private self with its internalized sense of virtue and worth separates itself from society and its status categories. The autonomous realm of the aesthetic, which enables value-judgements about Fielding and Richardson's novels, is an ideological means of resolving the moral and epistemological questions that the early novel muddles hopelessly. Aesthetic value is thus relocated and redefined; its function in the major novels is not primarily to give artistic and moral pleasure or to achieve a degree of cognitive value as truthful representation, but to enable the historical mission of the novel, nothing less in McKeon's words than to substitute the 'triumph of the creative human mind' (p. 418) for the cultural contradictions faced by the great novelists' hapless predecessors in the eighteenth century.

We are, in a sense, back where we started, since the significance of the non-canonical fiction that is the subject of my book is radically subordinated to the major, canonical works. McKeon and other recent commentators on the eighteenth-century novel have, in fact, even more invested in the superiority, aesthetic *cum* ideological, of the old masters than the previous generation of critics and literary historians. Day and McBurney find, after all, evidence of continuity and productive influence in the minor fiction they sift and study. But for McKeon and others there is nothing less to the story of the emergence of the novel than a rupture, a total break with the past and with predecessors. As my summary will have made clear, moreover, McKeon grants the novel, when it arrives in its fullness in the mid-eighteenth century, an immense cultural power and centrality. Texts, as critics say nowadays, are for him generative of cultural reality, not the other way round, so the texts that will interest the latest generation of commentators need to be pretty impressive.

Published in the same year as McKeon's blockbuster, John Bender's *Imagining the Penitentiary: Fiction and the Architecture of Mind in Eighteenth-Century England* (1987) makes equally grand, if rather more specific, claims for the novel. He asserts with great originality that the novel from Defoe to Goldsmith is part of the process of cultural production that enabled the turn from the traditional prison to the modern penitentiary, and more generally he argues that the novel is an active component of the regulating mechanisms that help to form the emerging modern state. Bender traces the decline of the older prison, a temporary space on the outskirts of the social order, a transitional or 'liminal' site through which the individual passed on his way to punishment, execution, or transportation, and he describes its replacement by the modern penitentiary and Enlightenment penal theories whereby the prison became an enclosing architectural entity and potentially reforming sequence in which individuals underwent a process of supervised incarceration as they served a sentence. Bender offers a subtle account of the ways in which, as he puts it, 'the novel enabled the penitentiary by formulating, and thereby giving conscious access to, a real texture of attitudes, a structure of feeling, that [he calls] the "penitentiary idea".' According to that idea, common to the realist novel and empiricist philosophy like Locke's and Hume's, the self is constituted by certain fictions grounded in material conditions that can be manipulated and recomposed for particular ends.[12] Bender, then, underscores even more heavily than McKeon the radical discontinuity between the fiction of the earlier part of the century and the new realist novel that participates in the profoundest of cultural and political changes. His texts, necessarily, are all impeccably canonical, Defoe and (especially) Fielding for the most part, and indeed his fascinating thesis depends upon those novels that fully achieve the realism on which his book dwells so intensely.

When it was first published, *Popular Fiction Before Richardson* was accused by some reviewers of being over-schematized, but next to books like McKeon's and Bender's its claims these days look very modest and, whatever else can be said about them, exceedingly specific.[13] I remain somewhat sceptical of the totalizing claims of critics like McKeon and Bender, and it seems to me that the question of the 'origins' of the novel is fundamentally an imponderable or unresolvable issue. My original thesis was only that popular fiction, in its various and diverse formats, was given a good deal of its ideo-

---

[12] *Imagining the Penitentiary* (Chicago, 1987), p. 38.

[13] Although it may be churlish to complain in the face of the theoretical richness totalizing literary critics like Bender offer, such work is often based on rather limited reading in the primary texts in question. McKeon has read everything, but clearly not very widely in the pre-Richardson material in which I immersed myself, and Bender treats only a very few novels, even though his range in secondary materials in various disciplines is extremely wide. Nancy Armstrong's incredibly ambitious *Desire and Domestic Fiction: A Political History of the Novel* (New York, 1987) develops an all-inclusive thesis about the ideological function of the novel: that it represents an assertion of middle-class power through a feminization of experience whereby individuals are defined in private and domestic terms. All of this seems to be based on a reading in her opening chapter of one eighteenth-century novel, *Pamela*.

logical force by participating in an eighteenth-century confrontation between traditional religious values and an emerging secularism that believers and public moralists in England at least found very sinister. Certain recurrent figures like the rake-seducer, the libertine-infidel, the libidinous courtesan, the amoral politician, the highwayman, the criminal, and the pirate pointed, it seemed to me, to a fascination with transgression that was invariably licensed by moralistic presentation. I still think such a broad characterization of the material's purposes and effects is valid, but I would venture that my book's real value now lies in its detailed examination of works that helped to constitute, quite simply, a new kind of market-place for a newly aggressive fictional product. To the extent that I was able to manage it within the prevailing critical and literary historical values of the mid 1960s, the book has the virtue of treating this material on its own terms, as more or less formulaic fiction that initiates the novel as a popular narrative format rather than a literary genre in the strict sense.

Whatever continuing value my book may have lies in its (largely implicit) assertion that these narratives are important precisely because they are ideologically transparent, 'entertainment machines and fantasy inducers' which deliver satisfactions that I then rather melodramatically called 'mythical'. It was precisely the technical ineptitude of these forerunners and predecessors, their slapdash, formulaic approach to narrative, their very awfulness, if you will, that interested me, or so I see now. In other words, fiction of the kind I labelled 'popular' in the early eighteenth century offered certain pleasures to its readers, much like those which formula fiction has continued to provide ever since. Their fullness is not the comprehensiveness and critical or moral intelligence of fiction written by privileged individual producers, but rather the unselfconscious articulation of ideology by writers paid to submerge themselves and write to order, re-working and repeating profitable formulae. Taken in clumps or in waves and trends rather than individually, narrative like this, by definition, has

all its purposes and designs in full and flagrant view. A revealing incoherence, ideology with all its contradictions hung out
in full view, is what it, now at least, uniquely offers. Popular
narrative, I conclude in the 'Epilogue' to the book, is 'essentially opportunistic; it sets out to flatter and exploit rather than
to challenge or redefine the assumptions of its implied audience' (p. 263). My purpose, I go on to say, has been 'to dismantle the apparatus' that delivered such satisfactions to its
original readers, although what I don't say (because at the
time it went without saying) is that such narrative is derived
from the ideology it serves; it is necessarily a means of dissem-
inating and reinforcing notions and formulations that origi-
nate elsewhere in the culture of the time. Not central, then,
not the source of ideology, and certainly not in any way a sub-
verter of it is how I still understand this fiction. And finally, it
is exactly in its capacity as the promoter of ideology that such
fiction initiates the tradition of what later becomes popular
fiction that truly deserves the name.[14]

The narratives of the kind I wrote about twenty-five years
ago effectively commence, in short, a commercially dominant
practice of fiction production within which the novelists still
read and assigned to their students by academics are best
understood as scattered and fitful attempts to elevate and per-
sonalize a popular format in which such individualized gestures were inappropriate. A commodity produced by cheap
labour hired by booksellers and publishers to satisfy a growing
market, popular fiction is nothing less than the central and initiating line of the novel. To varying degrees, the art novel
written by talented individuals is only an occasionally successful protest against this marketing strategy. As it flourishes
today in shopping mall and airport bookstores, such fiction is
made to order, marketed and packaged in sophisticated ways

[14] I have developed this point in an essay that reviews, using mostly different
examples from those in this book, the popular novel in the early eighteenth century. See 'Popular Narrative in the Early Eighteenth Century: Formats and
Formulas', in *The First English Novelists: Essays in Understanding*, ed. J. M.
Armistead (Knoxville, Tenn., 1985), pp. 3–39.

which were awkwardly, if accurately, adumbrated on a tiny scale by the publishers of early eighteenth-century popular narrative in England.

Now such an approach has a lot in common with recent disparagement of the idea of 'literature' in the traditional, honorific sense. And I suppose that my own reconsideration of the material I first read twenty-five years ago has been influenced by current scepticism about the absolute divide between high and low culture and art. But there are two directions in current work on the early novel, and perhaps in recent thinking about the novel in general, that my notion of the importance for the development of the novel of popular or, better, formula fiction may run counter to. Feminist critics and literary historians have sought to recuperate and re-evaluate forgotten, or at least neglected, women writers, among them, of course, important figures from the pre-Richardson years like Manley and Haywood. Much of this reassessment is, on its own terms, quite convincing, although to my mind some of this criticism makes gender far too central and determining a factor in literary production.[15] In attempting to add such writers to the canon, recent feminist critics grant them literary-moral value that largely negates their importance as part of the commercial beginnings of formula fiction, and returns us, curiously enough, to traditional literary history with its emphasis on the author as individualized creator and self-consciously moral entity.[16] That debate is just beginning, and I am sure that in the end the feminist revaluation will gain the ascendancy. Although I still think such fiction is best approached as a formulaic and commercial product, my own views on the meaning of the vast quantity of amatory narrative have modified slightly. Originally

[15] A valuable and representative book in this strain is Jane Spencer, *The Rise of the Woman Novelist: From Aphra Behn to Jane Austen* (Oxford, 1986).

[16] In 'Women and the Rise of the Novel: A Feminist-Marxist Theory', for example, Josephine Donovan complains that women have in fact been left out of the story of the rise of the novel by Lukács, Watt, McKeon, and Lucien Goldmann. Although she complains that I do not spell out my contention 'in explicitly feminist terms', she calls my book unique 'in drawing attention to early women novelists' (*Signs*, xvi (Spring 1991), 451.

I saw such novellas of invariably blasted female innocence as strictly in the service of hegemonic and patriarchal culture, as it is nowadays called: the virgin-martyr destroyed or sacrificed by a monstrous masculine world preserves moral order and individual integrity in her innocent inability to resist her seducer, and she also, of course, provides erotic-pathetic pleasure for readers. It now seems to me that formula fiction, in its very plenitude and variety, its inexhaustible supply of virtue/vice (male villains and female paragons), must have been in some way a challenge to an increasingly restricted and measured actuality. The realism of the canonical novels is, in this context, a refusal of that easy plenitude and bounding eroticism for the constraints of realism, with its regulatory emphasis on the slow and measured, the possible and the probable. The very looseness and artlessness, those guaranteed repetitions and recurrences of formula fiction, are to this extent, as the century wears on and the novel emerges, subversive features. Popular fiction, to reverse McKeon's emphasis, gains a new raciness and urgency when it has the canonical realistic mainstream to play itself off against.

The second direction in current work on the novel is the larger trend to which feminist criticism belongs, since it places literary production at the absolute centre of culture. Novels by these lights are no longer part of the cultural superstructure but generate in their representations the forms and structures of consciousness. The material base I was taught to believe in has been exposed, most literary critics now seem to believe, as a mechanistic fiction, itself a representation. What seems to have happened, as far as I can tell, is that literary production at all levels has been placed at the centre of cultural production, no longer part of the superstructure but generating in its representations the very materials for consciousness. As Michael McKeon's and John Bender's recent powerful studies make clear, the main question on the table is the novel's centrality to cultural and ideological change. Although Bender, especially, hedges the issue of causation and sees the novel as somehow both parallel to and influential upon the penitentiary and its related cultural changes, these critics and many others make the emerging novel nothing less than the cause rather than the effect of cultural and ideological changes.

Both of these trends raise problems of literary value and canonicity, and the more general question of the relationship between literature and social conditions and why the novel should have an especially intimate connection with the life that surrounds it. Value has been re-situated and redefined, I submit, so that for recent totalizing literary historians like McKeon, Bender, and others, it equals ideological fullness and cultural efficacy. Popular fiction in the sense in which I stumbled upon it twenty-five years ago in the British Museum is, in its energetic crudeness, a conservative and disruptive counterweight to such efficacy and fullness. It may be said to retard cultural change and to predict, in its irresponsibility, a similar blocking function in the commercial and popular fiction to come. In this sense it is also a body of work that invites re-examination in the light of our new understanding of the cultural power of literature.

I

THE RISE OF THE NOVEL
RECONSIDERED

THE casual reader of modern literary history might well conclude
that the English novel began abruptly in 1740 with the publication of Richardson's *Pamela* and that crucial preparation for the
event had been made in several of Defoe's narratives. This, at any
rate, is the paradigm which the textbooks present, and it is probably only antiquarian enthusiasm which can deny the aesthetic
justice of such bare simplicities. Defoe and Richardson are without question the two writers of prose fiction from the first forty
years or so of the eighteenth century who mean the most to the
twentieth century.[1] We value them quite rightly because they tell
us so much about the eighteenth century in artistic terms that we
can enjoy and understand readily.

Yet it is just this towering superiority of Defoe and Richardson
over their now-forgotten contemporaries that has led modern
criticism to distort to some extent the history of the English novel.
Since the late nineteenth century at least, critics have been only
too aware of the peculiar 'realism' that separates Defoe and
Richardson dramatically from previous writers and makes them
the first specifically 'modern' English novelists. Much literary
history has been simply content to document this critical distinction by recording with a kind of neo-Hegelian confidence the
historical progress from the factually careless and improbable
fictions called romances to the mimetically sensitive stories called

---

[1] I exclude Fielding (*Joseph Andrews* was published in 1742) because of his
massive irony. Fielding's first two novels are really anti-novels in that their
almost pervasive sense of parody makes them implicitly critical of the 'naïve'
realism by which Defoe and Richardson seek to induce a psychological participation which must be identified as the defining quality of the specifically modern
novel.

novels. The history of the novel has thus been handed down to us as the triumph of an enlightened realism over reactionary romance, the development or evolution of a superior literary instrument.

Older standard histories of the novel such as Baker's, for example, simply ranged through the predecessors of the eighteenth-century masters, from Sidney to Mrs. Behn, picking out scenes which struck them as vivid, realistic (full of low-life gusto and/or dialect), and circumstantial, and then ticketed them with meticulous hindsight as partial anticipations of the full-blown insight into the depiction of real life which Defoe and Richardson 'invented'. This sort of critical sifting and sorting resembled misguided neo-classical defences of folk literature such as Addison's remarks on *Chevy Chase*: such works, says the benevolent critic in effect, are valuable and interesting and not to be despised, for in their crude and vigorous ways they approach certain literary values of ours (which values, of course, were either unknown, irrelevant, or obnoxious to the author in question). Surprisingly, such an un-historical 'teleological' view of literary history still vitiates a good deal of modern criticism of the novel which aspires to more than appreciation.

Even so influential and impressive a book as Ian Watt's *Rise of the Novel* is weakened by a teleological bias. Watt is indeed incisively brilliant (if occasionally extravagant) in analysing the essentials of what he calls, as his title implies, a new genre: the use of circumstantial particulars to present a fictional world in which character is firmly rooted in and derived from the various environments (social, economic, biological, and psychological) which are recognized as the distinctive arena of modern experience.[1]

---

[1] Using the insights of the sociology of knowledge, which, according to Karl Mannheim, emphasizes the necessity of interpreting individual experience within the context of group experience (*Ideology and Utopia: An Introduction to the Sociology of Knowledge* (London, 1954), p. 27), Watt stresses the relationship between the development of the novel and such factors as the decline of patronage, the influence of middle-class female readers because of their increased leisure time through the development of urban industry (which provided the household with goods which in the past had to be manufactured in the home) and increased dependence upon servants, and the Protestant ethic of work. Watt's perceptive chapters on Defoe and Richardson make us see how

But as interesting and valuable as most of Watt's study is, it is a drastically selective work which makes, as he admits in his preface, only incidental reference to the immediate precursors and contemporaries of the three novelists he discusses. The point of the selectivity is, of course, that only in Defoe (*some* of Defoe) and Richardson can one find truly recognizable examples in any appreciable number of the process of development toward the modern novel that Watt tells us is taking place during the early years of the eighteenth century. The near-perfection of mimetic techniques by Defoe and Richardson and their rendering of the nuances of private experience in a direct and naturalistic style are the sources of their sociological richness and accuracy as well as the signs of their literary pre-eminence. In so far as a work lacks those realistic techniques, it would seem to be, we can infer from Watt's method, reactionary in an artistic and ideological sense.

If he were to deal with the minor fiction of the period, Watt would thus have to employ the same sifting and sorting machinery which older and less sophisticated literary historians such as Baker handled so thoroughly. He would have to convict the writers of the mass of fiction from the first forty years of the eighteenth century of ineptness and insignificance not simply because of their obvious failings from the point of view of modern realistic fiction, but because of their inability to communicate to us what we have decided is the proper *Weltanschauung* of their age.

It has been settled, one gathers, that popular literature in the eighteenth century (Defoe's best-known novels versus Pope's poetry is the usual inadequate means of developing the antithesis between popular and aristocratic literature) was produced for a public that wanted the real and the every-day in plain and straightforward language. The 'enlightened' bourgeois realism Watt and others are talking about when they trace the development of the modern novel demands, of course, a bourgeois audience with the appropriate ideological features.

they managed to produce characters and situations to which we can still respond because they are set in a world of things which is essentially our world. All references to Watt's book are to the Penguin paperback edition of 1963.

A study such as Watt's does, on a small scale, what Erich Auerbach's synoptic and seminal work, *Mimesis*, made possible; it finds the necessary relationship which exists between the assumptions of the age and the literary techniques which not only develop to match those assumptions but are shaped and determined by them. Yet, it is by no means certain that the early eighteenth century can be entirely summed up in terms of the advancing practicality and incipient democratic attitudes of the middle classes. It is, as well, questionable whether we can simply reduce so pluralistic an age as the eighteenth century to the fairly rigid scheme implied in the idea that the 'rise' of the novel is the triumph of the middle class in literature. What is involved is nothing less than a gratuitous imposition of the social and philosophical norms (summed up in such terms as bourgeois democracy and pragmatism) and the narrative effects (summed up in the term realism) we value most upon a body of writing which was at least partly unaware of, if not hostile to, them.

The identification of the characteristic and appropriate style of the age is, to be sure, only implicit in Watt's treatment, and it must be repeated that his analyses of Richardson and Defoe as realistic innovators yield brilliant critical results. We know when we finish Watt's book why we like Defoe and Richardson and how they anticipate the achievements of later and more self-conscious novelists, but we do not know as much as we should about why Defoe and Richardson wrote and why they were read so widely in their own time.

All of this is not to deny the value and necessity of criticism's accommodation of the works of the past to our contemporary frame of reference. But it seems possible, without lowering the stature of Defoe and Richardson at all, to object that criticism contributes to a distortion of literary history by attempting to identify the characteristic style and distinctive ethos of a period on the basis of what is really a quite rigorous selection of texts, those that have slithered through the fine nets of posterity.

Raymond Williams has recently warned of the difficulty of understanding the past according to what we have 'received' from it.[1] There is a natural and enormous process of selection which takes place, and the machinery of selection has been particularly ruthless with the prose fiction of the years 1700–39. Defoe, prolific and indefatigable as he seems to have been, was not the only practising hack writer of what we can now call fiction. It is undeniable that the great bulk of this pre-Richardsonian 'fiction' is artistically despicable. So much so that one might well ask, what is the use of bad art? Let us be done with the eighteenth century's literary rubbish, we have quite enough of our own.

The point is, however, that the development of prose fiction in the eighteenth century can only be understood if it is viewed as a significant step in the emergence of 'mass art' as modern critics have come to understand it, and if one remembers the psychological truism that all art is 'escapist' and provides fantasies which allow pleasurable identification and projection. The artistic highlights in prose fiction of the first forty years or so of the century, Defoe and Richardson, are examples of this art at a higher level of coherence and intensity than their now-forgotten contemporaries could muster. We cannot, therefore, understand Defoe and Richardson properly until we take into account their participation in this milieu, unless we understand that their contemporary popularity was the result of their being able to use or exploit much more capably the same raw materials (i.e. ideas, attitudes, 'myths') as their fellows. Their great achievement as realistic artists, it must be argued, is only part of the explanation of their great contemporary success.

To discuss this milieu and to describe it with some measure of objectivity, it is necessary to discard some of the traditional preoccupations of students of the period and of the genre usually called prose fiction. The most important and most restricting of these is the teleological bias, for it imposes an untenable pattern of growth and development upon the history of prose fiction. This preconception reduces any study of the material in question to the rather thankless, and to my mind meaningless, task of pointing out small 'advances' in realistic technique in various otherwise

[1] *The Long Revolution* (London, Penguin edition, 1965), p. 69.

hapless hacks. This procedure reflects what a Marxist critic might call the excessive concern of 'modernist bourgeois' critics for formal qualities, since the search for the exact biological history of the novel implies the existence of a Platonic ideal novel in which all prose fictions participate and towards which, with varying degrees of success, they all aspire.

One of the disastrous results of this preoccupation has been the obsession with generic terminology and definition which has infected most students of the beginning of the novel. Something as real as 'the novel' has seemed to require definition as precise as a Renaissance epic or neo-classical tragedy. And in general, the sheer formal variety (chaos perhaps) which exists among the prose fiction of the period has led scholars to attempt to impose some kind of generic pattern upon the chaos and to invoke traditional external categories such as picaresque, epistolary, romance, imaginary voyage, etc.[1] Often, such classifications merely produce fairly useless truisms, academic machines which give off heat but no light.

Yet the problem of definition is a real one, perhaps the most important obstacle to the proper study of the pre-Richardson fictional milieu. It is clearly useless to bandy about the old labels and to proliferate truisms, but one is still left with the inescapable

---

[1] A good example of this diversity is provided by Philip Gove's study of the 'imaginary voyages' of the seventeenth and eighteenth centuries. After a long and thorough survey of the history of the problem of distinguishing imaginary voyages from other prose fictions, Gove concludes somewhat wearily that 'what was obvious at the beginning has been consistently and persistently confirmed: the imaginary voyage closely relates to several other kinds of fiction. Any attempt to chart those relationships by interlocking circles necessitates the same dubious distinctions among unsatisfactorily defined and sometimes undefinable subdivisions into which earlier classifiers have been drawn' (see *The Imaginary Voyage in Prose Fiction* (New York, 1941), pp. 154–5). Gove's warning came too late for an older and much less daunted survey of English fiction from 1700 to 1740 which generated with Polonian vigour six separate categories: realistic narrative, letter novel, *chronique scandaleuse*, *voyage imaginaire*, framework *conte de fée*, and romance; seven sub-categories of romance: chivalric, pastoral, allegorical, religious, heroico-historical, informational conversational, and satirical; and four varieties of realistic novels: novels of manners, historical-psychological, picaresque, and psychological. See Arthur J. Tieje, 'The Expressed Aim of the Long Prose Fiction from 1579 to 1740', *JEGP*, xi (1912), 403.

root meaning of fiction—a *false* story, something which never happened, as opposed to an accurate biography, or travel account, or diary. But if this falsity is accepted as a minimum requirement for the admission of a prose narrative into the history of the novel, the facts uncovered by eighteenth-century scholars complicate matters considerably. Their findings show that many narratives of the period, presented as fact and accepted as such by many, were sheer fabrications. Many 'novels' were only thinly disguised *romans à clef*, gross mixtures of slander and scandal. It is, in short, extremely difficult to separate fact from fiction in a great many of the prose narratives of the period that are customarily called fiction. A patient and efficient scholar like A. W. Secord, for example, spent a lifetime untangling the various strands of truth and fabrication in some of Defoe's works.

The only way to deal with this Gordian knot of definition seems to be to cut away, to grant the usefulness of source studies like those of Secord and J. R. Moore on Defoe, but to insist that most extended narratives, whatever their origin and exact degree of veracity, become 'fictions' during the process of consumption. The narratives I am dealing with, in other words, are relevant because they stimulate to a greater or lesser degree some personal fantasy, some identification with the personages involved in the acts being related. One has, of course, to exclude from consideration grossly truthful or factual accounts, and to compromise in practice with the psychological truism that all narrative invites imaginative participation by accepting the corpus of fictional and semi-fictional narratives of the early eighteenth century as literary historians have more or less settled them. I have followed the most recent listing of the extant prose fiction from 1700 to 1739, W. H. McBurney's *A Check List of English Prose Fiction, 1700–1739* (Harvard, 1960), whose criteria for inclusion seem sensible.[1]

---

[1] McBurney claims that all the books on his list 'deal with characters and events which are largely or wholly imaginary, consciously invented by the authors' (p. ix). He supports this by his own examination and judgement of '86 per cent of the 391 works listed'. This claim leads to some anomalies, such as the inclusion of Defoe's *Robert Drury's Journal* and his *History of the Pirates*, which are not so much fictional as embellished with fictional or journalistic

But having delimited the area somewhat, I must return to the essential broadness of selection required. I cannot stop to quibble over the exact boundaries between fact and fiction in those narratives that have been accepted as probably fictional. Fiction, it seems to me, must be defined from a psychological rather than a literary or literal point of view. The narratives themselves must be scrutinized the way an anthropologist might examine the institutions of an exotic culture. To write literary history in this case, it becomes necessary to discard the customary pious gestures that 'literature' exacts and to treat fiction as a cultural artifact, a set of emotional and ideological stimuli, machines for producing pleasurable fantasies.

The great advantage of this approach is that it avoids the personalistic bias natural and perhaps appropriate to criticism of the products of high culture. One can speak with great profit of the 'mind and art' of such men as Pope, Swift, and Fielding. It may even be possible to approach writers like Defoe and Richardson from a deep involvement in their lives and conscious intentions as artists. But the material I propose to deal with can only be handled profitably on the primary level of 'audience use'. The investigation of writers' sources and authentic motivations is, in the long run, irrelevant in a journalistic milieu such as this.

Since we are concerned only with the narrative as finished product, the process of production is secondary; it does not matter whether a Defoe or a Mrs. Haywood wrote a particular account chiefly from a travel diary or local gossip or entirely from a quick and fertile imagination. The author's private conception of himself and his work, his sometimes inaccessible or inscrutable motive, spiritual or crassly commercial, is a matter for conjecture; the public presentation is there to be dealt with, transparent in its public function to amuse or thrill or edify.

Once again, the assumption behind my delimitation of the subject is that the beginnings of the novel must be approached as

techniques. McBurney has also wisely omitted 'short character sketches, jest books, topical pamphlets, dialogues, chap-books, and fictional pieces in periodicals' (p. ix).

essentially an event in the development of mass culture, a social phenomenon with important consequences for literature proper. What is required is not a critical hunt for lost minor masterpieces with which to delight modern audiences, but an effort of the historical imagination to understand the values which the eighteenth-century reading public attached to fiction, or, at least, the values which the most successful popular narratives advertised and delivered. The effort is not to establish literary genealogies but to reconstruct and explain a cultural phenomenon, what Raymond Williams has called the 'structure of feeling'.[1]

Of course, this eighteenth-century public is a huge and inarticulate mass which can no longer be consulted, a group very difficult to describe or identify with any kind of sociological precision. It is customary to see the early eighteenth century as a period of expanding middle-class culture and to point to periodical essays, bourgeois tragedy, sentimental drama, and the novel as evidence of that expansion. But despite the usual generalizations that the middle and lower-middle classes were reading as they rose to economic power, there are no meaningful statistics with which to chart this increase. We have principally the texts themselves, and it seems to me perfectly valid to generalize about this audience by treating these texts as evidence, by analysing them, and deducing their audience's features from them.

Certain facts seem clear and in need of emphasis. Prose fiction at a popular level essentially requires only a simple exercise of literacy, what Leslie Fiedler has very aptly called 'symbolic' or 'demonstration' literacy,[2] rather than the complicated enlightened response towards artistic structure and style involving an awareness of allusion and irony which neo-classic literature at its best demands. Put next to these standards, the fiction of the period can best be described as fantasy machines, which must have appeared to the educated literate élite of the eighteenth century precisely what comic books and television seem to the contemporary guardians of cultural standards. Prose fiction forms part of that steady

[1] Williams, op. cit., p. 64.
[2] *Waiting for the End* (London, 1965), p. 173.

expansion of popular literature in the eighteenth century which traditionalists like Pope and Swift could see only as a pervasive vulgarization of the arts.

It must be remembered that neo-classicism, as the textbooks define it, was represented by a tiny minority whose cultural position was largely defined by their opposition to an emergent and vehemently non-classical set of cultural values. The violence of Pope's *Dunciad* and much of the sullen ferocity of Swift can thus be partly explained: both are gloomy 'Tory satirists', defending what they thought was the doomed last bastion of classicism.

The early years of the eighteenth century are, in fact, dominated by an ethos which tends to value experience for its variety, curiosity, or intensity rather than for its status and propriety (taking these terms in a literary as well as a moral sense). Free forms such as the popular periodical essay (with its deliberately simplified style and careful vulgarization of current ideas), the loco-descriptive poem,[1] and prose fiction are the most obtrusive symptoms of this cultural change, most of the fiction obviously operating on lower cultural levels than the essays and loco-descriptive poems, but none the less significant for its low position in the cultural hierarchy.

Literary historians have usually been horrified by this growth of popular literature and have resorted to accurate but useless moral analysis, dismissing genuinely popular writers such as Mrs. Haywood and Mrs. Manley by calling their works scurrilous and licentious, or by exposing with magisterial scorn the moral claims of authors' prefaces as mere rationales for dealing in the sensational and the pornographic. Such self-righteousness and Popeian

---

[1] The term is, as far as I know, Marjorie Nicolson's. She uses it in her book *Mountain Gloom and Mountain Glory: the Development of the Aesthetics of the Infinite* (Ithaca, N.Y., 1959) to refer to extended poems, such as Thomson's *Seasons*, whose unity is provided only by the physical continuity of the landscape described rather than by any traditional literary occasion or formal shape such as an ode or a sonnet possesses. The unity is, in fact, personal or emotional; the neo-classic pleasure of pattern (accessible to the educated few) is exchanged for the non-classical pleasure of sensuous immediacy (available to the merely literate many). Thus, I call the extended landscape poem a free form and link it to prose fiction.

indignation seem unnecessary, especially now when we are re-evaluating low or popular culture and finding it important for understanding our own age.

It is perfectly true that much of the popular fiction in question is from the usual point of view morally indefensible. Yet it is all, no matter how scandalous or obscene, of historical interest because it depends for its effectiveness as popular entertainment upon its exploitation of what I will choose to call an 'ideology'. I use this word, normally restricted to the description of political and social commitment, because it suggests a body of assumptions and attitudes which commands immediate, emotional, and in-articulate assent, as opposed to a set of ideas which requires self-conscious and deliberate intellectual formulation. Fiction, in general, depends upon a community of such belief; the novelist (any story-teller) ruthlessly selects and inescapably shapes events when he presents them to his audience. This process of selection required by the act of narration itself expresses value judgements, even if no overt didacticism is involved and even if the novelist is concerned to avoid moralizing of any sort.[1] The great appeal of fiction at the popular level with which I am concerned was its ability to provide an over-simplification of the structure of society and the moral universe which allowed the reader to place himself in a world of intelligible values where right and wrong were clearly and unmistakably labelled. To read these popular narratives was, at least for the moment of belief and participation that even the most inept narrator can induce, to submit to an ideology, a neatly comprehensible as well as comprehensive pattern of reality.[2]

Modern critics, claiming to dislike ideologies, tend to dismiss the simplifications in which fiction inevitably deals as 'sentimentality'

[1] This point has been made at length in a very convincing fashion by Wayne Booth in *The Rhetoric of Fiction* (Chicago, 1963), p. 125 *et passim*.

[2] The narratives in question do not, of course, induce much participation and belief in a modern reader, especially the highly sophisticated kind of scholar or literary critic who might read them today. But, obviously, they did move and affect a great many of their eighteenth-century readers, many of them being on a much lower level of literary sophistication than our modern fastidious re-searchers.

and to look for aesthetic values in fiction to the exclusion of didactic ones. Or, on the other hand, they tend to treat certain novels as repositories of timeless wisdom which through the ironic scrutiny or mature moral vision of the author can deliver us from illusion without committing us to a positive position.

This analysis is certainly possible with later and more self-conscious fiction, imbued with a sense of the cultural mission and ethical responsibility of the novel, and almost obsessively aware of the problematical and the complex as the distinguishing features of existence. But even here a minimal ideological mobilization of forces is involved. Invariably, such a novelist (George Eliot, Joseph Conrad, James Joyce, for example) makes us identify with a character (or with his own narrative voice) who realizes that life is indeed complex and problematical. We who know and understand, the novel says to us, are united in our moral and intellectual superiority to those who do not see things as clearly. Such a procedure may be muted and only implicit, but even the greatest and most individualistic of novelists depends ultimately upon a community of ideas in which he is a member. Every novel, in short, is written with an audience in mind.

That audience is neither an ethical abstraction nor some Olympian posterity but a specific group during a particular historical period. A teleological bias or an excessive concern with explicatory criticism prevents us from seeing this social origin and essentially social purpose of all prose fiction as clearly and as constantly as we should. The writer of fiction, then, exists in relation to a body of generally accepted popular assumptions and attitudes, popular in that they are held, or he assumes that they are, by most of his audience. This relationship can be largely implicit rather than deliberate and contrived.

Now, to be sure, in the case of modern novelists, who may write for any one of many possible audiences and at various cultural levels, this truism of communication may be of very limited value; since we may have to postulate as many audiences as there are writers. But in the eighteenth century we are dealing with fewer cultural levels, and on whatever cultural level we choose with a much less fragmented audience. Furthermore, we are not distracted very much by the almost obsessive individualism and 'originality' that is one of the major rhetorical devices of modern literature. The content of works, the ideas and attitudes that we can abstract from them as their meanings, will therefore tend towards a certain uniformity, or, at the least, far away from the extreme cultural diversity characteristic of modern literature.

In fact, the main thesis of this essay is that the ideological key to the narratives I propose to deal with, their characteristic 'structure of feeling', is fairly limited and definable in its larger outlines. My reading of these narratives reveals that this structure tends to take the form of a dramatic confrontation between two opposing attitudes to experience. I will choose to call these two ways of existing in the imaginary worlds the narratives put before their readers 'secular' and 'religious'. I use these very broad and slippery terms to describe an even broader antithesis which is perhaps basic to any narrative, the contrast between active and passive actors implied in any description of an action. In eighteenth-century popular narrative, that is, action itself tends to be depicted as impious aggression against the natural or social order or against innocent and therefore virtuously passive characters. Popular fiction tends, I will suggest and illustrate in the following essay, to develop this basic conflict by means of a rhetoric and a frame of reference that make secular and religious the most accurate critical terms to describe the novelistic ideology at work. I do not, to be sure, claim that the minds or sensibilities of the readers of popular fiction were exclusively or obsessively aware of their age and the world in terms of this antithesis, but simply that the narratives indicate that they were moved (edified, thrilled, titillated) by the various embodiments of this conflict.

The presence and the relevance of this opposition for many eighteenth-century readers has been suggested by the recent re-evaluation of Defoe, notably *Robinson Crusoe*, which has questioned the now almost orthodox economic interpretation of that novel. M. E. Novak, for example, has lately pointed out that Crusoe is simply not convincing as a type of economic man. Crusoe, carefully considered as a character, does not really turn out to be the embodiment of capitalist principles that many critics would have him. He is, to be sure, inventive and industrious, but his penchant for travelling and what Novak calls his 'unprofitable desire to see foreign lands' make him rather someone who is impelled by a form of religious guilt, by his anxiety over disregarding his father's precepts about the moral value and security of the middle way of life into which God had set him.[1]

Defoe himself took great pains in the *Serious Reflections of Robinson Crusoe* to stress the religious significance of Crusoe's experiences and to point out that Crusoe's story was, like 'the historical Parables in the holy Scripture' and the *Pilgrim's Progress*, allegorical in that it was 'design'd and effectually turn'd for instructive and upright Ends'.[2] One can, as Gildon did in Defoe's own day, object that the 'religious and useful reflections' were craftily inserted in order 'to swell the bulk of Defoe's treatise to a five-shilling book'.[3] But even admitting the highly dubious assertion that Defoe was a pure opportunist, we must conclude that his public liked the religious 'padding', for it is at its most obtrusive and insistent here in Defoe's most popular work. Indeed, despite Gildon's malice, it is clear that the religious patterning is an integral part of Crusoe's narrative, effective and popular as such, whatever Defoe's ultimate motives may have been.[4]

Defence of what have usually been considered Defoe's somewhat disingenuous religious claims has come recently from G. A. Starr, who has pointed out that *Robinson Crusoe* follows the fairly conventional pattern of spiritual autobiography, and that the story

[1] *Economics and the Fiction of Daniel Defoe* (Berkeley and Los Angeles, 1962), pp. 32–48. Novak also points out that Defoe, far from being an instinctively advanced economic spirit, was in many ways quite reactionary in his economic thinking, and most often simply inconsistent and contradictory in his expressed economic views.

[2] *Serious Reflections During the Life and Surprising Adventures of Robinson Crusoe: With His Vision of the Angelick World* (London, 1720), p. 116.

[3] *Robinson Crusoe Examin'd and Criticis'd*, ed. Paul Dottin (London and Paris, 1923), pp. 110–11.

[4] A critical essay *contra* Watt which makes this point well is William H. Halewood's 'Religion and Invention in *Robinson Crusoe*', *Essays in Criticism*, xiv (October 1964), 339–51.

thus records Crusoe's awakening from a state of spiritual unconsciousness to a proper and keen perception of providential
purpose in the events of his life.[1] Defoe's achievement, Starr points
out, is that he leads his hero 'through a series of conventionally
meaningful actions' and thereby avoids the merely homiletic and
static unity of the ordinary spiritual autobiography by fusing
'a great deal of interpretation and comment into the narrative
itself'.[2]

The new emphases of Defoe's effect on his original readers seem
to me entirely just and true to the eighteenth-century importance
of the book. Crusoe consistently describes himself as a penitent
sinner and sees his story as an *exemplum* of the providential sources
of the random events of each man's life. It must be assumed that
his many readers agreed and responded to Crusoe's insistent
affirmations. As Starr has pointed out, Crusoe's island is for him
(whatever it was later for Marx) a providential trial intended to
awaken him from spiritual unconsciousness.[3] That unconsciousness is not, however, simply a negative condition; it is nothing
less than the secular individualism that has made Crusoe leave
home, go to sea, and eventually prosper in Brazil.

What must be added to the current revisionism in Defoe scholarship is that the moralizing in *Robinson Crusoe* and the *Serious
Reflections* has a very noticeable polemical edge; it is directed at
a counter-ideology of secular individualism which insists, in a
sense, upon the implications of modern experience, and thus
effectually denies providential control of the natural and human
orders. In its balancing of secular and religious experience and its
compensation for secular action and power by passivity and submission, *Robinson Crusoe* epitomizes the strategy of popular
religious ideology, not simply, as Watt would have it, Defoe's own
psychosis.[4] The same impulse that produced the many popular
proofs of the reality of the supernatural, anthologies of apparition
evidence gathered, for example, by Joseph Glanvill, George

[1] *Defoe and Spiritual Autobiography* (Princeton, New Jersey, 1965), p. 101,
and pp. 74–125.
[2] Ibid., p. 72.   [3] Ibid., p. 101.   [4] Watt, op. cit., p. 84.

Sinclair, Richard Baxter, and John Dunton,[1] is behind Crusoe's soliloquies and meditations.

This renew'd a Contemplation, which often had come to my Thoughts in former Time, when first I began to see the merciful Disposition of Heaven, in the Dangers we run through in this Life. How wonderfully we are deliver'd, when we know nothing of it. How, when we are in (a Quandary [*sic*], as we call it) a Doubt or Hesitation, whether to go this Way, or that Way, a secret Hint shall direct us this Way, when we intended to go that Way; nay, when Sense, our own inclination, and perhaps Business has call'd to go the other Way, yet a strange Impression upon the Mind, from we know not what Springs, and by we know not what Power, shall overrule us to go this Way, and it shall afterwards appear, that had we gone that Way which we would have gone, we should have been ruin'd and lost. Upon these, and many like Reflections, I afterwards made it a certain Rule with me, that whenever I found those secret Hints, or Pressings of my Mind, to doing, or not doing any Thing that presented; or to going this Way, or that Way, I never fail'd to obey the secret Dictate, though I knew no other Reason for it, then [*sic*] that such a Pressure, or such a Hint hung upon my Mind. ... I cannot but advise all considering Men, whose Lives are attended with such extraordinary Incidents as mine, or even though not so extraordinary, not to slight such secret Intimations of Providence, let them come from what invisible Intelligence they will, that I shall not discuss, and perhaps cannot account for; but certainly they are a Proof of the Converse of Spirits, and the secret Communication between those embody'd, and those unembody'd, and such a Proof as can never be withstood: Of which I shall have Occasion to give some very remarkable Instances, in the Remainder of my solitary Residence in this dismal Place.[2]

The last few lines of this passage remind us that this is, if one remembers the historical situation, a dialectical statement directed at those who claim that Providence has had nothing whatever to do with these events. The reiteration of the key theme that Providence is behind natural and human events points to one source of the

---

[1] Coleman O. Parsons, 'Phantom into Fiction', a paper read at the 1951 meeting of the MLA and summarized in *PMLA*, lxvii (February 1952), 144. Parsons makes the extremely interesting suggestion that the 'English short story originated as narrative proof of immortality and an overseeing deity'.

[2] *Robinson Crusoe* (London, 1719), pp. 207–8.

ideological tensions of the day: the defence of the traditional religious view of man against the new secularism of the Enlightenment,[1] the encroaching forces of infidelity. This defensiveness cannot simply be shrugged off as peculiar to the fringes of English Dissenting groups; it is an important and explicit part of such key works as Swift's satires, Berkeley's *Alciphron*, and Bishop Butler's *Analogy*. The philosophic argument and intellectual tensions of such polemicists, filtered through pulpit and pamphlet and supplemented by the usual Christian dialectic of man versus the world, the flesh, and the devil, produce a vivid if misleading impression of battle with a mobilized and powerful opponent.

Defoe's Crusoe, then, is for his eighteenth-century audience a hero who participates in this struggle. His validity as a character is not simply psychological but polemical; his discovery of religious meaning is in the context of the age a heroic and controversial act. We must add the role of religious hero to those of intrepid traveller and heroic castaway if we are to understand Crusoe's great appeal for his age. The great value of recovering the religious ideology behind an enormously popular work like *Robinson Crusoe* is that we can see how essential a factor that ideology was in its popularity.

Now, of course, it will not be argued that the enormously varied output of popular prose narrative can be neatly explained as pious

[1] This continuous polemic against secularism is well documented. God was, in Carl Becker's epigram, on trial in those years. See *The Heavenly City of the Eighteenth Century Philosophers* (New Haven, 1959), p. 73. The atmosphere, as a recent historian of the period has noted, was not one of languid doubt but of crucial and critical tension between opposing philosophies. See Ronald Stromberg, *Religious Liberalism in Eighteenth Century England* (Oxford, 1954), p. 1. Peter Gay has summed up the differences between our own day and the eighteenth century in just these terms: 'Theology was still important and still familiar; theological controversies had far more than academic interest—they went to the heart of daily concerns, to the very meaning of existence. It is no longer fashionable to speak of the warfare between science and theology, and in truth the seventeenth and eighteenth centuries produced a finely shaded spectrum of beliefs and tolerated close alliances between scientists and theologians, God and nature, the pulpit and the laboratory. Nevertheless, the notion of two parties, of believers against unbelievers, retains much validity.' See *The Party of Humanity* (London, 1964), p. 45.

In England orthodoxy felt itself attacked on all sides by deists, aetheists, and freethinkers, and the late seventeenth and early eighteenth centuries produced, as Ernest Mossner has shown, literally hundreds of defences of Christianity. See *Bishop Butler and the Age of Reason* (New York, 1936), pp. 69–70.

polemic in very effective disguise. There are, indeed, a significant number of works, such as the novels of Mrs. Aubin and the novellas of Mrs. Rowe, which owe their success to their use of this ideological framework, and part of the following essay will describe their works as the clearest and most explicit embodiments of an ideological pattern of beleaguered and necessarily 'helpless' virtue in a vicious and 'aggressive' world. But to say that all the narratives in question are at bottom, even unwittingly, religious parables is merely to substitute another reduction for the economic and political ones which must also be rejected. The object is not to reduce popular narrative to a single meaning; the point is that all this material, even the clearly pornographic or scandalous, depends upon a moral superstructure, a framework of sustaining assumptions within which compelling fantasies (of sex or power, for example) can be delivered safely and effectively. I will attempt to draw out those assumptions, to recreate what Kenneth Burke has called a 'scene', that is, the setting or background considered not as merely a backdrop or convenient locale but as a field of action which contains a certain number of possible actions, much the way a football field is no longer simply a plot of earth but a world of definite and limited achievements.[1]

The possibilities of this approach can be illustrated briefly with an extreme example. Mrs. Manley's *New Atalantis* (1709) presents its scandalous eroticisms through an allegorical fiction which is at least incongruous. Astrea has returned to earth to see if men have improved since she left and meets her mother, Lady Virtue, all in rags, who tells her that men are as corrupt as ever and shows her some notable examples. With the aid of another allegorical friend, euphemistically called 'Intelligence', she presents at length the story of the rise to power of Marlborough (Fortunatus) and the ruling Whig faction.[2] After hearing of the pathetic death of one of

---

[1] Burke outlines in the opening chapter of *A Grammar of Motives* (New York, 1952), p. xvi, his very suggestive method of analysis which he calls 'dramatism', and which he says 'invites one to consider the matter of motives in a perspective that, being developed from the analysis of drama, treats language and thought primarily as modes of action'.

[2] For a fuller treatment of the episode, see below, Chapter IV.

the ladies a certain duke has debauched and then left, Astrea moralizes:

I do not so much condemn the Duke for quitting as corrupting her; one is natural, and but the consequence of the other; methinks it shou'd not be the least inducement for Ladies to preserve their Honour, that let 'em be never so ill used by the Person that robs 'em of it, by any Art or Pretence whatsoever, tho' the World may condemn and call him a Villain, yet they never pity her; the reason is plain, Modesty is the *Principle*, the Foundation upon which they ought to build for *Esteem* and *Admiration*, and that once violated, they totter, and fall, dash'd in pieces upon the obdurate Land of Contempt, from whence no kind Hand can ever be put forth, either to rescue or to compassionate 'em. Men may regain their Reputations, tho' after a Complication of Vices, *Cowardice, Robbery, Adultery, Bribery*, and *Murder*, but a Woman once departed from the Road of Virtue, is made incapable of a return; Sorrow and Scorn overtake her, and, as I said before, the World suffers her to perish loath'd, and unlamented.[1]

Malice and lubricity, the chief attractions of her work for eighteenth-century readers,[2] are being presented within and upheld by the moral superiority of the heroine and the reader to the 'world', here specifically a masculine world which imposes a cruel double standard of morality.

Mrs. Manley's hectic narratives depend for their effects upon a stylized world of absolute masculine corruption, where all values are totally reversed and understood as such by the worldly. Only the heroine preserves her innocence, and we readers (who are sadly wiser but deeply sympathetic) look on in horror as she is deceived and then undeceived. The erotic simplicity which can cause the hapless heroines to desire their seducers at the risk of losing all social status is balanced by the complicated selfishness

[1] Mary de la Rivière Manley, *Secret Memoirs and Manners of several Persons of Quality, of Both Sexes from the New Atalantis, an Island in the Mediteranean* [sic], *Written Originally in Italian* (London, 1709), p. 83.

[2] G. B. Needham has drawn a convincing picture of Mrs. Manley as a political writer and provided a long defence and account of her secret histories as political tracts. See 'Mary de la Rivière Manley: Tory defender', *HLQ*, xii (1949), 253–88. Needham notes that Mrs. Manley's notoriety probably arose 'more from the allurement that her fiction gave to the recital of amours than from the scandal itself' (p. 287).

natural to the masculine ego. Thus, Mosco, who has had an affair with Zarah, is threatened by her when he grows cold.[1] He goes to see her:

> She was all Joy, and new Transport to see him; 'twas as if she had never been in pain. She told him he must lie there that Night: He said nothing to contradict her. They supp'd with her Mother, who afterwards withdrew to order the Linen for his Bed. All the good Nature he was Master of could not force him to shew Tenderness where he had so strong an Aversion. He ask'd himself whence it came, that a Person of her Youth and Charms, with all that's endearing in the Sex, excess of Truth and excess of Love, could not in the least sway his obdurate Heart to a return? He found the fatal Secret, he had been happy, and that prevented him from being still so; Satiety and Loathing succeeded, his Reason could not preside over his Appetite; he could eat no more, however delicate was the Banquet, and therefore it must be remov'd.[2]

These psychological-erotic truisms are supplemented by the social and economic 'realities' to which the male ego is attuned. Zarah drowns herself the night after Mosco tells her, in effect, that she is a primitive fool in a highly sophisticated and complex world.

> Alas! beautiful Zara! What can I answer? nothing, I fear, but will be disagreeable to your Expectations. You don't know the World; you are ignorant of Mankind. 'Tis in our power to marry ourselves but once, that is a fundamental establish'd Law, as long as that Wife shall live; I did not doubt but you knew this, and when I first gain'd the Pleasures of your Love, said the contrary, only to allow your Virtue that pretence for yielding; but we must be both utterly void of common Sense, to go to pass such a Marriage upon the World; me to abandon a Lady by whom I have so many Children, and other Benefits, to ruin my own Reputation and yours, for an airy Notion, by which we make our selves obnoxious to the Laws, and hated by mankind. You will object the Promises I made you, it would be much greater Madness to perform 'em, neither did I think you seriously expected it; no wise Woman

---

[1] Mrs. Manley is here drawing upon an old scandal of 1699 in which Spencer Cowper, younger member of an eminent Whig family, was accused of murdering one Sarah Stout, who seems to have committed suicide because she loved the married Cowper. The charges seem to have been unfounded, and Cowper (the poet's grandfather) was cleared. See *DNB*, xii.

[2] *The New Atalantis*, p. 239.

reckons upon the performance of those extravagant things that are said to gain her.[1]

Mosco has the letter of the law on his side, but he has played false, calculated and contrived a seduction. Zarah is technically an adulteress, but she has acted in good faith, betrayed not only by Mosco but by her own overpowering (and therefore blameless) impulsion to love. Having stooped to folly in a world which calls her spontaneity 'an airy Notion', she can only wring her hands and die. The eroticism which suffuses all of this is given shape by the moral antithesis of the cunning and worldly seducer and the innocent and unworldly victim, whose sexuality is rendered in elaborate periphrases and euphemisms which effectively 'spiritualize' it. Male sexuality is conceived as ruthlessly self-seeking, limited by economic and political realities (wives bring status, wealth, and stability, i.e. continuity of estates through children), and consistently degraded as simply another bodily appetite, regular and mechanical in its promptings rather than mysterious and spontaneous in the way of women's quasi-'spiritual' compulsions. I am not saying, of course, that the diffused sexuality of the heroine is an authentic religious feeling, but that the moral polarities within which she achieves her erotic-pathetic effects were designed (deliberately or instinctively) to evoke and exploit the moral-religious resonances of isolated innocence in a depraved and corrupt world.

Now this implicit moral antithesis has very little outward connection with the explicit ideology which informs a work like *Robinson Crusoe*. The *New Atalantis* is aimed at a different audience, or perhaps at different moods and needs of the same audience. Both these very popular books, however, may be said to exploit the same novelistic ideology; both resolve themselves into pictures of the embattled individual in a hostile and vicious world, and both dramatize the natural and spontaneous urgings of an inner spirit versus the mechanized and corruptly efficient institutions of the world. Both, although in entirely different ways, achieve their larger effects as narratives by confronting an opposing ideology

[1] Ibid., pp. 240-1.

which some in the eighteenth century recognized as the increasingly corrupt spirit of the times, the condition diagnosed by satirists like Swift and Mandeville which we can now, perhaps, call the secular spirit of the modern age.

It may well be that the moral and religious antitheses to be found in popular works like *Robinson Crusoe* and the *New Atalantis* derive ultimately from some sort of Protestant archetype of the individual's theological condition; the parallel seems striking and the hypothesis attractive. But this essay contents itself with the broad and more modest hypothesis that each of these ideological patterns reflects in its own way an eighteenth-century version of the traditional confrontation of the secular and the religious.

In outlining this opposition, I do not claim that I have found an ideological key to the age, the secret spring of the *Zeitgeist*. I say simply that such an antithesis obviously appealed to many readers of popular fiction, exercising the imaginations and emotions of people who doubtless lost little sleep otherwise worrying about the movements of secret secular forces.

My interests and perspectives are literary rather than theological, and these patterns are of interest because they illuminate the nature of popular narrative in the early eighteenth century before the great mid-century masters. These patterns constitute the ideological matrix, as it were, out of which Richardson's and Fielding's characters are to emerge and in which they obtain their significance. What will be attempted in the following essay is a description and analysis of the fictional and semi-fictional narratives from the period 1700–39 which will arrange a representative selection of these according to what can be called their ideological strategies.

II

ROGUES AND WHORES:
HEROES AND ANTI-HEROES

THE importance of the 'literature of roguery' in the development of the novel has long been recognized. The indigenous tradition of English criminal biographies traced long ago by F. W. Chandler in the *Literature of Roguery* (1907) incorporated elements of the continental picaresque tale and a native journalistic instinct for the notorious and the sensational. With their interest in the at once sordid and ordinary backgrounds of criminals and crimes and their journalistic need to provide at least an illusion of circumstantial fact, such narratives were clearly an important factor in the development of the modern realistic novel. Their eighteenth-century popularity, it can be argued plausibly, is a sign of a burgeoning market for reading matter that is bluntly free of any evasions or euphemisms. Here, obviously, we have the most blatant gesture of the merely literate masses for 'literature' which is as brutal as life itself can often be, for narratives which really provide (despite their pious prefaces) sheer diversion rather than decorous delight and instruction. Such narratives, says the literary historian with some justification, are important chiefly as documents in the evolution of realism.

Yet once this has been said, we really know that these works were not sent merely to prepare the way for the novel proper. We can if we like speak of the novel as partially fertilized by certain naturalistic elements in popular journalism such as criminal narrative, although one must wonder why the crop was so slow, those elements having been present in sensational journalism at least throughout the seventeenth century. But too much importance has doubtless been attached to the popular taste for journalistic realism and not enough attention has been paid to the ideological significance of popular literature, the social, moral, and religious values which it implicitly communicates and depends upon. Criminal fiction helps to perpetuate the criminal as a compelling and fascinating type-figure not simply because he and his environment satisfy a need for the recognizable rather than the ideal in literature, but also because his story and its significance evoke and exploit the deepest hopes and fears of his audience. Moreover, the 'realistic' world of underworld fiction and criminal journalism is, upon examination, an exotic place where mythological simplicities prevail. Criminal biography, in other words, is a species of fantasy which gives us access to part of the literary sub-culture of the early eighteenth century.

It is, of course, customary to shrug off the continued popularity of criminal narratives by drawing an analogy between them and modern tabloid journalism; both cater shamelessly to the apparently natural appetites of readers for the morbid and the gory. The uses of a sub-cultural form like criminal biography are thus lumped with the rough pleasures that attracted the many to public executions and blood sports. Yet it is a form of useless and antiquated self-righteousness to despise sub-culture as merely meaningless and degrading distraction for the masses. The sensationalism which played the largest role in attracting readers to criminal biography was not gratuitous but depended upon an ideological context for its force; the criminal's violence shocked because it violated the most important taboos of the social groups that read his story. An examination of the criminal narrative tradition as it existed during the early eighteenth century should help us to define that ideological context more clearly and exactly and to qualify the usual link between underworld realism and the development of the novel.

The most elementary form of criminal journalism was the casual pamphlet or broadside occasioned by sensational crime. This was presented with the same nervous indignation that still characterizes journalism of this sort. Thus, a 1703 pamphlet apologizes for its lurid exactness by a barrage of adjectives: *An Account of a most Barbarous and Bloody Murther Committed on Sunday last, by*

Mr. James Smith . . . on the Body of one Mr. Cluff . . . With an
Account of how he mangled his Body in a most Barbarous manner,
Cut off his Left Hand, and Stabb'd him in several places of the
Body, leaving him Dead upon the place, with other particulars relat-
ing to the occasion of that Inhuman Action. We are told how Smith,
angered by Cluff's request for fees for services rendered,

stabb'd him in several places of his Body, and repeated his Barbarous
Cruelty till he had cut him almost to pieces, notwithstanding the other
often beg'd his Life, but all in vain for he never ceased till he had
Murthered him in the most loathsom and barbarous manner as ever
was heard of . . . And thus was this Innocent Person made a Sacrifice
by those Hands who ought to have rewarded him with friendly Bounty
and Benevolence.

In breathless pamphlets such as this one the natural emphasis
falls on the act itself, the sensational news which is pinpointed in
time and space. The criminal himself matters much less than his
act in this sort of journalism. A somewhat more elaborate and fuller
journalistic product, an eight- or fifteen-page pamphlet costing
perhaps sixpence or so, enlarges the act to include its circumstances:
the motives and results of crime. The transition is from the mysterious and startling public act to the biographical completeness
which surrounds the sensational violence when it is seen as the
natural and logical result of a lifetime of moral miscalculation.
The criminal act here becomes testimony to the character of the
criminal; the burden of the sensationalism is carried by the
criminal himself rather than his deed. He becomes, albeit in a
crude and blunt way, the type of sinful man desperately confronting imminent death loaded with palpable guilt. The biographical
frame of reference, the 'system' into which events are fitted, is that
of popular religion with its simplifying and dramatizing tendencies.

Such emphases make many such pamphlets mild and inoffensive
to modern eyes. Typical is an eight-page pamphlet published in
1708: *The Whole Life and Conversation, Birth, Parentage and*
Education of Deborah Churchill; Condemn'd some time since for
the Barbarous Murder of Mr. William Ware in Drury Lane, and
now brought down to her former Judgment. As Also, Her Behaviour,

Confession, and last Dying-Words at the Place of Execution. This is
a straightforward narrative of the career of a whore, but salacious
details such as a modern tabloid can easily muster for any occasion
are few. The biographical scope promised in the title is hardly
fulfilled; the murder itself is referred to only in passing. Indeed,
the impact of the narrative, its sensational highlight, is that Mrs.
Churchill is the specific object of divine wrath: 'And now, like
most Mistresses of the Town, as she had been kept by several
before, she must now have a Paramour of her own, and Engag'd
her self with one Richard Hunt of the Life-Guard, with whom she
liv'd in unlawful Pleasure. But Heaven, that saw the Pride and
Wickedness of her sinful life, Providentially brought her thus to a
Shameful Death....'[1] Of course, this is partly a normal pious ejacu-
lation; all sinners are punished by God. But some are obviously, the
pamphlet makes clear, singled out and made examples to others:
'she was call'd down to her former Judgment, and with nine more
Malefactors received Sentence of Death, all which, as 'tis remarkable, were Repriev'd but herself.'[2]

This matter-of-fact interpretation of events as portents of
inescapable divine punishment for individuals is a commonplace
of popular eschatology and apologetics. The condemned criminal
faces the last things and confesses that he feels the finger of God.
He grows amazingly eloquent under the circumstances and feels
his own significance. *The Life and Penitent Death of John Mawg-
ridge, Gent. Who was Executed for the Murder of Captain Cape ...
With Reflexions on the Whole* (1708) thus ends with a long confession delivered by a soldier and man-of-the-town in the form of a
sermon, once again stressing the particular purpose of Providence:

And here, I desire to give a word or two of Advice or Warning, that,
if possible, it may lead some to Repentance: For they must not expect
to have any come from the Dead to warn them; but here is one that is
just going to the Dead, who bequeaths them this Legacy, lest some of
them, in like manner, be made Monuments of God's Wrath and Displeasure. For God has singled me out in this Case, and set me forth
to be an Example to you. He might have chose some of you, to have

been Examples to me, and other; but to the great Council of God, it has seem'd meet to take me, and leave you; and in taking me, has left you this solemn Warning; which, if you accept not, it shall be a Testimony against you at the last Day.[1]

Lacking credible supernatural visitors and extremely aware of the threatening atmosphere of unbelief around spiritual things, the eighteenth century was quite ready to see the sinner about to die as an awful reminder of the wages of sin, and popular religious sensationalism was quite ready to exploit the terror and uncertainty that surrounded the condemned man as proof of the reality of guilt and punishment in eternity. We notice the evangelical strategies and biblical echoes of the prose in this selection and the allegorical suggestions of 'Monuments of God's Wrath and Displeasure', and we can recognize the affinity of popular journalism to the more obvious turns of popular pulpit oratory. There are, of course, other examples of this casual or occasional criminal journalism which employ the theological pattern of sin, repentance, and imminent divine judgement in a much more off-hand and perfunctory way; but the pattern, whatever the degree of emphasis, is a standard one.

The sources for these various accounts and confessions were the commercially published Sessions Papers, which gave reports of the trials at the Old Bailey, and the descriptions of the last hours and executions of notorious malefactors published by the various Ordinaries of Newgate.[2] The former were sometimes summaries, sometimes apparently almost *verbatim* accounts of the various cases tried. The latter were undeniable 'scoops', on-the-spot accounts published the morning after the executions,[3] but in spite of their opportunistic eagerness unimpeachably devotional in presentation. Doubtless the Ordinary stood to gain something other than converts from his publishing efforts, but the pamphlets are quite honestly if monotonously concerned with describing his attempts

---

[1] p. 15.

[2] The Ordinary, of course, was the chaplain of Newgate, part of whose official duties was to prepare the condemned for death.

[3] In the *DNB* article (vol. xxxiv) on Paul Lorrain (Ordinary from 1698 to 1719), Thomas Seccombe notes that the pamphlets were issued at 8 o'clock in the morning following the execution.

to awaken the various malefactors to some sense of their guilt and the possibility and necessity of repentance.

Typically, the Ordinary explained briefly the nature of the crimes committed by the condemned, related in detail the spiritual strategies he employed—key texts quoted, Christian consolations repeated or explained, and auricular confession recommended—and reported the prisoner's response to these ministrations. Most repent, some brought, we are told, to almost beatified calmness in the face of death.[1] Here the excitement is clearly evangelical, the pamphlets building up to the execution as the climactic moment.

I laid before them the little Time that was between them and the Dark Night of Eternity, earnestly desiring them to improve every moment to their Souls [*sic*] Advantages, and to cry mightily to that God who was able to save them at the last Moment with true Repentance, through the Merits of a Crucified Saviour. I exhorted them to stir up their Hearts to God more and more to clear their Consciences, and to discover anything they knew might be of use to the World. They acknowledged they were Guilty of the Facts for which they were now to Suffer. They desired all Spectators to take Warning by them, and to pray for them; wishing that all that knew them would become wiser and surer by their shameful Death, so as they might not come to the same condemnation. . . . When I had perform'd the Offices requisite for my Function, and sung a penitential Psalm, I wished them a happy Passage out of this Life into a better, and recommended their Souls to God's boundless Mercy in Christ. Then they pray'd for some minutes by themselves, and then were turned off; calling upon God all the while to have Mercy upon their Souls, and open the Gate of Heaven to them.[2]

Sometimes, the Ordinary describes himself as victor in a struggle for the criminal's soul. The famous pirate, Captain Kidd, proves

[1] *Spectator*, no. 338, contains a humorous reference to the somewhat deliberate presentation of the execution scene. Complaining of humorous epilogues to tragic plays, 'Physibulous' concludes: 'One knows not what further ill Effects the Epilogues I have been speaking of may in Time produce: But this I am credibly inform'd of, that Paul Lorrain [see p. 27, n. 3, above] has resolv'd upon a very suddain Reformation in his tragical Dramas; and that at the next Monthly Performance, he designs, instead of a Penitential Psalm, to dismiss his Audience with an excellent new Ballad of his own composing.'

[2] *The Ordinary of Newgate's Account of the Life, Conversation, Birth and Education, of Thomas Ellis, and Mary Goddard. Who were executed at Tyburn, on Wednesday, the Third of March, 1708.*

lukewarm in his penitence, and arrives at the place of execution 'inflamed with Drink; which had so discomposed his Mind, that it was now in a very ill frame, and very unfit for the great Work, now or never, to be perform'd by him'. Kidd then refuses 'to own the Justice of his Condemnation, or so much as the Providence of God, who for his Sins, had deservedly brought him to this un-timely End'. But then, accidentally or providentially, the rope with which Kidd is tied breaks, and he falls to the ground alive.

When he was brought up, and ty'd again to the Tree I desired leave to go to him again, which was granted. Then I shew'd him the great mercy of God to him in giving him (unexpectedly) this farther Respite, that so he might improve the few moments, now so mercifully allotted him, in perfecting his Faith and Repentance. Now I found him in much better temper than before. But as I was unwilling . . . to offer any thing to him by way of question, that might perhaps have discomposed his Spirit, so I contented my self to press him to embrace (before it was too late) the Mercy of God, now again offer'd him, upon the easy Conditions of stedfast Faith, true Repentance, and perfect Charity. Which now indeed he did so fully and freely express, that I hope he was hearty and sincere in it; declaring openly that he repented with all his Heart, and Dy'd in Christian Love and Charity with all the World.[1]

Now, from our point of view, the Ordinary could have written much more interesting and convincing pamphlets if he had de-scribed the more secular aspects of the execution and told us more about the blasphemy and despair which he doubtless witnessed more often than hopeful resignation. That he did not write such accounts is not so much a testimony to his integrity as it is to the intrinsic sensationalism and immediate appeal which the spectacle of sinful man confronting certain death and faced with the terrible uncertainty of divine judgement still possessed for his readers.

Chandler notes that by 1730 this sort of separate criminal pam-phlet was on the wane, replaced by more elaborate collected chronicles of crime and by fuller and more circumstantial 'confes-sions', sometimes as long and involved as *Moll Flanders* and *Colonel*

---

[1] *The Ordinary of Newgate his Account of the Behaviour, Confessions, and Dying-Words of Captain William Kidd, and other Pirates, that were Executed at the Execution-Dock in Wapping, on Friday May 23, 1701.*

Jacque.[1] These longer and more complicated narratives are naturally more diverse in their attractions than the sensational pamphlets we have discussed so far; the historical facts are swelled by
anecdotes, jests, traditional 'trickster' pranks, and by sheer invention. But throughout this process of proliferation and complication,
one notices very little change in the basic procedure of criminal
biographies. They are written as if to a formula. All include the
journalistic essentials—details of parentage, education, early
employment, names of confederates, amount of proceeds from
crimes, record of arrests and punishments, and so on—and as
W. R. Irwin in his study of Fielding's *Jonathan Wild* and its
background points out after surveying the material, 'characterization of criminals contained in them was violent, but stereotyped;
their subjects were invariably incarnations of vice. Their sketch of
the criminal's social milieu was always the same. The pattern on
which they were constructed was conventional to the point of
monotony.'[2]

Such standardization was due partly to the inept and unimaginative hacks who ground them out, but also to the needs of the market
which consumed criminal biographies. What was involved was the
shrewd repetition of a highly saleable and successful pattern, a
pattern whose success owed as much to its manipulation of certain
fascinating and compelling themes as to its successful description
of a recognizable and convincing underworld milieu. The inefficiency of the sensationalism, the only intermittent bursts of specifically shocking particulars, the very monotony that Irwin complains
of, point to an imperfectly formed literary medium, closer to the
narrative point of view of the homily and the sermon than to the
modern ideal of journalistic objectivity. The longer and collected
chronicles of crime, in other words, share with the short reports
already described a fundamentally religious sensationalism which
sustains a good part of its attractive horror by the exploitation of
the drama of sin, repentance, and judgement.

The criminal tends to lose his secular individuality in such a

---

[1] F. W. Chandler, *The Literature of Roguery* (New York, 1907), p. 164.
[2] *The Making of Jonathan Wild* (New York, 1941), pp. 83-4.

situation, for the purposes of the story are best served not by separating him as a unique individual from the rest of mankind but by emphasizing the relevance of his career to the life of every man who reads his story. His ultimate psychological definition is in generalized moral terms rather than in the existential specifics we expect of all characters, no matter how poorly or inefficiently conceived. Indifference to the social and economic sources of criminal behaviour points, in this context, not to insensitivity but to a different conception of the nature of evil. The criminal's acts are, on this popular religious level, manifestations of Satan and his power. Evil is personified and described as an agent in the world, not as the tragic result of social injustice or oppression but as evidence of a menacing spirit who battles with men and God. The point of view of criminal narrative never essentially departs from the sermonizing of the Ordinary of Newgate. The criminal is led astray by an interior inclination to evil or by evil companions and loose habits, but those temptations and occasions are rendered not in psychological or sociological terms but in the broad rhetorical flourishes of pulpit oratory.

The criminal's cardinal sin, as he himself can come to see in his moment of repentance, is to ignore Providence (his desperate acts are aggressive challenges to the natural order represented by the social and economic order of society); and his salvation is to recognize the necessity and wisdom of submission to control from above. To put it another way, the criminal's sin is individualism; the shock of the narrative comes from realizing that this temporarily successful Satanic enterprise at self-determination has been doomed all along by the divine machinery of death and judgement. In literary terms, the thematic structure of criminal narrative by its very nature tends to exceed the realistic reportage as the effective part of the narrative, and the moral meaning thereby assumes almost allegorical status.

The importance of this religious allegorical tendency in popular literature has been neglected. It deserves study because these vestiges of the older religious frame of reference are as important for the achievements of Defoe and Richardson as their touch for the realistic rendering of events. Criminal fiction, by its very lack of fusion between the two narrative purposes of realistic depiction and moral generalization, allows us to see the latter all the more clearly, to understand the moral structure which is present in a more subtle and integrated way in real novelists.

Defoe himself was certainly aware of this mixture of the literal and the allegorical in fiction, and the secret of his success both in criminal narrative and in other types is his ability to fuse these two elements successfully. His 'theory of fiction', as M. E. Novak has recently called it, 'enabled him to treat his characters and their problems with a mixture of seriousness and humour and to add to the realistic descriptions of a work like *A Journal of the Plague Year* a sense of the social, religious, economic, political and moral implications of events which had no parallel in fiction until the nineteenth century'.[1] Novak may be claiming too much here, and he surely sees implications that Defoe and his audience could not. What we can be certain of are Defoe's strenuous and repeated protests that his stories were also intended to be read as parables and allegories, or at least that they were most worthily apprehended if such figurative meanings were kept firmly in mind. His prefaces consistently employ this sort of terminology in defence of fiction. The preface to *Colonel Jacque* (1722) can serve as a *locus classicus*, for it is indeed emphatic in stressing the exemplary uses of the book. The truth of the book, the preface concludes, is really irrelevant, since 'whether the Colonel hath told his own Story true or not; If he has made it a history or a Parable, it will be equally useful, and capable of doing Good; and in that it recommends itself without any other Introduction'.[2]

We are used to literary historians dwelling on the elaborate procedures of early eighteenth-century authors and booksellers to disguise fiction as fact, of the absolute aversion of stolid middle-class folk or pious Dissenters to fiction presented as such. Defoe, to be sure, insists that the people and the events are real, but he

---

[1] 'Defoe's Theory of Fiction', *SP*, lxi (October 1964), 668.
[2] *The History and Remarkable Life of the truly Honourable Colonel Jacque*, 'The Second Edition' (London, 1723), p. viii.

also insists with equal force, here and notably in the *Serious Reflections of Robinson Crusoe,* that the moral meaning is as important as the literal truth of the story. 'The Fable,' says Robinson Crusoe, 'is always made for the Moral, not the Moral for the Fable.'[1]

This awareness of a meaning other than the literal in his fiction, which seems at first glance a strange denial of that delight in the concrete for which we value him most, is certainly motivated by the great necessity popular narrative had of defending itself as a worth-while pastime. But it is not without significance that the rationale Defoe chose employed terms which sound curiously archaic to us, such as parable and allegory. His choice of terminology (or rather his use of the jargon of popular religion) reminds us, as E. R. Curtius once noted, that 'medieval forms of life subsist till about 1750'.[2] We are close to one of the literary survivals of those medieval forms in the allegorical possibilities that Defoe claimed for his narratives, and even closer in the almost allegorical clashing of forces which is implicit in criminal narrative.

The necessary connection between allegory and the justification of realistic narrative, and the crucial historical importance of the welding together of the two approaches has also been stressed by a recent study of allegory. Angus Fletcher has pointed to Bunyan's 'compromise' between realistic narrative and 'an abstract thematic art deriving from the Bible and the Moralities'[3] as the progenitor of Defoe's almost instinctive combination of these elements. Fletcher's keen reinterpretation of allegory as a 'mode' which cuts across traditional generic classes is extremely suggestive in its insistence that narrative tends to suggest 'powerful thematic conceptions'[4] which undercut the very realism that we presume the novelist seeks. These powerful themes tend to assume, in other words, the independence and reality which concepts are granted from the outset in traditional and explicit allegory.

Given the suggestion that all fiction has some latent allegorical

[1] *Serious Reflections of Robinson Crusoe* (London, 1720), sig. A2ʳ.
[2] *European Literature and the Latin Middle Ages* (London, 1953), p. 589.
[3] *Allegory: The Theory of a Symbolic Mode* (Ithaca, New York, 1964), p. 332.
[4] Ibid., p. 315.

content, we can point out a number of similarities between Fletcher's theory of allegory and criminal biography which reinforce the tendencies we have been attempting to isolate. The criminal of popular eighteenth-century narrative moves in a world which is brutal and degrading, but which is still the medieval one of spirits, witches, the devil, and the ubiquitous operations of Providence. The criminal's crucial act is to forget or defy those principles of external limitation and to insist on his right to what Providence has denied him.

Fletcher distinguishes between mimetic and allegorical drama using just these terms: realistic depiction always insists on a principle of internal change and questions control from above, where allegory always involves a *deus ex machina*. 'Allegory is structured according to ritualistic necessity, as opposed to probability, and for that reason its basic forms differ from mimetic plots in being less diverse and more simple in contour.'[1] This distinction reminds us of the invariability of the criminal's biography; the progress towards death and judgement, and the execution itself are clear examples of ritualistic necessity—crime *never* pays in criminal narrative. Similarly, criminal biography is reducible to the standard allegorical patterns which Fletcher calls progress and battle. The criminal is engaged in battle with society and the laws of God, and he progresses towards the devil and damnation. Finally, the criminal, in the violence of his career and in his desperate repentance before the scaffold, embodies the ethical extremes of hope and despair. The highlights of his career are potentially emblematic tableaux of those allegorical extremes.

To be sure, this discussion of criminal narrative can hardly claim that these religious allegorical tendencies are signs that the type is really a very clever form of devotional exercise. Criminal biography is obviously geared to gratify a need for vicarious violence and adventure, but those activities acquire their forbidden and therefore attractive value in a religious frame of reference. The criminal, it must be insisted, is both hero and anti-hero to his eighteenth-century audience. His career evokes the desire for

[1] *Allegory: The Theory of a Symbolic Mode*, p. 150.

secular freedom and economic self-determination which is a real part of the outlook of the age; but this latent social aggression is, at the same time, a source of guilt and anxiety which must be severely and decisively punished. The criminal, as a type figure, is a necessary social myth whose triumphs and abasements mirror the ideological tension between the new secular world of action and freedom and the old religious values of passivity and submission. Highwaymen and whores are heroes, in that their stories are gratifying fantasies of freedom—moral, economic, and erotic. But this freedom is necessarily desperate, for the social myth includes the fear that divine surveillance and mysterious retribution are inescapable. The criminal's end, whether stressed in the narrative or not, provides further gratification and completes the myth, as he suffers for the guilty power and independence which he and his readers have desired and enjoyed. He becomes, in effect, a scape-goat.

All of this is offered as a paradigm with an admittedly synthetic unity, a social myth which has no single or exhaustive source and cannot really be reduced to any definitive and final form. My argument is that each criminal narrative both contributes to and draws its force from the myth, which is thus clear in its main outlines if never quite static in actual existence. The following discussion attempts to illustrate the paradigm and to account for variations from it by considering the features of three fairly distinct types of popular criminal narrative: whore biography, picaro-prankster stories, and criminal biography proper.

The first is mainly comic, or at least begins in comedy. The whore, certainly the one successful and notorious enough in fact or fiction to be celebrated in popular biography, is the opportunist *par excellence*, the entrepreneur who exploits her fallen condition to rise in the world of men, who deliberately makes her spiritual ruin her material enrichment. She achieves power, pleasure (she takes great personal pleasure in her work; there are no suffering whores with hearts of gold and tender sensibilities), and independence impossible to eighteenth-century un-emancipated woman. Her success is an absolute denial of the theoretical definitions of society and of social worthiness, for her activities are really a form of radical social aggression. The resulting incongruity is inherently funny, for all men are reduced to the level of potential clients, helpless pawns in an erotic game controlled by the whore. The explicitly erotic, as the later *Fanny Hill* makes quite clear, was comic and sinful in that order to the eighteenth century. In the volatile careers of eighteenth-century whores, it is depicted as both, but the more frequent emphasis falls on the comic.

A good example of this comic emphasis is the 1723 *Authentick Memoirs of the Life Intrigues and Adventures of the Celebrated Sally Salisbury* by one Captain Charles Walker.[1] This is a mock-heroic account which ranks Sally with the most famous loose women of antiquity and comments ironically on the social usefulness of the profession to which she belongs: 'It must be allowed, that such Gay Volunteers as your Ladyship, give a young Fellow an handsome Prospect of the Town, lead him thro' all the inchanting Mazes, and even surfeit him with Delight; so that by the time he is come out of your Hands, he is grown very Tame and prepared for the dull Solemnity of Marriage.'[2]

This is followed by a series of scabrous and frequently brutal stories. The intent is humour of a very rough-and-ready sort, but the anecdotes are rather on a comic epic than a naturalistic scale— comic or brutal exaggerations depending on the delicacy of the reader. Some of these anecdotes, which are cleverly presented as letters from former customers of Sally, purport to be scandalous, relating her services to well-known aristocrats and politicians. The following, featuring the 'Eldest Son of a Son of a certain Nobleman', is typical of the book in its mixture of the brutal and the erotic delivered in an at least partially moralizing ironic style. The gentleman, having spent the night with Sally, is in bed with her when

. . . an Undertaker knock'd at the Door, and ask'd to speak with the Gentleman, the Servant answer'd, He was a Sleep, and could not be

---

[1] 'Captain Charles Walker' may have existed, but he has not survived in any of the biographical compendia available to me. The important point to make about the authors of ephemeral productions such as this is that they were probably pseudonyms most of the time for publishers' hacks.

[2] Sig. B4ᵛ.

Disturb'd, the Undertaker told him he must and would speak with him. This Dispute awaked the Gentleman, and he knowing the Voice, Cry'd D—n you Matt, What a P—x has brought you hither this Morning? Matt, in a sniveling Tone answer'd, My Lord, I am come to Condole with your Lordship, for the Loss of your Father; What a P—x (says the Lord) is my Father dead at last then? With that he jump'd out of Bed, took hold of the Bed-Cloaths at the Feet, and roll'd them up to the Head, which discover'd a most beautiful pair of Legs, Thighs, and so upwards, to the very Bubbies, for the Good'natur'd Creature had pull'd her Shift up to the Arm-pits that it might be no obstacle to their Diversion. This sort of Treatment very much ruffled her Temper, she sprung up, her Hair all flowing about her Shoulders, having lost her Head-Dress in the Encounter, and with a G—d D—n you! You a Lord, You a Pimp! says Sally, to use me in this manner; the young Peer gave her good Words, soon pacify'd her, and at length prevail'd upon her to get up, and take a Bottle with him and Matt, for says he, this Matt is the honestest Fellow in the World, and by G—d he shall Bury my Father. Matt continued bowing and cringing, reply'd, I am greatly oblig'd to your Honour, I am very thankful to your Lordship, 'till they had guzzled down Three or Four Bottles by way of Whet; the Wine had sufficiently warm'd Sally, and, all of a sudden, she flew at the Poor Undertaker, hit him an unmerciful Box on the Ear, D—n you, said she, for a Whining Carrion-hunting Son of a Bitch! What do you come to trouble us with your Cant for, and be D—d to you? Go mind your Insensible Flesh, and leave my Friend and me to enjoy our selves! Matt immediately took his Leave of the Nobleman, and stopp'd short at the Door, to tell my Lord he would go take Measure of the Corpse and so march'd off.[1]

The calculating servility of the undertaker and the callous joy of the new peer are presented in a moral light by the ironic style and the inherently grotesque aspects of the situation, but the anatomical survey of Sally and the leering comedy which takes over when the sexual encounter is described provide pornography as well.

The salacious and scandalous revelations of Sally are the staples of whore biography, but these are more often promised than delivered. The *History of the Life and Intrigues of that Celebrated Courtezan, and Posture-Mistress, Eliz. Mann* (1724), for example,

[1] pp. 47–8.

never gets past her early and quite innocent beginnings as a provincial Irish beauty, but the introduction continues the promises of the title. From it we gather that such biographies were addressed to an audience for whom the 'Hundreds of Drury' was an exotic rather than familiar area, for 'the Reader is to be inform'd, that these Haunts are not only frequented by Wretches of the meanest Condition, but by some Ladies that roll in a superior Orb, who, like the Divinities of Old, did not disdain to steal the soft Pleasures of Love in Mummery and Masquerade'.[1]

Whore biography is inhabited by social stereotypes from the polar extremities of eighteenth-century society and is aimed at those who consider themselves between the extremes. It soon becomes apparent that the stories of whores, like those of highwaymen, tend naturally toward the simple social satire of traditional folk-tales and rogue stories. Whores and highwaymen frequently become sympathetic figures, robbing or poxing with rollicking bravado and making brutal fun of conceptual monsters such as avaricious landlords, canting religionists, vicious aristocrats, or political extremists.

Scandal gives way to these traditional features in the 1729 *Life and Intrigues of the late Celebrated Mrs. Mary Parrimore, The Tall Milliner of 'Change Alley.* Mrs. Parrimore is a Hampshire girl of humble origins ('her Father kept a Slop-Shop') who is besieged by would-be seducers, successfully by one, a midshipman. The sailor goes to sea, but through her father's mercantile cunning she is passed off on the local parson as a worthy and chaste bride. Surprised by her husband soon after in adultery with the local squire, she is taken back when the squire promises the parson a benefice. After another affair in which she is enjoyed by a sea captain and all his officers, she runs away to London and sets up as a prostitute.

There she gulls various customers, notably two clerics of dubious worth: a Dissenting minister who seeks to convert her in order to seduce her, and a beneficed clergyman resident in London while his curates slave in the country. She has 'for some years a prosper-

[1] pp. iii–iv.

ous Trade'[1] which enables her to retire in comfort to the country,
a perfect parody of the successful and righteous merchant. Written
in the familiar mock-heroic style of whore biography, the book
ends with the tragic-comic death of the heroine, who grows bored
in the country and returns to trade again in the city, only to hang
herself when her old clients fail to appear. 'Thus fell the mighty
Parrimore, more worthy Admiration than Imitation; and whose
Talents (better employ'd) would have merited a much better Fate.'[2]
There is a moralistic hint in this conclusion, although hardly
enough to counter the tongue-in-cheek tone; Mrs. Parrimore remains simply the classic picara, and the implications of her story
are the conventionally satiric reversals of rogue literature.

Both the comic and the sinful possibilities of eroticism, amateur
and professional, are exploited in an ambitious collection published
in 1715 and 1716, a volume a year, by Captain Alexander Smith,[3]
the *School of Venus, or Cupid restor'd to Sight; being A History of
Cuckolds and Cuckold-makers*. This begins with a prefatory mixture of innuendo and pious protest which declares that although
the

Subject is wholly Amorous . . . a Vestal, or pious Recluse in a
Christian Nunnery, may safely read it, without danger of seducing a
Religious Probationer of Heaven; For hereby seeing the sudden Rise
and strange Fall of Women, who have proclaim'd themselves open
Enemies to Chastity, a miserable *Catastrophe* oftener attending them
than Prosperity, it plainly indicates that Vice stands not on the same
Level with Virtue, which always is its own Reward.[4]

We are hardly surprised to find that in spite of this claim Smith's
book is often quite as brutally and comically lascivious as others
we have quoted. Here is a sample of the style and manner at their
coarsest: describing the death of a famous whore, Smith tells us

---

[1] p. 77.   [2] p. 78.
[3] Again, nothing is known of 'Captain Smith' except that he was the author
of a number of collections of criminal narrative. It is quite likely that the name
is simply a pseudonym. Indeed, even if something more were known of him, it
would be irrelevant for my purposes, since a study of popular literature as such
has nothing to do with personalities in the biographical-critical sense common
to literary discussion. All references are to the 1716 edition of both volumes.
[4] i, sig. A3.

that she was 'as rotten as a Pear, by her carnal coupling with all Mankind that desired her conversation, which was not to be obtain'd for less than a Guinea, for she always kept up the Price of her Commodity, she departed her miserable Life in 1696, aged 29 Years'.[1]

But, in a way, the outrageous claims of the preface are justified. In spite of the leering vulgarity of the title-page, Smith goes on in his preface to describe the career of a harlot in biblical terms. He quotes Solomon on the result of whoring: 'But her end is bitter as Wormwood, sharp as a two-edged Sword. Her Feet go down to Death: Her Steps take hold on Hell.'[2] He paraphrases this with his own crude but undeniable vigour:

. . . a Strumpet is the Highway to the Devil; and he that looks upon her with Desire, begins his Voyage: He that stays to talk with her mends his pace; and whosoever enjoys her, is at his Journey's end. Her Body is the tilted Lees of Pleasure, dash'd over with a little Decking to hold Colour; but tast her she's dead, and falls flat upon the Palate. Her Trade is opposite to any other, for she sets up without Credit; and too much Custom breaks her. The Money that she gets is like a Traytor's, given only to corrupt her; and what she earns, serves but to pay Diseases. She is ever moor'd in Sin, and ever mending; and after Thirty, she is the Surgeon's only Customer: Wherefore Shame and Repentance are two Strangers to her; and only in an Hospital acquainted.[2]

The violence of the righteousness and its incongruous use of *double entendre* are of a piece with the 'comic' brutality of most of the stories. Once again, a social myth is involved. The inescapable end of any sort of illicit sex act by a woman, whether slyly seduced, raped, or the aggressor herself, is to rot to death in a whorehouse. One of the characters, kept close at home, argues for more liberty and says to her mother, 'it is impossible a Woman that is really Virtuous and remains so, should lose her Honour, unless she be Ravish'd indeed, and then 'tis a Question, whether she loses it or not'. Her mother replies that 'a Woman that is Murdered loses her Life as much as she that dies of a Fever'.[3]

Chastity, the myth insists with a brutal realism that we can only find appalling, is a valuable commodity, a spiritual essence which

[1] i. 185.   [2] i, sig. A4^r.   [3] ii. 151.

has been transformed by what Marxists call 'reification'. There is, in short, no glamorization of the results of sexual adventure; there is, if anything, an exaggeration of the inevitability of disaster for whores and adulteresses. The hard-headed secular reification of chastity has as its corollary the religious sentimentalizing of women, who can only be angels or devils. Once a woman has been ruined, her appetite for vice (which may have been virtually non-existent before the act) is automatic and insatiable. Madam Charlton, for example, is the barren and rigidly virtuous wife of Colonel Charlton. She is seduced only by trickery, 'but when once she came to relish those forbidden Pleasures and grow wanton in the Enjoyment of them, she grew as intemperate as Messalina; having the Impudence of a Bawd, and the Lasciviousness of a common courtezan'.[1]

Again and again the invariable moral pattern of whore biography, the descent into hell, is repeated whatever the comic or erotic attractions of the story. Low sexual comedy is the main feature of Smith's collection, which also features salacious scandal and sensational pseudo-history in its fictionalized accounts of royal and noble mistresses; but all of this is delivered with such brutal emphasis and within such an explicit moral frame of reference that religious sensationalism is an effective part of the presentation.

It is much less of a factor in the popular character of the highwayman or famous male criminal. Even more so than the famous whore or mistress, he may easily be transformed into the traditional rogue or trickster figure of legend and folk-lore. This comic and traditional rogue appears without disguise, for example, in a work published in 1706: *The Scotch Rogue: or the Life and Actions of Donald Macdonald A High-Land Scot*. The sub-title promises diverse entertainment indeed:

Relating his being found in the High-way, and carried home by Curtogh Macdonald to his Wife; and how he was brought up by them: His early Waggeries, and Villanies when he came to Riper Years. His Love-Intrigues, and how many various Fortunes he went thorow, and the Miseries that he endur'd: His Extraordinary Wit and Courage,

[1] ii. 116.

and how he extricated himself out of divers Difficulties, into which his Rogueries had brought him.

Here the legendary is the main ingredient. The hero begins, in fine mythological fashion, as a noble foundling of mysterious birth, left by the road side wrapped in 'a very rich Lac'd Mantle' and with a bag of gold by his side. These noble origins assert themselves spontaneously as he grows: 'I appear'd even in my poor Garments, as I have since been told, of a quite different Air from that of their other Children; so that I was admir'd by all that saw me; and they would frequently say, That I differ'd from all the rest of the Children. . . .'[1]

But one folk theme gives way to another in the confusion, and the noble foundling becomes the amoral trickster. At school, where his foster father has sent him with a view to his entering Aberdeen University, he avenges himself on his enemy, the usher, in Chaucerian fashion. Discovering that the usher and the master's young wife are lovers, he glues their eye-lids shut when they are asleep so that they awake in terror thinking they have gone blind. The master thus catches them *in flagrante delicto* and, to the infinite delight of Donald, the usher is whipped, the wife runs away with money, plate, and jewels, and the master dies of grief and chagrin.

From brutal trickster, Donald is transformed into the third of his mythological manifestations, the swashbuckling highwayman. After a series of rapid adventures and debaucheries, he alone escapes with a great deal of loot and watches as his companions are hanged. He then marries a girl he had seduced and ruined in his youth, but who has since prospered in the world. He leaves his wife after a time and turns highwayman again, promising a second part, which was either never written or does not survive.

The moral frame of reference is invisible here. *The Scotch Rogue* is an exuberant fantasy of freedom whose hero exists in a world of total irresponsibility where guilt never accompanies action. In a tightly hierarchical social and moral world such as that of the early eighteenth century, a character like Donald Macdonald

[1] p. 4.

is a projection of forbidden energies. His palpable unreality and his mysterious birth make it possible for his actions to be enjoyed in a moral vacuum, as 'sheer entertainment' which makes absolutely no pretence to documentation or moral purpose.

Usually, this sort of narrative required both of these. The author of a 1725 account of a no less fanciful hero called *Tom Merryman* does not hesitate to vouch for the truth and moral utility of his book:

It is the common Opinion of most People, that Works of this Nature are fictitious, and calculated rather for Diversion than Instruction. My Aim herein, is not only to divert, but to instruct the Reader; and I do affirm, That all the Facts herein recited, are literally true. There is not one Tale, which does not carry with it some Moral; and though every Story is related either in a Serious, Ludicrous, Tragical, or Comical Manner, yet we may draw good Instructions from them all.[1]

Tom Merryman proves to be as mercurial and daemonic as Donald Macdonald, but he has a firm base in the sordid realities we associate with the eighteenth-century underworld milieu. Instead of assuming the traditional roles of the rogue, Tom passes through various standard contemporary situations, all the while remaining as magnificently unreflective as any traditional rogue.

He begins as the son of a prostitute, orphaned after she is hanged, and brought up by a captain, who is probably his father. He is apprenticed to a mercer, seduces his daughter but refuses to marry her when she becomes pregnant. Turned out by the mercer, he becomes a gigolo, a certain countess paying him liberally for his favours. He is caught by her husband, wounds him in a duel, and runs away in disguise as a captain. In this guise he seduces a goldsmith's wife, comes into an inheritance of £3,000, spends it in three years, and becomes a sharper and swindler. Committed to Newgate for debt, he learns more dissolute habits and marries a Drury Lane whore. The comic gusto of all of this is underlined and turned against any serious exemplary implications

---

[1] *The Matchless Rogue: or, an Account of the Contrivances, Cheats, Stratagems, and Amours of Tom Merryman, commonly called Newgate Tom* (London, 1725), pp. iii–iv.

when Tom's wife expresses a desire to repent. He opposes this and declares himself Baron of Bridewell, Viscount New Prison, Earl of Holborn Hill, Marquis of Newgate, and Duke of Tyburn.

Yet soon after, Tom has a dream in which he is brought to justice and punishment, and the tone changes abruptly as a 'grave Old Gentlewoman' warns him of the dream's significance:

That how incredulous soever he might be and tho' Men of Learning are apt to despise and laugh at Dreams, believing them to be nothing else than the Effects of a vitiated Imagination, occasioned by Fumes, arising from Indigestion; or that they are the Produce of those perplexing Thoughts which incumber and sit heavy upon the Mind at the Hour of Rest: yet, says she, I have found by Experience, that many Occurences of human Life are predicted by Dreams, which, when likely to be attended by evil Consequences, we may with Prudence avoid, and obviate those Dangers that hang over our Head. This, I think, ought to convince and confirm all Mankind, that there is a Divine Providence, which presides over the World, and knows all our Thoughts and Actions, and searches into the deepest Recesses of our Heart, and beholds those Thoughts and Actions even before we ourselves have formed and brought them to Perfection. And it is a manifest Token of the divine Goodness, that he will give us timely Caution to prepare and arm ourselves against those Dangers that impend over our Heads, and which we may frustrate by making a right Use of his kind Admonition, by having due Regard to his Salutary Forewarnings.[1]

Tom merely laughs at all this. We, presumably, do not, for this passage carries the serious ideological burden of the work. If Tom's escapades provide the diversion (from one point of view the guilty, vicarious joys of absolute freedom and irresponsibility), then this passage and several more scattered throughout, pasted in at intervals, provide the instruction. Directed at the sceptical modern élite from the deeply reactionary wisdom of the masses, the passage is the explicit reverse of all that is implicit in the narrative; for it makes of Tom's story a pious *exemplum* of the wages of heedless sin.

Of course, the book is nothing of the sort most of the time. Tom

[1] pp. 52–3.

continues to prosper, for a while legitimately as the owner of a brandy shop. He returns to crime, however, and is caught stealing some plate. Condemned to die, he goes cheerfully, regretting nothing and making no edifying speech, having learned nothing from it all. In Tom the type figure has been upgraded slightly; the rogue has been given a local habitation and a name that sounds almost authentic. But the sheer joy of the trickster remains totally separate from the context of popular religious ideas in which the criminal is usually presented and which crops up at intervals in *Tom Merryman*.

Somewhat different in its justification is a brief criminal biography which appeared in 1723, *The Highland Rogue: or, the Memorable Actions of the Celebrated Robert Mac-gregor, commonly called Rob-Roy*. This purports to be an absolutely veracious account, 'Impartially digested from the Memorandums of an authentick Scotch Manuscript', which is scornful of other obviously imaginary criminals who are appearing in print. 'It is not a romantic Tale that the Reader is here presented with, but a real History: Not the Adventures of a *Robinson Crusoe*, a *Colonel Jack*, or a *Moll Flanders*, but the Actions of the *Highland Rogue*; a Man that has been too notorious to pass for a meer imaginary Person.'[1] The preface continues self-righteously about the crass commercial lies which other criminal biographies indulge in: 'Had I assumed the Liberty of charging Mac-Gregor with Robberies that he was never guilty of, 'tis possible it might have been more for the bookseller's Advantage; for the many are better pleased with the Pageantry of Falsehood, than the simple Attire of Truth.'[2] The specific object of this abuse is then discovered. 'What an Object of Contempt and Ridicule is Captain *Alexander Smith*, alias Will. Hawkins, alias *B---ge*, alias, etc. His Works are a confus'd Lump of absurd Lies, gross *Obscenity*, awkward Cant, and dull Profaneness.'[3] The author is attacking a rival commodity, in fact, the most popular collection of criminal annals of the time, the two-volume *History of the Lives and Robberies of the Most Noted Highway-Men, Foot-Pads, House-Breakers, Shop-Lifts and Cheats of both Sexes in*

[1] p. iii.   [2] pp. vi–vii.   [3] p. vii.

and about London and Westminster, which ran to many editions and was expanded to three volumes.[1]

These popular volumes lie somewhere between the chap-book level of *The Scotch Rogue* and the quasi-documentary approach of *The Highland Rogue*. Smith strikes a shrewd balance between the documentary and the legendary; he pilfers facts from journalistic accounts and adds, deletes, and alters to make his material saleable. He retains as part of this successful recipe the religious context which is so important in criminal journalism. His books, to be sure, remain popular entertainment and, as such, lack the unity and sense of purpose that we expect of art. They are, therefore, miscellanies, variety shows whose tone can vary from the jocular and the lubricious to the earnestly religious.

By contrast, a short book like *The Highland Rogue* is restricted to one tone, one angle of presentation—documentary heroics. Rob-Roy turns outlaw only when his creditors refuse to wait for their money after the Duke of Montrose unjustly deprives him of some of his land; venal usurers and vicious aristocrats combine to force the simply virtuous hero to resort to justified violence. The story is told boldly and rapidly, as befits its nervous pretence to truth, and ends with a shrewd reinforcement of that pretence. We hear, at the end, of a barbarous murder committed by two of MacGregor's clan on two British soldiers. Rob-Roy has them punished or turns them over to the justice of the state. Since the author is not sure and not willing, he protests, to embellish his source, the uncertainty is left unresolved.

Such objectivity is not the defence that Captain Smith offers for his work. His presentational apparatus (and I think this sort of pseudo-technical phrase is necessary here to save us from the

---

[1] First published in 1713, a third volume appeared in 1720. In 1734 it was published in an elaborate folio edition with copper engravings along with Captain Charles Johnson's *Genuine Account of the Voyages and Plunders of the most Notorious Pyrates* (see Chapter III). This is the bound version of a weekly serial publication issued in seventy-three numbers during 1733–4, the same work being published serially in 1742. See R. M. Wiles, *Serial Publication in England Before 1750* (Cambridge, 1957), p. 293. References in this essay are to volumes i and ii of the 'Second Edition' published in 1714, and to volume iii of the first edition of that volume.

irrelevant question of Smith's sincerity) is entirely moralistic. His main rationale is that he is following the noblest examples of the past in recounting for his readers the 'Actions of Criminals and Wicked Persons, that by the dreadful Aspects of Vice, they may be deterr'd from embracing her Illusions' (i. i). Such a protest strikes us as entirely conventional, yet like the blurbs on modern dust jackets it indicates that Smith's audience may not have been as disingenuous as we presume (perhaps cynically) he was. Some doubtless believed that this exemplary use was a valid reason for reading such stories, and some (probably the greater part) used the preface's moral claims more or less as a rationalization for reading such material. The exact individual uses of the moralistic claims remain matters open only to conjecture; but their presence argues at least some commercial recognition of the need of a *moralitas* as part of the finished product.

The heavy-handed moralizing does not, of course, exclude the comic and the social grotesque that we noted in whore biography and that is the chief attraction of picaresque narrative. Smith mixes the horrific admonitions of divine vengeance and the rough humour of popular jest with great dash. A perfect example is provided by the story of Thomas Wynne, who 'became so expert in Housebreaking and other sorts of Theft, that he was then reckoned the most notable Thief of that time, which was in the Reign of the most glorious Queen Elizabeth' (iii. 32). Reprieved from Newgate by a general pardon, he becomes a scullion in the household of the Earl of Salisbury. He makes addresses towards and is repulsed by the Countess's gentlewoman, which leads him to take the following grotesque revenge:

. . . one Night lying on the great Stairs in Salisbury House in the Strand, before it was pull'd down, and as the Gentlewoman was coming from her Lady, when she had been undressing her for Bed, he runs his Head under her Coats, and getting hold of her *Tu quoque* in his Mouth, she roar'd out like a Bull that was baited; he in the mean time pull'd and tugg'd at his Game as fierce and eager as any Mastiff, not in the least breaking his Hold, till some Servants came to the Gentlewoman's Assistance, who were forc'd to put a Stick into his Mouth to open it, before they could get him off her. (iii. 33)

Wynne is whipped and runs away, robbing the household before he goes. After eight years of stealing, he murders an old retired draper and his wife by cutting their throats in bed and robs them of £2,500. He runs away to Virginia and an innocent person is hanged for his crime. Twenty years later he returns as a prosperous Virginia planter for a short visit. But seeing a crowd running after a thief one day, he is stricken with guilt and confesses to the authorities.

Thus the just Judgment of God at last overtook him for his shedding innocent Blood, tho' a great many Years had been past and gone after the Commission of that Barbarity, so that he thought himself secured then from the Stroak of Justice; neither was divine Vengeance wanting to punish his Wife and Posterity, as being privy to his Wickedness, and living upon the Reversion thereof. . . . (iii. 38)

The vulgar comedy of the early career and the exemplary admonitions of the last scene are complementary rather than contradictory elements in Smith's recipe; their presence indicates the continuity, albeit on a popular and very debased level, of the inclusiveness and human completeness which cultivated neo-classical taste excluded. It may, in fact, startle us to admit that Smith's audience could find delight in such extremes, but this paradox, it seems to me, must be accepted and understood if we are to understand the meaning of criminal biography.

Often, this moral underlining is much less organic to the story, simply pasted on at the end of an account which has presented the criminal as an attractive folk hero rather than as a horrible example of the wages of sin. Smith's opening story, for example, tells of the very successful 'Golden Farmer', who lived ostensibly as a farmer for forty years while carrying on a prosperous career in crime as a highwayman. The Golden Farmer, we notice, commits no murders, and those he robs are not the objects of pity but of satiric scorn of a rather brutal sort. Masked, he robs his landlord of the rent he and his fellow tenants have just paid and responds to the landlord's indignation by telling the truth which, it is implied, the sanctimonious world denies:

What, have you no Religion, Pity, or Compassion in you? Have

you no Conscience? Nor have you any Respect for your own Body and
Soul, which must certainly be in a miserable Case, if you follow these
unlawful Courses? D—n you (said his Tenant, unknown to him) don't
talk of Age or Barbarity to me, for I shew neither Pity nor Com-
passion to any. D—n you, what, talk of Conscience to me! I have no
more of that dull Commodity than you have; nor do I allow my Soul
and Body to be govern'd by Religion, but Interest; therefore deliver
what you have, before this Pistol makes you repent your Obstinacy.
(i. 8–9)

The picaro-prankster of folk-tale provenance has had ideological
self-consciousness added to his egoistic energies. He is, as well,
more realistic a figure than the noble Rob-Roy, who attacks the
same hypocritical viciousness of the 'legal' world but from the
quixotic pose of the robber knight. The highwayman, like Gay's
characters in the *Beggar's Opera*, admits his depravity and increases
his moral usefulness thereby. This levelling of thief and merchant
is not applied with any satiric toughness or thoroughness, since
the highwayman is also a character in a morality play, a Vice who
must and will end badly. Yet in scenes such as this one his moral
pretensions to the same kind of freedom from the theoretical
religious and moral restraints that the world hypocritically swears
to implicitly condemn that world. The audience is expected to
laugh, for example, at the Anabaptist preacher who begs another
highwayman, Ned Bonnet, to desist.[1] Ned's reply is at the expense
of religious cant but in the name of the irreligious cant of the men
of the world.

Pray, Sir, keep your Breath to cool your Porridge, and don't talk of
Religious matters to me, for I'll have you to know, that, like all other
true bred Gentlemen, I believe nothing at all of Religion; therefore
deliver me your Money, and bestow your laborious Cant upon your
Female Auditors, who'll never scold at their Maids without cudgelling
them with broken pieces of Scripture, which flows very fluently from
'em on all Occasions. (i. 72–3)

[1] It should be noted that Dissenters in general are objects of ridicule and
contempt throughout Smith's volumes. This is worth noting, not because it
makes the author a good stout Tory, but because it shows the religious con-
servatism natural to popular literature.

But in spite of the attractive swashbuckling of some of the high-waymen, the brutal realities of crime are never totally suppressed. We are told of a highwayman, named Jack Bird, who had in his first attempt at robbery been subdued by a sailor with no hands. Jack meets resistance another time from a Welsh drover and

. . . being enrag'd at the Drover's Resistance, he leap'd nimbly out of his Staff's Length, and, saying, 'If a Son of a Whore once could take me without any Hands, I shall not venture my Carcass within the reach of one that has Hands, for fear of another Conviction', so he shot him thro' the Head: Then rifling his Pockets, in which he found Eighteen-pence; Ay (quoth Jack again) this is a Prize worth killing a Man for at any time; and so went about his Business as orderly as if he had done no Hurt at all. (ii. 127–8)

Even more savagely shocking is Jack Withers who, after taking eight shillings from a penny postman, 'took a Butcher's Knife out of his Pocket, and not only most barbarously cut his Throat, but also ript out his Guts, and filling the poor Man's Belly full of Stones, threw him into a Pond, where he was found the next Day, but none could give any Account of this Inhumane Murder . . .' (i. 93). Withers is caught eventually and executed, and his story ends with a formal moral: 'Thus may we see God's Goodness in bringing Murder always out: For tho' a Murderer may escape for some short time, nay, sometimes for many Years, yet will God's Judgment overtake the Bloody Offender at last, and bring him to condign Punishment' (i. 93).

Now, this sort of conventional moralizing in the expected place means very little by itself. The moral tone which returns inevitably to put the criminal into 'proper' focus and to challenge the attractive fantasies he generates is not wholly explained by the explicit moral comments, for they come at predictable places and are often perfunctory and automatic. We must, rather, speak of an ambience which surrounds the criminal, a context in which even his most hilarious and attractive deeds are accomplished. The frame of reference of popular religion imposes its sensational system of causality very easily and naturally, and we are still in the luridly spiritual world of the Newgate pamphlets. The biographical 'point of view' (to use the phrase in its widest sense) is fundamentally religious in the broadest and most reactionary way and reduces the criminal's career at times to plain evidence of the presence of evil in the world.

Jocelin Harwood, for example, is born 'of well reputed, honest, and reasonably estated Parents', but in spite of these advantages he is seduced by Satan: 'the great Deceiver of Mankind taking Notice of his early Ripeness, was resolv'd to corrupt the Root, and blast the Fruit that might be expected thence, which he effected to Purpose' (iii. 106). At school Jocelin leads his school fellows into all manner of Rudeness and Debauchery', and when he is punished runs away to London. There he turns thief, but so horrifies his own comrades by killing four people they have robbed that they turn him in themselves. A monster to the end, a palpable manifestation of the devil's power, he spits in the face of the jury that condemns him.

But the Matter of Fact being plainly prov'd against him, he received Sentence of Death to be hang'd first till he was Dead, and then for a publick Spectacle to be hang'd up in Chains; however this made no Impression upon him, he was no Changeling but still the same, cursing and swearing and drinking to the very Morning he was to die, when being brought to the Place of Execution, he said with an unchangeable Countenance, That was the Murder to do again, he would act it, which being all he would say at the Gallows, he was turn'd off the same in 1692, aged 23 Years. (iii. 110)

Harwood is nothing less than patently unregenerate man; his story is a verbal equivalent of his carcass in chains by the roadside. That brutal custom of exposing the bodies of criminals as public warning lingered as an archaic survival into the eighteenth century. Analogously, an anatomy of the compulsive criminal such as Harwood, with its biblical echoes and evangelical risings and fallings, exploits the style and tone of traditional popular homiletics and makes (the last scene especially) a macabre monitory tableau of damnation out of the facts of the criminal's career.

This is even more explicit in the story of William Holloway, who deserted hard and honest work in the country for debauchery and crime in the city. His story is told with appropriate biblical allusions as a progress towards hell:

> This wretched criminal, William Holloway, was born at Newcastle-under-Line in Staffordshire, and was bred up to Husbandry; but liking not his Occupation, he came up to London, where falling into such Company who had rather be the Devil's Soldiers than fight under the Banners of Honesty, he soon became such an Enemy to Vertue, that being absolutely possess'd with Sin, he would cry out with the Demon-iack in the Gospel, 'What have we to do with *Thee* Jesus thou Son of God? Why art Thou come to Torment us before our Time?' So giving himself up to all manner of Wickedness, no sort of Theft miss'd his Inclination, to support himself in the Extravagancies of a most licentious Course of Life. (i. 94)

This homiletic style, with its casual allegories and cavalier neglect of details that would be realistically profitable and contribute arresting sensationalism ('where falling into such Company . . . giving himself up to all Manner of Wickedness . . .'), continues and is combined with a lament of the times, another stock sermonizing turn. Holloway kills a turnkey while in prison and is hanged for it. He admits that he did not know what he was doing, having been drunk at the time.

> Thus we may evidently see the fatal Consequences of Drunkenness; which odious Vice is now become so fashionable, that we may too often behold Sots contending for Victory over a Pot, and taking the measure of their Bravery by the Strength of their Brains, or Capacity of their Bellies. Taverns and Alehouses are the common Academies of Sin, where Drunkards make themselves expert in all those Arts whereby they gratify Satan, and as it were, in so many open Bravadoes, challenge the Almighty into the Field, and dare him to do the worst he can. Doubtless Satan hath but too much Power over these Men when they are most sober, they need not give him the Advantage of finding them so often Drunk; except in a Bravado they desire to shew the World how boldly they dare defy Heaven, and how much they scorn to owe their Ruin to any but themselves. (i. 102–3)

Here in one paragraph are the recurrent themes of criminal narrative, the essence of the ideology they embody. The criminal's revolt is against social and moral restraints, against any sort of control from an external source. His drive is towards self-determination, primarily and overtly economic, but inescapably spiritual and ideological as well, as this passage clearly recognizes. Providence, the concept that invokes the hierarchical orders which support eighteenth-century life from the arrangement of the cosmos to the distribution of wealth among social classes, is being challenged and defied. Popular ideology senses that this is monstrous and reacts by undercutting the entire validity of such a revolt, reducing the criminal's behaviour to the stirrings of Satan, either directly or through his efficient earthly manifestations in organized corruptions of human society, such as taverns and alehouses in the passage above. The criminal's individualism is declared an illusion, his triumph over Providence merely and ironically a capitulation to Satan. It is a logical but perhaps unsteady assertion, for the criminal cannot be left to his own fate and almost invariably comes to at least formal repentance and renunciation of his ambitions before the scaffold.

Satan's power is, of course, frequently equivalent to the natural pressure of social and economic reality. The highwayman and the thief became earth-bound creatures of their environments when we translate Satan's power into modern terms. To the eighteenth century the causes are different but the social patterns are equally clear. Holloway is a standard moral character of the age described in social terms—the countryman corrupted in the city. Another is the idle and erring apprentice. Thomas Savage, apprentice to a vintner, is led on by a whore to rob his master. He goes home and finds the maid in the room where the gold is kept. His crime is described with an admirable and restrained naturalistic accuracy:

The Maid then upbraiding him with having been at a Bawdy-House, which would be the Ruin of him in the End; he was much vex'd at her, and while he was at Dinner, the Devil enter'd so strongly into him, that he was resolv'd within himself to kill her: So when his Master and all the rest of the Family were gone to Church, leaving only the Maid and him at Home, he goes into the Bar and fetches a Hammer, with which knocking on the Billows as he sat by the Fire, the Maid chid him for making a Noise. He says nothing to her, but went to the

Kitchen-Window and knockt there with the Hammer, at which the Maid then saying nothing at all, he, to provoke her, walks on the clean Dresser-Board with his dirty Shoes forwards and backwards several times together; which Piece of Malice incensing the Maid to scold at him, he suddenly threw the Hammer with such Violence at her, that hitting her on the head, she presently fell down shrieking; then he went and took up the Hammer, and laid it down again twice, not daring to strike her any more; but at last taking it up the third time, the Devil was so great with him, that he gave her many Blows with all the Force he could, and quickly dispatch'd her out of the World. (iii. 42–3)

The natural hesitation after the initial impulse to violence is perfectly rendered by his laying down the hammer twice, and his deliberate provocation of the maid to anger in order to provide a stimulus or rationalization for violence impresses with its psychological accuracy and subtlety. This finesse looks very strange coupled with the Devil in capital letters twice at crucial moments; but for Smith's audience this is hardly an inconsistency or a breakdown in intensity but a necessary supplement to the external action. We are still in a world where evil is rendered more real and menacing by being personified and made palpable rather than by being reduced to its psychological components. Indeed, the choice of 'realities' does not exist; for realism includes the supernatural, that being as real for Smith's audience as anything else, more real certainly than the social and economic conditions of the time which strike us as the 'real' reasons for crimes of violence by apprentices.

Savage, who is soon apprehended, confesses that 'breaking the Sabbath . . . was the first Inlet to all his other Vices, especially Whoredom, Drunkenness, and Theft' (iii. 42). The devil can only enter when the normal pious defences have been discarded, and an important part of the sensationalism in accounts such as this one lies in the conventional pious analysis of the sources of crime. Anyone who neglects the normal fortifications against evil is liable to be overwhelmed by it, for crime begins in ordinary sin.

These popular religious implications are continued after Savage is brought to repentance in jail and confesses that his remorse is made worse by the fact that he has not only committed murder, 'But for any thing I know, have sent her Soul to Hell' (iii. 46). Two

nights before he is to be hanged, he grows eloquent in his repentance:

After he had receiv'd Sentence of Death, he was visited by Mr.
Baker; and the Saturday before his Execution, he said to the same
Person, being also then with him, Oh! my dear Friend, come hither,
and opening his Coffin, look here, said he, is the Ship in which I must
launch out into the Ocean of Eternity; and is it not a terrible thing to
see one's own Coffin and burial Cloaths, when at the same time I am
every whit as well as you? On the Sunday, he expecting to be executed
on the Monday, he desired to be alone, and spent it in Prayer, and other
religious Duties. (iii. 47)

Such conventional eloquence is rarely found among the
highwaymen and famous professional criminals featured in Smith's
collection. They repent, for the most part, but in a much more perfunctory way. The professional criminal's deliberate commitment
to evil, however, is capable of provoking a terrified incoherence
which is the antithesis of the apprentice's systematic preparation
for the execution. Tom Sharp, for example, is a highwayman who
suddenly changes from swaggering impiety to absolute terror:

But such was his Impiety, whilst under Sentence of Death, that
instead of Thanking such who had so much Christianity in 'em as
to bid him prepare for his latter End, he would bid them not to trouble
his Head with the idle Whimsies of Heaven and Hell, for he was more
of a Man than to dread or believe any such Matter after this Life. But
when he came to the Place of Execution, which was at the End of Long-
Acre in Drury-Lane, and the Halter was set about his Neck, he then
chang'd his Tone, and began to call out for Mercy, with such a sorrow-
ful Voice, which could not but awake the most lethargick Conscience
that ever the Devil lull'd asleep. One there might plainly see by the
Deluge of Tears which fell from his Eyes, what Convulsion-Fits his
poor Soul suffer'd, whilst his own Mouth confess'd how grievously his
afflicted Spirits were stretch'd on the Rack of horrid Despair. Now was
the Time that the voluminous Registers of his ill Conscience, which
formerly lay clasp'd in some unsearch'd Corner of his Memory, were
laid open before him; and the Devil, who hitherto gave him the lessen-
ing End of the Perspective Glass to survey his licentious Courses,
turn'd the magnifying End to his Eye, which making him now implore

Heaven for a gracious Pardon of his manifold Transgressions, he was turn'd off the Cart. . . . (i. 212–13)

These extremes of penitential behaviour serve the same exemplary end: illustrations, negative and positive, of the art of dying. They are, as well, entirely appropriate reactions for the highwayman and the revolted apprentice, the most fitting conclusions to their respective stories. The highwayman and the revolted apprentice are mythical opposites: the highwayman, at his best, embodying an honest and noble independence, but the apprentice gone wrong summarizing furtive and unnatural longings for disruptive revolt. But the apprentice tends to die much better than the highwayman. He repents in time and meditates profitably for the public good; whereas the highwayman's penitence is often merely a desperate reflex such as Tom Sharp's, exceedingly useful to those who watch it but of dubious sincerity and limited validity. The myth endorses the flamboyant independence of the highwayman because it is unreal enough to serve as a pleasant fantasy which has no direct social relevance, but it immediately condemns the apprentice's revolt because of its plainly revolutionary character. The historical highwayman is easily assimilated by the picaro-prankster tradition, but when he approaches the scaffold his blameless amoralism, now seen in the light of the penitential drama of which he is suddenly the centre, is changed into deliberate and monstrous sin.

The apprentice, on the other hand, is a character whose entire criminal career is enacted against a background of guilt and apprehension; his revolt is never glamorized or romanticized but made as sordid and unspeakable as possible. Yet he is allowed an effective repentance, since this is the high point of his career, the moment when he confirms the guilt which the myth has insisted must have compromised his every illegal act of independence. With his repentance and death, the story of the bad apprentice can end happily, for he has resumed his rightful subordinate place and reaffirmed, in a kind of penitential apotheosis, the existing social and moral order. The highwayman has had his glory and his reward in his guiltless freedom. His end is shrouded in uncertainty, and he trips into eternity with suggestions of damnation.

There are times, of course, when the facts cannot quite be accommodated to the myth. The best example is the featured story in another collection of criminal biographies which appeared in 1726 under Smith's name, *Memoirs of the Life and Times of the Famous Jonathan Wilde, Together with the History and Lives of Modern Rogues.*[1] Crime, the preface to this collection declares, is epidemic. The laws against theft are being prosecuted with inefficiency and neglect, and criminals once caught are treated with scandalous mildness. Jonathan Wild's prosperity is blamed on this permissiveness, and the abuses connected with organized theft are exposed and condemned. Wild's story is told with gleeful sarcasm without any of the serious moral overtones we have discussed, for he is presented as a cold-blooded entrepreneur in crime rather than an instructive victim, like the apprentice, of evil inclinations or forces. His calculating treachery reveals a degree of amoral efficiency which cannot be reconciled to the capricious freedom of spirit with which the highwayman or glamorous criminal is endowed. Wild's freedom consists in the systematic and self-conscious exercise of power to destroy the freedom of others: a version of freedom which approaches its real social meaning in eighteenth-century England. This deep social relevance of Wild's career and *modus operandi*, as Fielding later recognized so well, makes him an enemy of the spirit behind the popular myth of the criminal. Wild's sin is that he is not a sinner but a businessman; he has made crime simply another secular profession. His is not a revolt against the theoretical bases of society but a thorough-going co-operation with the actual machinery of society, a business which ignores ideological considerations.

---

[1] This is, of course, only one example of the voluminous popular literature dealing with the infamous thief-taker which appeared after his execution in 1725. These narratives are described in some detail by W. R. Irwin (op. cit., pp. 4–29), who lists eight other full-scale biographies of Wild which appeared in 1725, Defoe's being one of these. Irwin concludes that Wild became in the popular mind not so much a man as 'a symbol of human infamy' (p. 30). I have used Smith's account as representative of this popular literature and the attitude towards Wild which it reflected and preserved. I consider this sort of selectivity a legitimate limitation which allows scope for valid analysis without the distracting bulk of an academic *catalogue raisonné*.

But only a sophisticated satire like Fielding's *Jonathan Wild* can allow its readers to see Wild as the embodiment of social actuality that he really is. A popular narrative can yield nothing but an attack on him as a perverter of the legal machinery of society. His story here is a debunking rather than a mythologizing, and his end is not the occasion for a homily or an *exemplum* but for destructive ridicule. He is not allowed to strike the conventional edifying postures and is reduced to puny comic proportions by his simple fear of the pain attached to death rather than the penitential dread of eternal punishment usually portrayed in the condemned criminal.

Then Jonathan being decently seated in a Cart, he was convey'd from Newgate to Tybourn, amidst innumerable Spectators, who went to see the Last of him, who was abhorr'd by the better Sort, loath'd by the middle People, and despis'd by the Mob, who so much insulted him as he rid, that they pelted him with Stones and Dirt all the Way, broke his Head in several Places, and revil'd him with the most opprobious Language, for having sold more human Blood at forty Pounds per Head, than would fill the Canal in St. James's Park. When he was arriv'd at the Place of Execution, being dos'd beforehand with Liquors, he made no Speech, nor did he trouble himself to make any Confession of his Sins to Mr. Ordinary, because he could not think of 'em all; but requested the Hangman to adorn his Neck with the Halter, place the Knot exactly under the left Ear, and put him out of his Pain as soon as he could; then the Cart drawing away, he was, to the universal Joy of all that beheld his last Exit, turn'd off, and in the twinkling of an Eye, sent out of this World into another, where how he will Fare I will not pretend to Judge. . . .[1]

The simple tendentiousness of the style matches the secular content of Wild's story. He is a monster with whom the usual devices of criminal biography cannot cope. Those devices, as we have seen, require the brutal and sordid realities of crime as raw materials. Smith's volumes are collections of the scattered annals of crime to be found in broadsides and pamphlets. These facts, presented baldly in other collections such as the *Chronicles of Tyburn* (1720), the *History of Executions* (1731), and the *Newgate Calendar*

[1] pp. 18–19.

(1773), remain, but they are supplemented by the comic, erotic, and satiric possibilities of rogue legend and picaresque narrative.

Given the moral and social context of the age, the popularity of criminal narrative thus processed justifies us in interpreting the criminal (especially the heroic highwayman, relatively innocent of cruel and bloody acts) as a mythical figure of great significance: an embodiment of the secular energies of the age which chafe under the traditional system of social and moral limitations and their religious foundations. The criminal, generally speaking, obtains his compelling stature because he violates the specific taboos of the age, and it will not do simply to resort to psychological truisms, to say only that violent crime has always been fascinating to the many. We must add to this truism another one: crime in each age and society has a specific and distinct historical meaning. This survey of criminal narrative of the early eighteenth century has shown that it is a miscellaneous type, capable of a whole range of entertaining postures, but that these attractions and mythical implications are superimposed upon the biographical pattern created by the religious rubrics of fall, sin, and repentance or damnation. Documentation and circumstantial detail are only minor if occasional factors in this successful formula. In fact, whatever objective realism or journalistic particularity there is in these accounts tends to be absorbed by this religious pattern; the sensational particular, the violent events of the individual criminal's career, depend for their sensational value and effect upon the moral abstractions which they illustrate so vividly. The strenuous moralistic claims of criminal narrative are valid to the extent that the criminality of its subjects is described in a language which in somewhat debased and diluted popular form exploits the style and frame of reference of sermon and traditional religious allegory. But more important, the criminal is more of a mythical than a statistical reality in popular criminal narrative because he begins and ends as sinful man, God's enemy as well as society's.

III

TRAVELLERS, PIRATES, AND PILGRIMS

I. THE PIRATE: FAUSTIAN RUFFIAN

IT is one of the ironies of literary history that the most durable
survivor from the mass of travel literature that flooded Europe
during the seventeenth and eighteenth centuries was meant to
satirize the genre. *Gulliver's Travels* was inspired in part by Swift's
contempt for the vulgar credulity that nourished a popular form
like the travel account. The initial joke which ignites his huge
satiric engine is an elaborate parody of the documentary apparatus
which accompanied the travel book. But Swift's satire, it can be
argued, goes deeper than the mock framework; his book is in spirit
an attack upon the ethos that produced the travel book and caused
its enormous vogue. As modern scholarship has made clear,
Gulliver's Travels is a profoundly 'reactionary' work whose main
satiric thrust is against the insane (to Swift) modern optimism
which disregards the limitations natural to man. His apt choice of
the voyage as initial target demonstrates that Swift was aware of
the peculiarly modern, and therefore to him hateful and dangerous,
implications of travel literature and its popularity.

Those implications have recently been brought out with new
clarity by a wide-ranging survey of seventeenth- and eighteenth-
century travel literature by P. G. Adams, who shows in some detail
just how travel books provided entertainment and education which
fit the controversial and inquisitive spirit of the age: a source of
delight for all with their exotic and sometimes marvellous places
and stories, and a mine of information and controversial ammuni-
tion for theologians, philosophers, and poets.[1] As Adams's survey

[1] *Travelers and Travel Liars 1660–1800* (Berkeley and Los Angeles, 1962),
pp. 223–35. R. W. Frantz's *The English Traveller and the Movement of Ideas
1660–1732* (Lincoln, Nebraska, 1943) is a much more restricted and conservative study, but provides a wealth of basic information and an invaluable bibliography.

makes abundantly clear, this popularity was nothing less than a sign of the extension of the geographical and cultural frame of reference of Europe. The possibilities of human achievement seemed to expand as a 'Copernican' rearrangement of the world revealed new fields for action and provided fresh perspectives for European self-study. Europe, it may be said, responded so eagerly to travel literature not simply out of curiosity about the new and strange, but because the travel book served the ideological needs of an emerging modern world.

In the broad sense, that is, the form and spirit of the travel book embodied the cultural values and assumptions summed up in such words as movement, variety, change, and originality, as opposed to the opposing conservative religious orientation suggested by ideals such as passivity, submission to authority, permanence, self-effacement, and voluntary restriction. The travel book could easily invoke a world where joyful and profitable movement was potentially unlimited; where there were, ideally, no boundaries; where there were many human and natural dangers, but where great rewards might be earned by those who moved with skill and speed. If the favourite story of the Middle Ages was the fall of princes (the assertion of the inevitable, the dance of death for all), the characteristic fable of the modern age was to be the rise of merit (that is, ability, agility, skill, cunning: the denial of the inevitable, the march of progress).

And what more spectacular test and reward of merit than the voyage? Just as for modern philosophy after Descartes the world was a measurable and absolutely malleable quantity, so too, for travel literature, the world as philosophical entity tended to be reduced, in effect, to specific geographic and cultural facts; it became a field for action and conquest rather than a mysterious and controlling totality. The eighteenth-century hero-traveller often embodies this ethos of change and conquest, and his story is a metaphor of modern possibilities. Swift's irrepressible Gulliver, resourceful and ingenious but bumptious and egregiously optimistic, is a malicious caricature of this ideal hero-traveller.

Travel literature, then, had acquired a peculiarly and

aggressively modern emphasis by the early eighteenth century, for these modern implications of travel directly contradict some of its most important traditional literary and mythical associations. Ulysses was, after all, sent wandering for his sins against Poseidon, and his tour was a painful if exciting exile from his homeland and domestic joys. Alexandrian exegesis made the *Odyssey* an allegory of the soul's exile from God, and travel in the Old Testament featured exile and residence for a weary time in the land of bondage. Medieval Christianity, by and large, continued this tradition and considered travel as an allegory of life itself, a hard pilgrimage or arduous quest, but never explicitly and positively the open road or the high seas of adventure. It is not too much to say that travel still retained many of these overtones and associations into the eighteenth century, just as actual travel was still full of 'travail', a hazardous and occasionally fatal business in fact.

It is this older meaning of travel that tends to survive with peculiar force in the popular 'novels' of the early eighteenth century which use travel as a basic plot device, peculiar because they seem at first glance to be firmly committed to the new and exciting possibilities of travel. The stories in question partake of the modern ethos of travel; they glitter with the attractions of exotic locale and action and frequently give us heroes who are capable of 'daemonic' and free-wheeling exploits. But this diversity of scene and event is often balanced by a narrative voice which tries to see in the random and the coincidental the mysterious workings of Providence. We are sometimes assured by narrators or promised by titles that the events being described are luminous with moral significance and fall naturally into an exemplary pattern. The illuminations, however, are fitful rather than steady, and the pattern is often imposed and ill fitting. Much of the rhetoric is perfunctory and conventional, the result of pious commonplaces of speech and thought. Yet the protests are an important sign that the infinite possibilities and new perspectives which secular travel can imply were automatically and implicitly qualified by the ideological limitations and restrictions which traditionally defined travel as a sobering pious metaphor for life.

This mixture of implicit meanings in the travel narrative-novel bears out Lucien Goldmann's point that the novel reflects essentially not so much the surface content of life as what he calls its 'structure'.[1] Now 'structure' is perhaps a fairly opaque term which may suggest to some the strained ingenuity which modern criticism is often capable of in misguided efforts to find architectonic consistency in every work. But Goldmann's use of the term is historical rather than exegetical, and by the structure of life he means simply the characteristic ideological pattern of the age. This may vary, obviously, according to one's point of view and historical perspective. Goldmann sees the conflict between real or 'use' values and the artificial ones induced by capitalism as the pervasive underlying meaning of human conflicts. For my purposes, the confrontation of the secular and the religious views of experience constitutes one aspect of the dialectic reality of the early eighteenth century, at least at the ideological level exploited by popular fiction. The popularity of the travel narrative and of those 'novels' organized around travel records a historical process, what Goldmann calls the 'destructuring of old structures and the structuring of new totalities likely to create balances which will satisfy the new demands of the social groups who formulate those demands'.[2]

We have already seen in criminal narrative an example of the process that Goldmann describes. The criminal—archetypal sinner, unregenerate man facing death and judgement—is a vivid emblem of the wages of sin. His story is, as eighteenth-century 'blurb' writers insist, a moral *exemplum*, and its presentation retains some of the allegorical resonances of a more completely religious age.

---

[1] *Pour une sociologie du roman* (Paris, 1964), p. 20. Summarizing the conclusions of Georg Lukács and René Girard, Goldmann describes the modern novel as the story of a search for authentic values in a world given over to inauthentic ones. From Goldmann's Marxist perspective, the commercial values of capitalism are the inauthentic values which pervade the modern world and lead to the hopeless search for real values. The normal dialectic of the novel, the search, the quest for reality in a world of illusions, is the novelistic counterpart of the structure of everyday life, where what seem to be the qualitative values of bourgeois society are actually the purely quantitative and dehumanizing ones of capitalism. It is this distinction between content and structure and his insistence that the latter is the true object of literary analysis that are instructive.

[2] Goldmann, p. 214 (my translation).

But at the same time, the criminal is a journalistically authentic and therefore partially attractive figure, who in so far as he is life-like acquires our sympathy, understanding, or hatred—what modern journalism might call 'human interest'. The reportage which deals in the concrete facts of his career tends to contradict the moral generalizations he is supposed to make us think on, and he becomes instead a specific being, trying through a programme of illicit self-reliance to assert a violent and precarious selfhood. His secular energies begin to transform the old religious structures of allegory and the strict social and moral hierarchies which allegory requires; his independence and anti-social behaviour co-operate with a journalistic realism which prizes individuality and specific intensity. But the criminal's self-assertion is necessarily limited. His violence is of an archaic and unimaginative sort which violates the moral and social order without seeking to destroy it. The revolutionary implications of crime, the blasphemous logical extension of the secular habit of mind, appear in the pirate, whose use of the truly revolutionary ethos of the travel book enables him to transcend the narrow world of criminal narrative.

The great success of the pirate as a journalistic commodity in the early eighteenth century can be measured by the popularity of the collection of criminal biography first published in 1724 by one Captain Charles Johnson, now generally assumed to have been one of Defoe's pseudonyms. This work was expanded and enlarged in 1726, and reprinted often thereafter.[1] It has been, as J. R. Moore has pointed out, so widely read since then that it remains to this day the source of the popular conception of pirates.[2] Moore has

[1] During the period we are concerned with, the book reached a 'Fourth Edition' in 1726 in two volumes. All further references in the text are to this edition. The collection was combined in 1734 with Smith's *History of the Lives and Robberies of the most Noted Highwaymen* under the title of *A General History of the Lives and Adventures of the Most Famous Highwaymen*. The only other collection of pirate narrative was a translation from the Dutch of A. O. Exquemelin, *The History of the Bucaniers of America*, first translated in 1684. It reached a 'Fifth Edition' in 1771.

[2] *Defoe in the Pillory and Other Studies* (Bloomington, Indiana, 1939), p. 126. One might object that the great popular source of the legend for our time comes from Stevenson's *Treasure Island*, but Moore has shown that Stevenson had read and praised Johnson's book, and that there are convincing parallels

shown that the collection is really a remarkably accurate work, a
first-rate historical document for the study of piracy. But Moore
also makes the revealing comment that to 'the casual reader' the
most noticeable aspects of the book are 'the bizarre incidents and
the undercurrent of humorous exaggeration'.[1] It is, of course,
precisely the casual reader and his reactions that are of interest to
this study. We can assume, I think, that the book was read for the
most part by amateur rather than trained historians. Moore's
historical awareness and modern sophistication mislead him into
underestimating the imaginative appeal of pirate narrative.

There may have been some who read the *History of the Pirates*
as a work of history, but the appeal of the book, the reason for its
great success, lay in the bizarre and exaggerated (*pace* Professor
Moore, rarely humorous) scale of its characters. The pirate emerges
from this collection as a compelling mythical figure who combines
the attractions of the merchant-traveller with the seductive vigour
of the criminal, a legendary figure at last rather than a historical
figure of common dimensions. It is true enough that actual pirates
were often very dull and cautious entrepreneurs, disorganized and
inefficient, attacking small ships hardly worth the taking and running away from any sort of resistance. Very little is said of all this
in the *History of the Pirates*, although the book fairly bristles with
'documentation': lists of pirates captured, executed, and reprieved,
lengthy court proceedings in great detail, statistics of booty taken,
casualties inflicted and endured, and several long travelogues of
exotic places. The pirate remains a mercurial personality whose
movements are not really measured by these statistics, and the
cumulative effects of these details is to provide a factual base on
which to erect imposing and terrifying heroic statuary. I will
attempt to reconstruct that composite personality which the *History
of the Pirates* evokes and to outline the ideological implications it
exploits.

The *History of the Pirates* begins with a long introductory account

between both *Treasure Island* and *The Master of Ballantrae* and *The History of
the Pirates*. 'Defoe, Stevenson, and the Pirates', *ELH*, x (1943), 35–60.
    [1] *Defoe in the Pillory*, pp. 130–1.

of the growth and suppression of English piracy in the Caribbean. The author speculates sensibly in the preface about the origins of piracy in mass naval unemployment after war and recommends that England establish a national fishery to absorb idle sailors, 'to prevent Pyracy, employ a Number of the Poor, and ease the Nation of a great Burthen, by lowering the Price of Provision in general, as well as of several other Commodities' (i, sig. A₂ᵛ). This sobriety of tone is followed by a declaration that he himself has seen some of the events to be narrated and has had the balance from those who apprehended the pirates, and indeed from some of the pirates themselves. Not only, he continues, are the contents of the book true, but quite worthy of extended and serious treatment. He proves his point by a historical analogy suggesting that pirates are potentially formidable opponents, dangers to the safety of a nation by their very coherence and united strength. The pirates are not simply a 'Parcel of Robbers', for it is 'Bravery and Stratagem in War which make Actions worthy of Record; in which Sense the Adventures here related will be thought deserving that name' (i, sig. A4ʳ). Had the 'Progress of our Pyrates . . . been equal to their Beginning, had they all united, and settled in some of those Islands, they might by this Time, have been honoured with the Name of Commonwealth, and no Power in those Parts of the World could have been able to dispute it with them'. (i, sig. A₄ʳ).

Rome itself, the introduction proper continues, was threatened in just such a way by organized pirates and this provides an example of 'the great Mischief and Danger which threaten Kingdoms and Commonwealths from the Increase of these Sort of Robbers; when either by the Troubles of particular Times, or the Neglect of Governments, they are not crushed before they gather Strength' (i. 17–18). As it happened, the narrator goes on to say, the pirates were defeated by Pompey the Great because they were taken unawares when their ships were scattered all over the Mediterranean. But had they had 'Time to draw their scattered Strength into a Body . . . it is likely they would have made greater Attempts, and Rome, which had conquer'd the whole World, might have been subdued by a Parcel of Pyrates' (i. 23).

The analogy is strained and Roman history is, needless to say, somewhat distorted in the bargain. The effect of it all, however, is to highlight and underline the political suggestions of piracy. The pirate, '*Hostis humanis generis*, a common Enemy, with whom neither Faith nor Oath is to be kept, according to Tully',[1] is no ordinary criminal because his enterprise is a carefully planned and constituted undertaking, a deliberate legal and moral separation from any established human community. The pirate aboard his ship suggests a microcosm of society, and the pirate legend derives part of its fascination from the radical political independence and moral isolation that such self-sufficient communities involve. The pirate is capable of utopian achievements and retires occasionally to tropical paradises, but, more frequently, he creates fierce and menacing criminal kingdoms whose political features are related to the conditions of eighteenth-century society.

Both of these possibilities are, in fact, examined in the first biography, 'Of Captain Avery, and his Crew'. Avery, we are told, has acquired a legend which goes something to this effect:

. . . he was represented in Europe, as one that had raised himself to the Dignity of a King, and was likely to be the Founder of a new Monarchy; having, as it was said, taken immense Riches, and married the Great Mogul's Daughter, who was taken in an Indian Ship, which fell into his Hands; and that he had by her many Children, living in great Royalty and State; that he had built Forts, erected Magazines, and was Master of a stout Squadron of Ships, mann'd with able and desperate Fellows of all Nations; that he gave Commissions out in his own Name to the Captains of his Ships, and to the Commanders of his Forts, and was acknowledged by them as their Prince. . . . and these Accounts obtained such Belief, that several Schemes were offered to the Council for fitting out a Squadron to take him; while others were for offering him and his Companions an Act of Grace, and inviting them to England, with all their Treasure, least his growing Greatness might hinder the Trade of Europe to the East Indies. (i. 45–6)[2]

[1] From 'An Abstract of the Civil Law and Statute Law now in Force, in Relation to Pyracy', 'appendix', i. 439.

[2] This summary matches a 1709 pamphlet account of Avery, *The Life and Adventures of Captain John Avery, the Famous English Pirate (rais'd from a Cabbin-Boy, to a King) now in possession of Madagascar*, which makes him a folk hero, the victim only of his own courageous ambitions and a scheming world.

The narrator proposes to tell the truth about Avery, since 'while it was said, he was aspiring at a Crown, he wanted a Shilling; and at the same Time it was given out he was in Possession of such prodigious Wealth in Madagascar, he was starving in England' (i. 46). As a result of this discrepancy between fact and legend, we are given an account of Avery which is a deliberate debunking, careful to strip him of any ability, courage, or even capacity for real evil. Instead of the exuberant and straightforward aversion to honest submission to work we expect of the pirate, Avery begins as a mutineer 'of more Cunning, than Courage' (i. 47) who engineers the theft of the ship he is sailing in by pulling anchor while his captain is drunk and asleep. He comes to Madagascar with the ship and joins forces with other pirates in a smaller sloop. The first ship they blunder into turns out to belong to the Great Mogul, and when she seems 'to stand upon her Defence; Avery only cannonaded at a Distance, and some of his Men began to suspect that he was not the Hero they took him for' (i. 47).

The ship is captured, but by Avery's allies in their sloop. The narrator notes carefully that Avery's notoriety ensued when the Great Mogul threatened to drive the English from India in reprisal: 'the great Noise this Thing made in Europe, as well as India, was the occasion of all these romantick Stories' (i. 51). The pirate community of the legend and the frightening bond between thieves which is its social cement, dissolve into sordid facts as the narrator describes Avery's betrayal of the sloop's men. His crew all agree 'to bilk their new Allies, the Sloop's Men; nor do I find that any of them felt any Qualms of Honour rising in his Stomach, to hinder them from consenting to this Piece of Treachery' (i. 53). After various wanderings and more betrayals, Avery comes to a sordid end not in Madagascar or the West Indies, but penniless in Bideford in Devon, on his way to Bristol, where he had been cheated of the remains of his Indian treasure by unscrupulous merchants.

Avery, we are not allowed to forget, is little better than a lucky sneak-thief, and the ominously efficient pirate empire with its satanic pirate king is merely a European nightmare. The real thing is described for us after we have heard of Avery's death. His betrayed allies make for Madagascar, and there they establish a colony, or rather, conquer one, for their establishment is a matter of subduing and enslaving the native population. The result is not a commonwealth but a Hobbesian state of war in which each of them fears not only the hostile natives but each other. They soon separate, 'each living with his own Wives, Slaves and Dependants, like a separate Prince; and as Power and Plenty naturally beget Contention, they sometimes quarreled with one another, and attacked each other at the Head of their several Armies; and in these civil Wars, many of them were killed' (i. 58–9).

Our last view of this pirate colony emphasizes its degraded anarchy and reminds us that its pirate princes are merely the refuse of society, whose only similarity to royalty lies in their seraglios. A ship calls and the pirates trade large numbers of their subjects for clothes, knives, tools, and shot. After avoiding the clumsy attempts of the pirates to corrupt the crew and commandeer the ship, the captain sails away and the narrator concludes with heavy sarcasm:

Thus he left them as he found them, in a great deal of dirty State and Royalty, but with fewer Subjects than they had, having, as we observed, sold many of them; and if Ambition be the darling Passion of Men, no doubt they were happy. One of these great Princes had formerly been a Waterman upon the Thames, where having committed a Murder, he fled to the West Indies, and was of the Number of those who run away with the Sloops; the rest had been all foremast Men; nor was there a Man amongst them, who could either read or write, and yet their Secretaries of State had no more Learning than themselves. This is all the Account we can give of these Kingdoms of Madagascar, some of whom it is probable are reigning to this Day. (i. 63)

The de-mythologizing is complete and self-conscious but temporary. Captain Avery's story is, in fact, one extreme, and by its repeated insistence upon the ideological insignificance of its subject and its contemptuous rejection of the legend of Captain Avery reveals the power of that legend and its ideological implications. Indeed, the narrator goes on in volume ii to construct what is apparently his own version of the pirate legend in the person of the mythical French pirate, Captain Misson,[1] whose story is told in such familiar detail that the narrator begins with the customary explanation that he is simply presenting 'a French Manuscript, in which he himself gives a Detail of his Actions' (II. i).

The result is a deliberately constructed counter-myth, a fable which exploits to the full the ideological implications of the pirate legend while purging it of its grosser aspects of violence. Misson is a Frenchman of good family and education but a younger son in a large family. Having therefore to make his own way, he goes to sea, 'as he was of a roving Temper, and much affected with the Accounts he had read in Books of Travel' (ii. 2). While in Rome he observes the corruption of the Roman clergy and the papal court and is confirmed in his disaffection from religion by a disillusioned Italian priest, Caraccioli. They go off together and eventually turn pirates as a means of asserting their philosophical and moral integrity. Caraccioli first convinces Misson at length of the falsity of established religions by an essay in comparative religion and anthropology.

I shall only observe, that Signor Caraccioli, who was as ambitious as he was irreligious, had, by this Time, made a perfect Deist of Misson, and thereby convinc'd him, that all Religion was no other than human Policy, and shew'd him that the Law of Moses was no more than what were necessary as well for the Preservation as the Governing of the People; for Instance, said he, the African Negroes never heard of the Institution of Circumcision which is said to be the sign of the Covenant made between God and their People, and yet they circumcise their Children; doubtless for the same Reason the Jews and other Nations do, who inhabit the Southern Climes, the Prepuce consolidating the perspired Matter, which is of a fatal Consequence. In short, he ran through all the Ceremonies of the Jewish, Christian and Mahometan Religion, and convinced him those were, as might be observed by the Absurdity of many, far from being Institutions of Men inspired; and that Moses, in his Account of the Creation, was guilty of known Blunders; and the Miracles, both in the New and Old Testament, inconsistent with Reason. (ii. 8)

[1] Misson is discussed by M. E. Novak in *Economics and the Fiction of Daniel Defoe*, pp. 109–10.

Caraccioli's knowledge of the world is wide and expansive; it gives him the same perspective that a contemporary philosopher such as Bayle used to dispose of the gods. His opinions, carefully labelled as dangerous by the narrator but allowed to proceed at great length, are a product of the comparative method of knowledge popularized by the proliferation of travel literature. If Defoe was in fact the author, the mild warnings against the dangers of such opinions are in violent contrast to the fulminations against free-thinkers in a work such as the *Serious Reflections of Robinson Crusoe*. The lesson is that pirate narrative called for an ideological openness that the closed world of the devotional essay prohibited.

Thus, Caraccioli and Misson are presented as essentially sophisticated ideologues rather than men of action. They take their stand with deliberate and eloquent precision. The world as it now exists, Caraccioli argues, is clearly corrupt, for it has declined from a primeval state where only natural paternal government existed, where 'every Father was the Head, the Prince and Monarch of his Family, and Obedience to such was both just and easy' (ii. 11). When the captain of their ship is killed in battle and Misson saves the day with his courageous leadership, Caraccioli urges him to declare himself captain and themselves free men. His argument here is from expediency and opportunity rather than abstract justice:

. . . he had his Fortune in his Hands, which he might either keep or let go; if he made Choice of the latter, he must never again expect she would court him to accept her Favours: That he ought to set before his Eyes his Circumstances, as a younger Brother of a good Family, but nothing to support his character; and the many Years he must serve at the Expence of his Blood before he could make any Figure in the World; and consider the wide Difference between the commanding and being commanded: That he might with the Ship he had under Foot, and the brave Fellows under Command, bid Defiance to the Power of Europe, enjoy every Thing he wish'd, reign Sovereign of the Southern Seas, and lawfully make War on all the World, since it wou'd deprive him of that Liberty to which he had a Right by the Laws of Nature: That he might in Time, become as great as Alexander was to the Persians, and by encreasing his Forces by his Capture, he would every Day strengthen the Justice of his Cause, for who has Power is always in the Right. (ii. 12–13)

Here, then, is the key fantasy behind pirate narrative: the self-sufficient rise to incredible power and influence of the man who has only his talents as a patrimony. Shrewdly and perhaps instinctively, Misson and Caraccioli are made distant and strange to English experience and reality as 'foreigners' (the only foreign pirates in the collection). They and their outlaw community are free to dramatize the utopian possibilities of piracy without any dangerous direct relevance for English institutions.

The artificial and deliberate nature of their revolt is emphasized by the great deal of careful polemicizing that Caraccioli and Misson seem to find necessary. Caraccioli, for example, objects to sailing under a black flag, for 'they were no Pyrates, but Men who were resolved to assert that Liberty which God and Nature gave them, and own no Subjection to any, farther than was for the common Good of all' (ii. 14). Governments have everywhere, he continues, perverted the laws of Nature and God. Ordinary pirates are simply men 'of dissolute Lives and no Principles' who, it is implied, do not understand their own alienation from the world. Misson and his men thus choose to sail under a white flag with 'Liberty' and the motto *a Deo a Libertate* painted on it, taking ships as politely and fairly as possible. Misson himself exhorts his men to behave to each other in a spirit of brotherly love, for they constitute a unique band of free men, as opposed to the masses of men, 'who ignorant of their Birth-Right and the sweets of Liberty, dance to the Musick of their Chains' (ii. 17). A slave ship is captured and Misson declaims against slavery as proof that the religion of the Europeans is 'no more than Grimace, and that they differ'd from the Barbarians in Name only', and then makes the slaves 'free' members of his crew. The Dutch sailors from the slave ship he makes his prisoners, and reprimands them for the various vices they have almost infected his virtuous crew with. He lets them go off at last in a ship, they 'not a little surprised at the Regularity, Tranquillity, and Humanity, which they found among these new-fashioned Pyrates' (ii. 31). Misson founds a pirate colony in

Madagascar, 'Libertalia', a utopian and utterly democratic experiment which is totally destroyed by a native attack rather than by any inherent flaws in its constitution. Misson himself dies soon after in a storm at sea.

Captain Misson's story has lately been reprinted by M. E. Novak, who sees it as an interesting example of the vigour of Defoe's mind, which in this case dramatized 'proletarian ideals', the 'growing revolt of the poor against a useless nobility'.[1] Novak considers the story evidence that Defoe was 'especially fascinated by the comparison between businessmen and thieves'.[2]

But Novak's choice of words is unfortunate, I think, for it restricts us to a simple cause-and-effect relationship between Defoe and his material: Defoe was attracted to this subject and stimulated to fabricate this elaborate story because he delighted in the ironic counterpoint it created with existing society. That may well have been the case, but it seems much more important and accurate to me to treat the story of Captain Misson primarily as evidence of Defoe's awareness of the power of the satiric commonplace of the age which played upon the alarming similarities between the amoral individualism of the criminal and the secular individualism required for survival in modern society. Defoe and his publishers responded to the pirate legends which developed spontaneously, as he himself attests in debunking the legend of Captain Avery, by producing the elaborate *History of the Pirates* and by creating Captain Misson as his own composite version of the myth, a clever combination of it with well-known and attractive utopian ideas.

What is important about Defoe's fable is that it reveals the ideological context in which it was conceived: the liberating possibilities of travel and the radical critique of Western society which travel's new perspectives afforded. Just as Gay's Macheath transcends the satiric occasion provided by Tory propaganda against Walpole's government, all of the pirates are more than simply Defoe's 'commentary on the injustice and hypocrisy of

---

[1] Introduction to *Of Captain Misson*, Augustan Reprint Society, no. 87 (1961), p. iii.
[2] Ibid., p. i.

contemporary English society'.[1] In effect, the decorous and conventional utopian speculations out of which Misson's story is made are an attempt to contain the fantasy of social aggression and secular independence which is implicit in the pirate myth; but the satiric commonplaces of the rogue turned culture hero possess a subversive vigour which Defoe is elsewhere unable or unwilling to control. Another of the pirates, Captain Bellamy, states those commonplaces with more rude gusto than Misson and Caraccioli are allowed to muster.

D—n my Bl—d, says he, I am sorry they wont let you have your Sloop again [when Bellamy's lieutenants decide that a captured ship cannot be returned to her captain], for I scorn to do any one a Mischief, when it is not for my Advantage; damn the Sloop, we must sink her, and she might be of Use to you. Tho' damn ye, you are a sneaking Puppy, and so are all those who will submit to be governed by Laws which rich Men have made for their own Security, for the Cowardly Whelps have not the Courage otherwise to defend what they get by their Knavery; but damn ye altogether: Damn them for a Pack of crafty Rascals, and you, who serve them, for a Parcel of hen hearted Numskuls. They vilify us, the Scoundrels do, when there is only this Difference, they rob the Poor under the Cover of Law, forsooth, and we plunder the Rich under the Protection of our own Courage; had you not better make One of us, then sneak after the A—s of those Villains for Employment? Capt. Beer told him, that his Conscience would not allow him to break thro' the Laws of God and Man. You are a devilish Conscience Rascal, d—n ye, replied Bellamy, I am a free Prince, and I have as much Authority to make War on the whole World, as he who has a hundred Sail of Ships at Sea, and an army of 100,000 Men in the Field; and this my Conscience tells me; but there is no arguing with such sniveling Puppies, who allow Superiors to kick them about Deck at Pleasure; and pin their Faith upon a Pimp of a Parson; a Squab who neither practices nor believes what he puts upon the chuckle-headed Fools he preaches to. (i. 220)

Bellamy knows that he is honestly wicked in a world of hypocritical knaves and obsequious fools. He recognizes that his brand of practical atheism and amoral independence is a superior version

---

[1] Novak, Introduction to *Of Captain Misson*, p. i.

of the moral anarchy that prevails in the world. His honesty redeems his solipsistic world from the nihilism that is the real result of hypocrisy; in a world which is in fact given over to the swift and the strong, the pirate exemplifies strength and speed in heroic proportion. He is, as William Empson has said of Macheath, 'like the hero because he is strong enough to be independent of society (in some sense), and can therefore be the critic of it'.[1] Empson makes the very shrewd point that the rogue was vaguely felt to be the most appropriate judge of society because there was 'a feeling that the unity of society had become somehow fishy . . . and the independent individual—the monad, the gravitating particle—was now the only real unit'.[1]

Empson's suggestions can lead us to see that the independence of the pirate king is much more than a simple satiric inversion: the criminal and the pirate (even more so) have a fascination all their own, for they embody the most dangerous and revolutionary forces of the age—the radical individualism which summarizes the totally secular view of experience. In Captain Misson's case, this secular isolation and ideological independence lead to a theoretical improvement of human nature and human institutions, his career being a sophisticated working out of the political and philosophical implications of that independence. Captain Avery and his allies, we remember, provide the dialectic opposite—piracy reduced to nothing more than social incoherence and human degradation. The other pirate narratives in the *History of the Pirates* exist between these two deliberate and carefully executed reactions to the pirate myth, and in them the typical pirate's legendary features assert themselves often enough to evoke a compelling figure whose secession from the normal human community involves an invocation of demonic forces and energies, demonic, I submit, because of their uncompromisingly secular basis.

Most of the pirates, that is, are presented as the greatest of sinners, whose revolt from law and morality, while not often as coherent and articulate as that of Misson, is total and uncompromising, but whose independence is always ringed about with attractive

[1] *Some Versions of Pastoral* (London, 1935), p. 200.

satanic suggestions.[1] The narrator is often careful to stress the utter blasphemy of their acts, a commitment to self-seeking which is frequently quite undiluted by a sense of guilt or by last-minute repentance. The result, as the following passage from 'Of Captain Bartho Roberts' makes clear, is a melodramatic set piece in which the pirates strike postures of stylized defiance:

They tore up the Hatches and entered the Hold like a Parcel of Furies, and with Axes and Cutlashes, cut and broke open all the Bales, Cases, and Boxes, they could lay their Hands on; and when any Goods came upon Deck, that they did not like to carry aboard, instead of tossing them into the Hold again, threw them overboard into the Sea; all this was done with incessant Cursing and Swearing, more like Fiends than Men. They carried with them, Sails, Guns, Powder, Cordage, and 8 or 9000 £ worth of the choicest Goods; and told Captain Cary, That they should accept of no Act of Grace; that the K— and P——t might be damned with their Acts of G— for them; neither would they go to Hope-Point, to be hang'd up a Sun drying, as Kidd's and Braddish's Company were; but that if they should ever be over-power'd, they would set Fire to the Powder, with a Pistol, and go all merrily to Hell together. (i. 238)[2]

The absolute defiance of all authority and the categorical refusal of quarter from anyone are complemented by the demonic analogies, a casual but constant part of the narrator's rhetoric. Not only are they like fiends and furies in action and desperate to the point

---

[1] The popularity of satanic hero-villains in the late eighteenth- and early nineteenth-century Gothic 'tale of terror' is well known: characters like Mrs. Radcliffe's Schedoni in *The Italian* (1797), Matthew Gregory Lewis's Ambrosio in *The Monk* (1796), and Charles Maturin's Melmoth in *Melmoth the Wanderer* (1820) are familiar type figures. All of these creatures inhabit a world so strange and palpably unreal that their stories can only be understood as opportunities for erotic and sadistic fantasy. As popular versions of the alienated Byronic hero of the Romantics, they satisfy a craving for the exotic and the supernatural put on the defensive by the prosaic, utilitarian, and mechanical tendencies of the age. Gothic hero-villains are daring anachronisms; they dare to live in a world of spells, devils, and magic power. The pirate, on the other hand, is by definition a modern revolutionary. His satanism is the new diabolism of the emerging secular age, and he achieves it by refusing to leave the realities of the new world of unconditional competition.

[2] An Act of Grace had been promulgated in April of 1699 offering pardon to all pirates who surrendered themselves.

of deliberate damnation before surrender, but they add an extra shudder by violating the sacred decorum of trade, destroying wantonly those goods of no interest to them. Theirs is in effect a gratuitous violence which exceeds the needs of the transaction.

The extreme example of gratuitous violence is Captain Edward Low, whose career is a succession of blood-curdling atrocities—disembowellings, ear and nose splittings, lip hackings, and mass murders. On one occasion Low takes a Portuguese ship, and when he learns that the captain has thrown a fortune in gold overboard rather than lose it to pirates, he 'swore a thousand Oaths, and ordered the Captain's Lips to be cut off, which he broil'd before his Face, and afterwards murthered him and all the Crew, being thirty two Persons' (i. 377). This and other similar incidents in Low's career display brutality on an epic scale; the ferocity of Low goes far beyond the prudent elimination of witnesses. Most of the other pirates, with a few notable exceptions,[1] are occasionally capable of this fantastic cruelty. The pirate legend, it becomes clear as we read along, requires a large element of recognizable sadistic fantasy. But this brutality evokes a demonic rather than modern pathological state, for the violence is accompanied by the narrator's chorus of demonic analogies.

The career of the famous Captain Edward Teach, 'Blackbeard', shows us just how deliberately and self-consciously the pirates can assume these demonic overtones. Blackbeard's adventures are related with all of the documentary apparatus we noticed earlier as a part of the 'history' which the narratives aspire to be, but we are given along with the statistics a picture (an engraving as well as a

---

[1] Notable among these kind and generous pirates is Captain Thomas White, a Barbadoes merchant who is forced into piracy by sheer circumstance. Captured by French pirates, he escapes and is stranded in Africa. Rescued by English pirates, he has eventually to join them. One day they take a ship with some money which they discover belongs to two children on board. 'Captain White made a Speech to his Men, and told 'em, it was cruel to rob the innocent Children; upon which, by unanimous Consent, all was restor'd to them again; besides, they made a Gathering among themselves, and made a Present to Stacy's [the captain of the captured ship] Mate, and other his inferior Officers, and about 120 Dollars to the Children; they then discharged Stacy and his Crew, and made the best of their Way out of the Red Sea' (i. 136–7).

verbal description) of Blackbeard which makes those carefully enumerated piratical activities contributions to a legend:

Captain Teach, assumed the Cognomen of Black-Beard, from that large Quantity of Hair, which, like a frightful Meteor, covered his whole Face, and frightened America more than any Comet that has appeared there a long Time.

This Beard was black, which he suffered to grow of an extravagant Length; as to Breadth, it came up to his Eyes; he was accustomed to twist it with Ribbons, in small Tails, after the Manner of our Ramilies Wiggs, and turn them about his Ears: In Time of Action, he wore a Sling over his Shoulders, with three brace of Pistols, hanging in Holsters like Bandaliers; and stuck lighted Matches under his Hat, which appearing on each Side of his Face, his Eyes naturally looking fierce and wild, made him altogether such a Figure, that Imagination cannot form an Idea of a Fury from Hell, to look more frightful. (i. 87)

The 'daemonic' energies of the hero-traveller-merchant when allowed to be extended too far lead naturally to the demonic. The traveller may be said to create himself by sailing deliberately into the possible; the pirate like Teach expands those possibilities past the tacit legal limits and tries like Faustus to make anything possible. In Teach's case the Faustian implications are made explicit as he plays the role of fiend incarnate with self-conscious and extravagant bravura:

. . . some of his Frolicks of Wickedness were so extravagant, as if he aimed at making his Men believe he was a Devil incarnate; for being one Day at Sea, and a little flushed with Drink—Come, says he, let us make a Hell of our own, and try how long we can bear it; accordingly he with two or three others, went down into the Hold, and closing up all the Hatches, filled several Pots full of Brimstone, and other combustible Matter, and set it on Fire, and so continued it till they were almost suffocated, when some of the Men cried out for Air; at length he opened the Hatches, not a little pleased that he held out the longest. (i. 88)

Teach is presented as a formidable and impregnable tyrant, whose own crew suspect him of mysterious and horrible alliances with evil. The night before he was killed, we are told, one of his men asked him if in the event he died his wife knew where he had buried his money: 'He answered, That no Body but himself and

the Devil, knew where it was, and the longest Liver should take all'
(i. 89). And some of the crew relate that the devil was amongst
them once.

That once upon a Cruize, they found out that they had a Man on
Board more than their Crew; such a one was seen several Days amongst
them, sometimes upon Deck, yet no Man in the Ship could give an
Account who he was, or from whence he came; but that he disappeared
a little before they were cast away in their great Ship, but, it seems,
they verily believed it was the Devil. (i. 89)

The legend makes Teach aware, in other words, of the absolutely
desperate nature of his enterprise, nothing less than a bargain
with the devil, or more accurately, an identification with the
devil. The pirate's loud and insistent *non serviam* is a consistent
feature of his personality, and like Lucifer he is regarded as a fallen
angel, or at least a potential angel. Teach's end, for example, is
the occasion for a brief lament: 'Here was an End of that couragious
Brute, who might have pass'd in the World for a Heroe, had he
been employ'd in a good Cause' (i. 84). Here and elsewhere the
paradox the narrator sets before us is the undoubted capability of
many of the pirates, such that we wonder what could have led
them to such courses:

It is suprizing that Men of good Understanding should engage in a
Course of Life, that so much debases humane Nature, and sets them
upon a Level with the wild Beasts of the Forest, who live and prey
upon their weaker Fellow Creatures: A Crime so enormous! That it
includes almost all others, as Murder, Rapine, Theft, Ingratitude, etc.
and tho' they make these Vices familiar to them by their daily Practice,
yet these Men are so inconsistent with themselves, that a Reflection
made upon their Honor, their Justice, or their Courage, is look'd
upon as an Offense that ought to be punished with the Life of him that
commits it. ('Of Captain Edward England', i. 113)

The invective reminds us that the individual pirate's demonic
independence must be qualified by the political requirements of
the pirate communities he requires for existence. But the demonic
features of individual pirates make their communities totter on the
brink of self-destructive anarchy. The terrible efficiency of the

legendary pirate empire is made impossible by the elementary democracy that must prevail outside of any established society. The only thing that can save a pirate enterprise from this weakness is the presence of an autocratic captain who can by sheer force and personality subdue his men. Brutal democracy and brutal dictatorship are the only possibilities, the narratives imply, when the traditional moral and legal systems of society are abandoned. To many of the readers of the *History of the Pirates*, the possible analogies with the now widely despised Puritan Commonwealth were probably quite clear and ideologically satisfying.[1] To all its readers the typical pirate community was clearly visible as a social microcosm somewhere between the extremes of organization and ideological awareness seen in the stories of Avery and Misson.

The most detailed description of the workings of a pirate gang comes in 'Of Captain Bartho Roberts', the longest of the narratives and, according to the preface, the most typical.[2] Here piracy begins realistically in the manner of Captain Avery when Roberts, captured by pirates while serving as second mate aboard a trading vessel, agrees to join them simply 'to get rid of the disagreeable superiority of some Masters he was acquainted with, and the Love of Novelty and Change, Maritime Peregrinations had accustom'd him to' (i. 272). He is soon nominated for captain, but the pirate

[1] Popular opinion of Cromwell and the Commonwealth is summed up by Caroline Robbins in *The Eighteenth-Century Commonwealthman* (Harvard, 1959), p. 3: 'In the eighteenth century the majority of the ruling oligarchy and the greater part of their fellow countrymen emphatically denied any continuity or connection between the innovators and Levellers of the Puritan Revolution (1641–60), and the philosophers and Whiggish statesmen of the struggle (1679–1710) to exclude James Stuart and secure the Glorious Revolution. An eccentric antiquarian might hang a copy of Charles the First's execution writ in his closet and speak slightingly of kings and superstitions, but in general all talk of '41 alarmed Englishmen as much or more than the sight of Jacobite toasts "over the water". Any proposed tampering with the fabric of the Church and state produced dismal recollections and dire predictions.'

[2] The preface declares that Captain Roberts's story is longer than any of the others, because 'being resolved not to weary the Reader, with tiresome Repetitions: When we found the Circumstances in Roberts' Life, and other Pyrates, either as to pyratical Articles, or any Thing else, to be the same, we thought it best to give them but once, and chose Roberts' Life for that Purpose, he having made more Noise in the World, than some others' (i, sig. A4ʳ).

who suggests him for the office reminds his audience of its constitutional limitations:

That it was not of any great Signification who was dignify'd with
Title; for really and in Truth, all good Governments had (like theirs)
the supream Power lodged with the Community, who might doubtless
depute and revoke as suited Interest or Humour. We are the Original
of this Claim (says he) and should a Captain be so saucy as to exceed
Prescription at any time, why down with him! it will be a Caution after
he is dead to his Successors, of what fatal Consequence any sort of
assuming may be. However, it is my Advice, that, while we are sober,
we pitch upon a Man of Courage, and skill'd in Navigation, one, who
by his Council and Bravery seems best able to defend this Commonwealth, and ward us from the Dangers and Tempests of an instable
Elemint [*sic*], and the fatal Consequences of Anarchy; and such a one
I take Roberts to be. (i. 209)

In an eighteenth-century context this speech is identifiable as
'levelling' cant, plausible but pernicious because it traces all
political power to a practical secular source—the will of the community. Pirate society is put in its ideological place as an example
of the consequences of such totally secular orientation. Roberts's
articulate supporter locates the will of the community in self-
interest and caprice, motives sure to lead to instability or anarchy.
And anarchy is indeed the undoing of this 'roguish Commonwealth', for its members allow their captain only nominal authority
in the time between battles.

After a short time Roberts's crew deserts him and he is left with
only a sloop and forty men. He regroups and draws up a constitution to which all agree, a thoroughly democratic pact which provides equal shares and rights for each man. Yet the narrator wonders at Roberts's faith in such a compact: 'How indeed Roberts
could think that an Oath would be obligatory where Defiance had
been given to the Laws of God and Man, I can't tell, but he thought
their greatest Security lay in this, *That it was everyone's Interest to
observe them, if they were minded to keep up so abominable a Combination*' (i. 230). We are warned that the articles are not reprinted in
full, since the pirates 'had signed and taken Care to throw overboard

the Original they had sworn to', and, it is hinted sensationally, 'there is a great deal of Room to suspect, the Remainder contained something too horrid to be disclosed to any, except such as were willing to be Sharers in the Iniquity of them' (i. 233). All newcomers, it is explained, had thenceforth to swear 'an Oath taken upon a Bible' to these articles. The narrative cannot do without the pirate legend, and Roberts's otherwise chaotically organized crew retains some of the mystery of the blasphemous conspiracy against the world which is a part of that legend.

Even this solemn agreement and horrid ritual do not quite temper the extravagant individualism of Roberts's pirates. The captain is given the great cabin of the ship and certain privileges, but 'every Man, as the Humor takes him, will use the Plate and China, intrude into his Apartment, swear at him, seize a Part of his Victuals and Drink, if they like it, without his offering to find Fault or contest it' (i. 234). Despite a number of subsequent successes, Roberts finds that 'there was no managing of such a Company of wild ungovernable Brutes, by gentle Means' (i. 248). If any resent his new authority, 'he told them they might go ashore and take Satisfaction of him, if they thought fit at Sword and Pistol, for he neither valued or feared any of them' (i. 248).

But Roberts and his crew never quite achieve the all-encompassing power of the archetypal pirates. Their end is a combination of the clumsy realities of piracy and the graceful panache of the mythical pirate kings, revealing in its uncertainty and ambiguity of tone the peculiar fascination of the pirate. Cornered by a man-of-war, Roberts resolves, 'like a gallant Rogue, to get clear or die', and meets the enemy with courage, even though 'the greater Part of his Men were drunk, passively couragious, unfit for Service' (i. 271). But Roberts himself dresses appropriately and dies in full feather:

Roberts made himself a gallant Figure, at the Time of the Engagement, being dressed in a rich crimson Damask Wastcoat and Breeches, a red Feather in his Hat, a Gold Chain round his Neck, with a Diamond Cross hanging to it, a Sword in his Hand, and two Pair of Pistols hanging at the End of a Silk Sling, flung over his Shoulders (according to the

Fashion of the Pyrates;) and is said to have given his Orders with Boldness and Spirit; coming, according to what he had purposed, close to the Man of War, received her Fire, and then hoisted his black Flag. . . . (i. 271)

Roberts is killed by grape-shot, and the narrative ends with an account of the trial of the survivors, and a report of the last speeches and actions of those condemned, the narrator declaring that he is 'not ignorant how acceptable a Relation of the Behaviour, and dying Words of Malefactors are to the Generality of our Country-men' (i. 326). Some repent, some do not: 'They walk'd to the Gallows without a Tear, in Token of Sorrow for their past Offences, or shewing as much Concern as a Man would express at travelling a bad Road; nay Sympson, at seeing a Woman that he knew, said, "he had lain with that B—h three times, and now she was come to see him hanged" ' (i. 327). These stock gestures of the condemned criminal call forth the conventional invective and moral amaze-ment: 'I mention these two little Instances, to shew how stupid and thoughtless they were of their End, and that the same aban-doned and reprobate Temper that had carried them thro' their Rogueries, abided with them to the last' (p. 327). This invective is merely a familiar repetition of the moral chorus, as it were, which follows the action and comments at appropriate moments in all of the pirate narratives. The compelling demonism of the pirates in their moments of violence requires this moral under-lining, for the pleasing horror is increased by the moral context thus invoked and the necessary rationale for reading of such atrocities is provided by the self-righteousness.

The story of Captain Roberts and his crew emphasizes once again the ambiguous appeal of the pirate—that mixture of scorn-ful debunking, shocked self-righteousness, and grudging admira-tion or even compelling fascination that has already been discussed. Pirate narrative, highly acceptable popular entertainment as it obviously was, bears out Marshall McLuhan's aphorism that such entertainment must 'flatter and exploit the cultural and political assumptions of the land of its origin'.[1] Thus, the pirate community

---

[1] *Understanding Media* (London, 1964), p. 311.

is examined as a political institution and found to be self-destructive and therefore relatively harmless in the long run. On this level, the conscious political prejudices common to most men of the time are satisfied: total democracy leads to total chaos. A workable society requires authority, but in the pirates' 'open' society that authority is tenuous, because it rests on force and compulsion rather than on traditional, sacred rights and duties of both governor and the governed. Moreover, both curiosity and scepticism about the pirate myth are encouraged and served by the occasional debunking tone and the plentiful statistics and official documents reproduced. But at the same time on another and deeper or less explicit level, the ruthless and expansive self-seeking of the pirate in his open society fascinates because it mirrors many of the actual forms of life in an increasingly secular and competitive society.

The pirate in his community is a relevant and highly meaningful fantasy for such a society, meaningful because he aggressively denies the religiously oriented values of inter-dependence and social unity. Perhaps his totally secular commitment could have acquired such horrific features only to an audience still partially oriented by the old Christian frame of reference but conscious that it was really steering by new stars.

These satisfactions of pirate narrative can be observed in coherent novelistic form in *Captain Singleton* (1720), in which Defoe, again with customary sensitivity to the requirements of the age, produced a compromise between the compelling egoism of the pirate-adventurer and the self-effacement and submission of the repentant sinner.[1] Singleton is a picaro who makes good; his career is a perfect example of the assertion of personality and the achievement of status by a totally disenfranchised character. He is kidnapped as a small boy, sold to a beggar woman for twelve shillings, sent to sea at twelve, and captured by Turkish pirates, who are in turn captured by a Portuguese man-of-war. He then

[1] Many of the events in *Captain Singleton* are based on the life of Captain Avery. All citations in the text are from the Everyman edition, which is a reprint of the 1720 first edition.

serves a tyrannical Portuguese pilot and sails to the East Indies by way of Brazil. Having been involved in an unsuccessful mutiny, he is left with a number of other conspirators on Madagascar. The group eventually blazes a spectacular trail across Africa, and Singleton makes the first of his fortunes here by finding gold. After squandering the money in England, he goes to sea again, and after another mutiny (this time successful), he turns pirate. We are then given a long and detailed description of his buccaneering activities much like the accounts Defoe was later to put together in the *History of the Pirates*.

The disorder and discontinuity of the events being narrated are held together in the latter work, as I have suggested, by the pervasive mythical personality of the pirate. Here, of course, concentration and focus are provided by the central character's personality and narrative voice. This is a calmly retrospective voice which is very careful to stress the differences between the central character of the narrative and the older and wiser person who is looking back upon his youth: 'Education, as you have heard, I had none; and all the little Scenes of Life I had passed thro', had been full of Dangers and desperate Circumstances; but I was either so young, or so stupid, that I escaped the Grief and Anxiety of them, for want of having a Sense of their Tendency and Consequences' (p. 14). Singleton presents himself as a completely disenfranchised and free-floating person, capable of understanding nothing but simple survival. Escaping from Madagascar and making for Africa, he recalls, affected him in a superficial way:

As for me, I had no Anxieties about it; so that we had but a View of reaching some Land or other, I cared not what or where it was to be, having at this time no Views of what was before me, nor much Thought of what might, or might not befal me; but with as little Consideration as any one can be supposed to have at my Age, I consented to every thing that was proposed, however hazardous the thing it self, however improbable the Success. (p. 54)

Given this kind of unreflective but observant centre, the narrative flows along easily and quickly; the sheer variety of scene and event carries us along without obstructive moralizing. The march across Africa is described as a desperate struggle against the impossible and sustains itself as a triumphant exploration rather than a painful exodus: flora, fauna, and topography are faithfully observed, and hordes of native warriors flee as they are fired upon by our intrepid and embattled white men.[1]

And to add to the Exclamation I am making on the Nature of the Place, it was here, that we took one of the rashest and wildest, and most desperate Resolutions that ever was taken by Men, or any Number of Men, in the World; this was, to travel over Land through the Heart of the Country, from the coast of *Mozambique*, on the East-Ocean to the Coast of *Angola* or *Guinea*, on the Western or Atlantic Ocean, a Continent of Land of at least 1800 Miles; in which Journey we had excessive Heats to support, unpassable Deserts to go over, no Carriages, Camels or Beasts of any kind to carry our Baggage, innumerable Numbers of wild and ravenous Beasts to encounter with, such as Lions, Leopards, Tigers, Lizards, and Elephants; we had the Equinoctial Line to pass under, and consequently were in the very Center of the Torrid Zone; we had Nations of Savages to encounter with, barbarous and brutish to the last Degree, Hunger and Thirst to struggle with; and, in one Word, Terrors enough to have daunted the stoutest Hearts that ever were placed in Cases of Flesh and Blood. (p. 58)

The heart of darkness yields a fortune in gold for each man at the journey's end. The subsequent piracy provides opportunity for another fortune, which is carefully listed in long inventories of ships taken. And all along Singleton avoids that deliberate engagement against the conventional world and its implicit values that we noticed as the key ideological feature of the pirate. The fable and the possibilities for vicarious freedom are the same, but Singleton remains a remarkably passive figure who simply has had to accommodate himself to the needs of the moment. His piracy, like his trek across Africa, is presented as an almost involuntary

[1] Gary J. Scrimgeour has reconsidered Defoe's use of his sources and pointed out that Defoe is always careful to confine the wanderings of Singleton's party to those parts of Africa that were completely unexplored, thus underlining the 'original' dangers they face. See 'The Problem of Realism in Defoe's *Captain Singleton*', *HLQ*, xxvii (November 1963), 23. Comparing the details in *Singleton* to Defoe's sources, Scrimgeour concludes that the exotic details are there primarily to serve as obstacles to survival and opportunities for wealth. The emphasis, in other words, is on the hero's daemonic personality.

gesture of survival. When he ships out for the second time, he is seduced into a mutinous conspiracy by a fellow sailor named Harris, who corrupts him and seals the bargain in these terms:

When we were together, he asked me if I had a Mind for an Adventure that might make amends for all past Misfortunes; I told him yes, with all my Heart; for I did not care where I went, having nothing to lose, and no Body to leave behind me.

He then asked me if I would swear to be secret, and that if I did not agree to what he proposed, I would nevertheless never betray him; I readily bound myself to that, upon the most solemn Imprecations and Curses that the Devil and both of us could invent. . . . this was his Plot, and I without the least Hesitation, either at the Villany of the Fact, or the Difficulty of performing it, came immediately into the wicked Conspiracy, and so it went on among us; but we could not bring our Part to Perfection. (pp. 169–70)

They thus turn pirates and join forces with another renegade crew, and Singleton continues this preface to his piratical career by invoking the sinister attractions of the pirate myth, the natural ease with which piracy suits the uncommitted and disengaged modern personality: '. . . being well prepared for all manner of Roguery, bold, desperate, without the least Checks of Conscience, for what I was entered upon, or for any Thing I might do, much less with any Apprehension of what might be the Consequence of it' (p. 170). And then he carefully notes again the mindless and conscienceless desperation which led him into crime: 'I that was, as I have hinted before, an original Thief, and a Pyrate even by Inclination before, was now in my Element, and never undertook any Thing in my Life with more particular Satisfaction' (pp. 170–1).

To be sure, Singleton himself is never allowed the gratuitous savagery of a Blackbeard nor even the expedient occasional atrocity that a pirate such as Roberts can be capable of. When his crew is all for murdering the Dutch crew of a captured ship who refuse to join them, Singleton intervenes at some risk to himself and his whole enterprise and saves the men. In fact, Singleton is made to stand apart from his crew, an efficient leader but otherwise above reproach and beyond the normal vices that would seem to accompany piracy such as drunkenness and whoring. At one of the Dutch East Indies, for example, a battle with the natives is caused by some of his men 'having been a little too familiar with the *Homely Ladies* of the Country; for Homely indeed they were, to such a Degree, that if our Men had not had good Stomachs that Way, they would scarce have touch'd any of them' (p. 264). The tone of this makes clear that Singleton is not given to such irregularities but tolerates them in his brutish sailors. He is so much the virtuous schoolmaster and officer that in this particular case he 'could never fully get it out of our Men what they did, they were so true to one another in their Wickedness; but I understood in the main, that it was some barbarous thing they had done' (p. 264).

Singleton's desperation is, in other words, directed purely towards survival, and the conquest of the world is forced upon him by the extenuating circumstances of his life. Now within a Christian frame of reference, the necessary is, in a sense, the providential, the irresistible. But the irresistible in *Captain Singleton* leads to action of a spectacular and liberating sort rather than to a blessed passivity and suffering of the inevitable. The importance of necessity has been correctly stressed by M. E. Novak,[1] who sees that Defoe's various heroes are pushed to the unlawful only by a choice between personal destruction and action. This choice is for Defoe, Novak argues, no choice at all and absolves the individual of blame. But Novak tends to discuss Defoe's characters as if they were somehow parts of Defoe's almost systematic 'theory' of man. It is more accurate to see them, I think, as reflections of social reality (as Defoe saw it) and novelistic necessity. Precisely because of Defoe's narrative skill, that is, the characteristic ethical impasse which his characters confront is the difficulty of acting morally (that is, in line with the values of passive acceptance, communal interdependence, and self-effacement before authority) in the world their creator evoked so well, a world committed to the com-

[1] 'The Problem of Necessity in Defoe's Fiction', *PQ*, xli (October 1961), 513–24.

mercial values of competition, independence, and self-assertion. Defoe's characters are thus forced to live in a world which precludes meaningful choice.

In Captain Singleton's case the submission to the inevitable is implicit. The circumstance of his life and the lack of moralizing comment in the narrative create the impression that he is simply reacting rather than initiating movement. (What makes Defoe so congenial to modern readers is precisely his ability to suggest a world of controlling circumstances, which we can recognize as real, in which at the same time extravagant fantasies of success and conquest can take place.) The narrative is free to portray the rise to social and economic status through sheer ability, agility, and cunning; and it is free to provide vicarious enjoyment of a totally secular adventure and enterprise of the sort we have seen in pirate narrative, for it need not affirm those values explicitly.

Moreover, Singleton is telling his story from the vantage point of penitential wisdom. He has arrived at repentance and a new wisdom about his past life. But the effect of this change in his personality is to emphasize just how unaware he had been of the implications of his acts in the past, and therefore just how incapable of ethical choice. He tells us that he came to reflect only during a violent storm when his ship and his life were in danger.

I was all Amazement and Confusion, and this was the first Time that I can say I began to feel the Effects of that Horrour which I know since much more of, upon the just Reflection on my former Life. I thought myself doom'd by Heaven to sink that Moment into eternal Destruction; and with this peculiar Mark of Terror, *viz.* That the Vengeance was not executed in the ordinary Way of human Justice, but that God had taken me into his immediate Disposing, and had resolved to be the Executor of his own Vengeance. (pp. 236–7)

This is only a temporary insight, and Singleton goes on with piracy for some time. 'Nor can I deny but that we were all somewhat like the Ship, our first Astonishment being a little over, and that we found the Ship swim again, we were soon the same irreligious, hardened crew that we were before, and I among the rest' (p. 238).

He does, at length, come to repentance through the counsel of his Quaker accomplice, William Walters. William tempers the normal ideological extravagance attached to piracy by treating it as a limited commercial venture: 'I would ask, whether, if thou hast gotten enough, thou hast any Thought of leaving off this Trade; for most People leave off Trading when they are satisfied with getting, and are rich enough; for no body trades for the sake of Trading, much less do any Men rob for the sake of Thieving' (pp. 309–10).

William, the cunning Quaker, is doubtless partly a comic figure, but it is his comic status which makes it possible for him to draw the analogy between trade and piracy without making the book subversive. He is really pointing out as well that Singleton is for the first time in his life capable of choice. He has acquired the social stability through piracy that is necessary for effective moral operation and can now indulge in the luxury of ethical consciousness.

Indeed, Singleton repents so far as to suggest to William that they attempt to make restitution. William points out the gross impracticality of that, and advises instead that they must simply submit to the irresistible facts of their case. Since they cannot possibly return any of the goods, William points out that they are clearly meant to wait for Providence to complete the design it has obviously begun:

... we ought to keep it [their loot] carefully together, with a Resolution to do what Right with it we are able; and who knows what Opportunity Providence may put into our Hands, to do Justice at least to some of those we have injured, so we ought at least to leave it to him, and go on, as it is, without doubt, our present Business to do, to some place of Safety, where we may wait his Will. (p. 322)

For us, there is an inescapable irony in this passage. William is invoking the values of submission after a career of the most violent self-creating activity possible. But our irony is doubtless an imposition; the repentance is not merely an insincere palinode but an affirmation of the religious values which the narrative has never explicitly denied. The usual whoops of delight at debunking the piety of the commercial man are irrelevant, since money has created a totally new situation wherein Singleton can now acquire the distinct personality that he lacks throughout his headlong career. This personality, it can be suggested, is not *developed* in any recognizable novelistic way during the course of the events but is *asserted* by the 'confessional' convention Defoe uses to tell the story. With its affinity to the popular devotional genre of spiritual autobiography, this convention has, as G. A. Starr has suggested,[1] the formal effect of making a narrative told in this retrospective manner as much a search for spiritual significance and progress in the events of the narrator's life as the presentation of a secular success story or the development of a personality to cope with new experiences.

Instead of being the gravitating particle to whom things happen, Singleton is now made capable of the coherent response to experience that is the excuse for composing the narrative and that causes him to declare that he never had any joy of his wealth after his conversion. The formal devotional construction of the narrative and Singleton's repentance act as the necessary ideological balance to the piracy. Where the pirate normally uses his stridently asserted independence to maintain his egoistic separation from the moral community, Captain Singleton uses his newly won freedom to acquire the guilt which gives him membership in that community. He returns to England incognito with a huge fortune and marries William's sister. The daemonic energies of the pirate have led to domestic and suburban identity; the fluid and destructive element in which the pirate moves (literally, the sea) has been exchanged for the stability of permanent land settlement and marriage. Viewed in these terms, *Captain Singleton* is more of an extravagant and satisfying popular fantasy than a convincing novelistic study of character development. We can if we like see parts of it through the psychological lenses of our own age, but for Defoe's audience its hero was an engaging protagonist because he moved successfully within the novelistic dialectic of the secular and religious.

---

[1] *Defoe and Spiritual Autobiography*, p. 50 *et passim.*

2. CRUSOE AND AFTER

If the pirates supply popular literature with its demonology, hagiology is provided by travellers whose momentum is often accompanied, if never really checked, by an inward reluctance or sense of guilt in one form or another. If the pirate is invariably aware of the radical isolation of his career and glories in it as the only true expression of his being, this sort of traveller shows himself equally aware of his self-propulsion but chooses to interpret the movement as towards spiritual exile. He inhabits books which exploit the whole range of implicit meanings and opportunities for fantasy suggested by modern travel literature. But this new secular content is qualified by the old religious context and symbolic possibilities of travel. The effect is that one can discern beneath the sharp journalistic discontinuity of events a pattern of religious and almost allegorical meaning of a rudimentary sort which seeks to assert itself.

Robinson Crusoe is the classic and familiar example. Everyone now recognizes Defoe's instinctive genius in fashioning it perhaps better than he knew, for Crusoe on his island is for modern critics a figure of mythical proportions whose story is the epic of resourceful Western man conquering nature through technology. But, as we have seen, it is equally clear that Defoe intended his hero's career to serve its readers as a pious *exemplum*, or at least to attract them as such in part.

Defoe makes Crusoe soliloquize often and at length about the religious implications of his misfortunes and deliverances. Crusoe thinks of himself as a renegade from God, a prodigal son (the analogy is his)[1] serving out a painful exile. He sees his fate as a just punishment for disregarding his father's pleas to remain at home in the 'middle station of life', and he looks back on his own obtuseness in not recognizing the various warnings which Providence had sent to keep him from roaming. Crusoe has chosen freedom and possibility, or, as he sees it, has been driven by an inner compulsion to travel: 'that Propension of Nature tending directly

---

[1] *Robinson Crusoe* (London, 1719), 4th edition, p. 14. All subsequent references in the text are to this edition.

towards the Life of Misery which was to befal me' (p. 2). His father's description of those who follow the sea reminds us of the radical implications of Crusoe's decision: such men are 'of desperate Fortunes on one Hand, or of aspiring, superior Fortunes on the other, who went Abroad upon Adventures, to rise by Enterprize, and make themselves famous in Undertakings of a Nature out of the common Road' (p. 2). As Crusoe sees it, the alternative is traditional submission to the will of God (delivered by Crusoe's venerable and Jehovah-like father), remaining in the state in life to which God had called him.

> I have been, in all my Circumstances a *Memento* to those who are touch'd with the general Plague of Mankind, whence, for ought I know, one Half of their Miseries flow; I mean, that of not being satisfy'd with the Station where in God and Nature hath plac'd them; for not to look back upon my primitive Condition, and the excellent Advice of my Father, the Opposition to which, was, as I may call it, my *Original Sin*, my subsequent Mistakes of the same Kind hath been the Means of my coming into this miserable Condition. . . . (p. 330)

For Crusoe the island is pre-eminently a place where he learns that he cannot escape the dispensing providential hand and that his success as sailor and planter has been only superficially an act of independence. He comes, in time, to regard his island as a punishment for his sins.

Yet in spite of all this, critics like Ian Watt who have stressed the enduring vitality of *Robinson Crusoe* as a modern myth of economic man, have their point. Defoe's energetic prose and real involvement in the artifacts and techniques of modern life communicate a joy in the business of living and working which contradicts the penitential soliloquies and confessions of abject helplessness and dependence he has his hero indulge in. But the point must also be made that Crusoe on his island captured the popular imagination of his day and became a legendary character because his story exploited to the full the interplay of religious-passive and secular-active values that has been discussed in pirate biography. He combines perfectly on his island the passive recognition of theoretical helplessness in the hands of God and the active involvement in self-creating activity noticed as present in separate parts of *Captain Singleton*. Crusoe's eventual integration of these two states of being makes him a secular saint whose blessedness flows from his achievement of ideological equilibrium.[1]

Crusoe learns the technique of observing events from two points of view. The first of these is the perspective of popular apologetics which scrutinizes each and every event for the evidence it gives of providential intervention. Crusoe tells us that he only really experiences repentance as he lies ill and meditates upon the operations of Providence in his life. He discovers specific instances of divine influence and intervention, including marvellous coincidences which testify to providential workings:

> First, I had observ'd, that the same Day that I broke away from my Father and my Friends, and ran away to Hull, in order to go to Sea; the same Day afterwards I was taken by the Sallee Man of War, and made a Slave.
>
> The same Day of the Year that I escap'd out of the Wreck of that Ship in Yarmouth Roads, that same Day-Year afterwards I made my Escape from Sallee in the Boat.
>
> The same Day of the Year I was born on, (viz.) the 30th of September, the same Day I had my Life so miraculously sav'd 26 Years after, when I was cast on Shore on this Island; so that my wicked Life and my solitary Life began both on a Day. (p. 157)

The intensity of these searches for God's mysterious ways is matched by Crusoe's incredible application to practical projects such as baking bread and making pottery. He has to re-experience

---

[1] If we read past the island episode, it is clear that Crusoe has learned to react properly to good fortune. In the following speech to the ship's captain who finally rescues him from his island, Crusoe speaks firmly and without hesitation about the significance of what has happened to him: 'I told him, I look'd upon him as a Man sent from Heaven to deliver me, and that the whole Transaction seem'd to be a Chain of Wonders; that such Things as these were the Testimonies we had of a secret Hand of Providence governing the World, and an Evidence, that the Eyes of an infinite Power could search into the remotest Corner of the World, and send Help to the Miserable whenever he pleased.

'I forgot not to lift up my Heart in Thankfulness to Heaven, and what Heart could forbear to bless him, who had not only in a miraculous Manner provided for one in such a Wilderness, and in such a desolate Condition, but from whom every Deliverance must always be acknowledged to proceed' (p. 324).

the conquest of nature through technology, to examine natural phenomena from the secular, utilitarian viewpoint with the same precision employed in finding their divine configurations. Real castaways like Selkirk became bestial, absorbed by their environment. Crusoe painstakingly separates himself from the island, building ramparts and digging caves. He achieves absolute independence on that level even while participating in a real way, the sincerity of which cannot be questioned, in spiritual dependence and involvement with God.

This is only possible because of Crusoe's unique location. The secular energies required to survive in the world necessarily involve destructive competition with others. Crusoe contends with nature pure and simple, and his exertions thus take place in a moral vacuum. His physical isolation paradoxically guarantees his connection with the explicit moral values of his audience. Since he is alone and against nothing but nature itself, there are no antagonists to darken the image of Crusoe's heroism or to prevent the reader's direct identification with him.

Moreover, as Rousseau perceived, his heroic self-determination can act itself out in a natural state free of the dehumanizing abstractions of commercial society.[1] Crusoe lacks the inhumanity of *homo economicus* because there is no split in his case between the economic and personal roles he plays; what he does to sustain life is perfectly consistent with the religious values he professes. The Machiavellian split between life and theory is irrelevant on Crusoe's island, for power is only the result of honest labour and endurance.

All of this is implicit. Crusoe, it is true, rejoices in his technological triumphs, but thinks of his life on the island as a punitive exile, the result of his sins. When at the very end of the book he recovers a large fortune from his Brazil plantation, his comment draws what is to him the obvious analogy: 'I might well say, now

[1] *Robinson Crusoe* is Émile's first book. Robinson's condition on his island, says Rousseau, will not be Émile's, 'but he should use it as a standard of comparison for all other conditions. The surest way to raise him above prejudice and to base his judgements on the true relations of things, is to put him in the place of a solitary man, and to judge all things as they would be judged by such a man in relation to their own utility.' See *Émile*, Everyman edition (London, 1961), p. 147.

indeed, That the latter End of Job was better than the Beginning'
(p. 338). Job had submitted; he was the very type of submission
to what seemed the arbitrary and capricious edicts of Providence.
Crusoe's summarizing epigram underlines the pervasive and
explicit religious frame of reference of the book. Crusoe may be
said to have purified the secular values which are implied by the
spirit of the book through the religious values which are its letter.
The letter, in this case, does not kill, but rather bestows a benedic-
tion upon the efficient movements of the modern spirit. Watt is
quite wrong, then, when he refers to the 'relative impotence' of
religion in Defoe's novels,[1] for in the central island episode of
Robinson Crusoe, at least, it provides a crucial set of motives for
the protagonist, a way of looking at action so that it becomes redeemed of its purely worldly direction and consequences.

The prominence of this aspect of Crusoe for his age can be
illustrated by a work which appeared in 1727 called *The English
Hermit*[2] and which crudely exploited the most successful part of
Defoe's story and presented its hero in the most attractive and
enduring of Crusoe's various roles—the holy and self-sufficient
hermit. In a sense, a work such as this gives us access to the

---

[1] *The Rise of the Novel*, p. 84.

[2] *The English Hermit, or The Unparalell'd* [sic] *and Surprizing Adventures
of one Philip Quarll; Who was lately found in an Uninhabited Island in the South
Sea, near Mexico; where he has liv'd fifty Years unknown and remote from humane
Assistance, and where he still remains and intends to end his Days.*

*With an Account of his Miraculous coming there, and most wonderful manner of
Living ever since; of his Dress, Habitation, and Utensils, as also of his being
accidentally found out by an English Merchant and an Inhabitant of Mexico,
Fishing at the Foot of the Rocks that surround the said Island.*

*With his Conversation and extream kind manner of Entertaining of the said
Persons, to whom (having shew'd several wonderful Rarities) he gave at Parting a
Mapp of the Island of his own Drawing, and a Memorial of his Birth and Education,
of all the strange and most unaccountable Transactions of his Life from the Age of
Eight Years, to that of Seventy Eight.*

*Likewise of the surprizing and unheard of Events happened in the Island since
his being there, carefully gathered out of the above said Memoirs in three Books, by
P. L. Gent.* Two versions of this work appeared in 1727, the other slightly more
literate and coherent. Arundell Esdaile speculated that this one represented an
'edited' version revised by the publisher's hack, while the one above was the
original which the author brought out as a protest against the edited version.
See 'Author and Publisher in 1727 "The English Hermit"', *The Library*,
4th series, ii (1922), 185–92. All references in the text are to the 'original'.

mythical stereotype of which Crusoe is the chief source but which differs in certain ways from Defoe's hero. These differences between Crusoe (seen more or less objectively) and the mythical figure he inspired can help us to understand more clearly, I think, the ideological strategy which makes his simultaneously active and contemplative life one of the key stories of the age.

The English Hermit is a confused and rambling narrative, but it is always careful to recommend itself primarily as a devotional exercise. It is always alert to the exemplary nature of the events it describes: the author tells his story,

chiefly to excite his Devotion and rouse his Gratitude to a due Sence of the many Favours, unaccountable Mercys that have been so liberally and often extended upon him, throughout the whole course of his Life, which has sundry times been rescued by kind Providence from appearantly [*sic*] unavoidable Perils and Dangers, as tho' decreed by Fate to a predestinated Ruin; and then, that if his Memoirs should after his Decease happen to fall into any Bodys Hands, they might be an Emulation to Vertue and an Encouragement to the Unfortunate and Distressed, never to depair, tho' in the greatest of Extremity. (p. vii)

Some wretched verses complete the preface, celebrating the contemplative joys of isolation and the wisdom of Providence, and making the hero and his story nothing less than symbols of Christian eschatology:

> Here, in these lonely Shades he just uprose,
> A Type of Resurrection to disclose;
> A Resurrection from a Wat'ry Hell,
> Where Shoals of Terrors strove which should excell.
> A Resurrection, Emblem of the Last,
> Which will recal our ev'ry Guilt that's past;
> Drawing a Grave of Conscience to our View,
> Of Horror for our Sins, both old and new;
> But so unspotted in his present State,
> I'd wish myself as happy; not more Great:
> I'd know no Change but when God calls obey,
> Prepar'd in my Accompt for Judgment-day,
> Then happy, rise from Cares and worldly Toys,
> To more substantial and eternal Joys. (p. x)

The narrative itself, somewhat more grammatical than the preface, combines those contemplative advantages of solitude with the active pleasures of founding an estate. Book I is told by a narrator who stumbles upon the hermit's island off the coast of Mexico while fishing with his companion, a Mexican named Alvarado, when their fishing-boat drifts into it. The narrator marvels at the neatness and cleanness of the hermit and his establishment. The hermit speaks of his island as an Eden and reinforces his analogy by taking them to a grotto where his voice and its echoes produce a choral effect which frightens Alvarado away. The Mexican, like all Catholic foreigners, is a stranger to the mystery, an ideological outlander who is automatically incapable of understanding the spiritual meanings of these things, and sees all according to his idolatrous lights as proof of the hermit's traffic in spirits. The narrator, an Englishman and therefore one to whom the idea of solitude and its technological mastery *cum* spiritual communion relationship to nature is a natural and blessed one, stays and is ravished by the music and its situation.

The Melody did so transport me that I willingly would have spent not only the Remainder of the Day, but the succeeding also, the Extasy having quite put out of my Mind the Necessity of my going, and the Danger of delaying: But the good Man, having sung an Evening Hymn after the Psalm, which he said he sung every Night, he takes me by the Hand: Now, said he, is not this Emulation, who but would sing with such a Chorus of Choiristers as you might imagine was there. Indeed Sir, said I, this has so great Resemblance to the Relation we have given us in Holy History, of the celestial Joys the blessed do possess in Heaven, that I thought my self already there; for which reason, I would willingly end my Days here. (p. 140)

But unlike Crusoe, this hermit never leaves his island, and the narrator's practical function is to carry back his story to England. In fact, Quarll, as we learn from Book II, differs radically from Crusoe in that he has not been a sailor or a merchant and is, indeed, a traveller only by accident. He is castaway when the ship sinks which is 'transporting' him to Barbadoes as punishment for his crimes in England. He has been first sentenced to death and then to transportation for bigamy. His biography before the ship-wreck is a bizarre story of a poor boy who survives in the world by the same fine singing voice that has ravished the narrator's soul. But Quarll is also the victim of rather turbulent passions and his own innocence, and marries four times without becoming a widower once. At last, his second wife catches him with his fourth, and he is tried and condemned upon her accusations.

Unlike the aggressive son of the bourgeoisie, Crusoe, who has seen the world and survived calamities to attain prosperity as a planter in Brazil, Quarll is a proletarian who has risen to become a professional man (singing master), a servant of the upper classes— a meaningful rise but one which still preserves him as one who waits upon others and is controlled by others. His marriages also reflect his growing desire for stability and status. His first wife is a whore who seduces him, but then leaves when she is in turn seduced by a rich and amorous knight. Then he marries a chamber-maid who aspires above their social and financial station and ruins him by her expensive aping of the quality and her voguish hypo-chondria. He marries his landlady next, and she provides security and stability for a time until she bankrupts herself by drunkenness and jealousy. His last alliance is with the proprietress of the tavern where he sings for money.

Although he progresses from innocent amorist to calculating and successful careerist, Quarll is still carefully presented as some-one who is dependent upon others, who is essentially a victim rather than an aggressor in life. The facts of his life are contradicted by the rhetoric of despair and prostration into which the narrative now lapses. His complaint to his first wife as she visits him in jail while he is under sentence of death establishes the emotional mood which afflicted virtue demands. Crusoe has earned his disasters; Quarll's disasters, the story insists, come sadly undeserved.

What joyful News, says he, can you bring a Man under my wretched Circumstances? can any thing elevate the Mind whom Heaven itself has contriv'd to depress? Am not I the very Out-cast and Scorn of Providence? Have not I been unfortunate from my Infancy? And why will you still add to my Misery? 'tis you that now make me wretched;

Had you not so compassionately assisted me in this my dismal Calamity with so much Tenderness, I then should willingly have left this hateful World. (p. 149)

This tone naturally continues when his ship is wrecked, and he (the lone survivor of course) is tossed up on a rock. Book II concludes with the rhetorical commonplaces of affliction and near-despair as Quarll looks about and sees 'the deadful Effects of the late Tempest, dead Corps, broken Planks, and batter'd Chests floating' (p. 155) on one side, and on the other 'the Prospect of . . . Hunger and Thirst, attended with all the Miseries that can make Life burthensome' (p. 155). He is saved from these alternatives by the religious perspective which reinterprets calamity and converts it into a providential arrangement: 'but why should I complain? and have so much Reason to be thankful! Had I been cut off, when the Cares of saving this worthless Carcass intercepted me from seeking the Salvation of my Soul, I should not have had present Opportunity of taking care of it' (p. 155). It is only after this perspective is established and Quarll's passivity is reasserted after a brief suicidal wish—'looking on the dead Corps, whom the Sea now and then drove to the Rock, and back again. Oh! that I was like one of you, said he, past all Dangers; I have shar'd with you in the Terrors of Death, why did I not also partake with you of its Relief?' (p. 156)—that the narrative can allow the hero to discover the fertile island which lies behind his back.

Here the subtle and psychological connection developed in *Robinson Crusoe* between a proper disposition towards God's inscrutable purposes and a proper enjoyment of the advantages of solitude is made obvious and immediate. The island becomes effectively Quarll's secular reward for his spiritual interpretation of events; he is free to enter into his demi-paradise because he has not despaired of God's Providence. Although he suffers some spiritual relapses later on, he has achieved without trying at all the ideological balance between secular 'survival' and religious 'preservation' which Crusoe had to strive for so long and earnestly.

Once again, as in Quarll's earlier life, the struggle to survive and the victory which follows are described in terms of dependence.

Where Crusoe impresses us by his skill at practical tasks, this hermit is sustained in a more direct way. Starving at first, he has a dream which instructs him to go back to the rock whereon he was first thrown. There he finds a codfish trapped in a hole in the rock: 'where Providence rescu'd my Life from the grim Jaws of Death, there it has provided me withal to support it' (p. 160). Like Crusoe, he farms and domesticates animals, but his staples remain roots which he simply gathers and fish which he catches easily. We recall Crusoe's laborious and triumphant efforts to bake bread and to make pottery. Quarll makes rudimentary articles such as tables and chairs, but his dishes and kettle are provided by large and beautiful turtle shells. Crusoe's discoveries of providential purpose are gradual and internal; Quarll's are external and spectacular. When a ship appears his content vanishes and he signals madly for help. But the rocks around the island prevent the boat which is sent for him from landing, and the ship sails away. Quarll despairs now, having betrayed Providence which sustains him here on the island and lost all hope of rescue by the outside world. The antithesis between the world, where individual movement and self-help are possible, and his island, where all movement is only by providential permission, is deliberate and explicit:

. . . his full Dependance upon a Retreat made him to abandon all further Reliance on Providence, whom then he could implore; but now having ungratefully despis'd Heaven's Bounties, which had been so largely bestow'd on him, he has forfeited all hopes of Assistance from thence, and expects not from the World: Thus destitute, and in the greatest Perplexity, he cries out, where shall I now fly for help? the World can give me none, and I dare not crave any more from Heaven. (pp. 216–17)

He prepares to throw himself into the sea, 'but a vast large Monster, raising out of the Water, with its terrible Jaws wide open, looking at him in a most dreadful manner, stop'd the Execution of his desperate Design' (p. 217). The subtle 'signs' of Providence which Crusoe learns to extract from the flow of events are here magnified into palpable and sensational manifestations of overseeing deity. Quarll's monster may, of course, be taken as a vivid hallucination, for when he attempts to draw a picture of it, he traces an apocalyptic creature with features from every beast imaginable. This possibility does not lessen its supernatural implications, for 'visions' and prophetic dreams are frequent occurrences for Quarll. Crusoe dreams as well, and he was later made to have visions, but Quarll's dreams are more frequent and more clearly prophetic, like the dream about the codfish already mentioned. Crusoe's dream reflects his spiritual and psychological guilt, and Defoe's description of it captures the uncertain and vaguely remembered terror of real nightmares.

I saw a Man descend from a great black Cloud, in a bright Flame of Fire, and light upon the Ground: He was all over as bright as a Flame, so that I could but just bear to look towards him; his Countenance was most inexpressibly dreadful, impossible for Words to describe; when he stepp'd upon the Ground with his Feet, I thought the Earth trembled . . . and all the Air look'd, to my Apprehension, as if it had been fill'd with Flashes of Fire.

He was no sooner landed upon the Earth, but he moved forward towards me, with a long Spear or Weapon in his Hand, to kill me; and when he came to a rising Ground, at some Distance, he spoke to me, or I heard a Voice so terrible, that it is impossible to express the Terror of it; all that I can say, I understood, was this, Seeing all these Things have not brought thee to Repentance, now thou shalt die: At which Words, I thought he lifted up the Spear that was in his Hand to kill me. (p. 102)

Quarll's dreams lack this psychological verisimilitude, are crudely allegorical, and can concern external events. He dreams of an ugly and ill-tempered old man who is being petitioned by a beautiful lady with three pairs of breasts. The old man drives her away by having his servant blow snow and ice on her. Quarll awakens and interprets: 'certainly this old Man is Time, laying up a Store of Frost and Snow against next Winter, and that goodly Woman is Nature, who being tender over all her Creatures, interceded for Moderation; and his surly Refusal and rough Usage prognosticates a forward and hard Winter, to whose Severity I must lie expos'd, being altogether unprovided' (p. 165). Another dream, after he has been visited and robbed by Indians and French fishermen, is even more artificial and allegorical: a lady appears and introduces herself as Patience, restoring his serenity by granting him 'Content, which you throw away after worthless Things' (p. 228).[1]

These dreams are perhaps the most obvious sign of this instinctive modification of the mythical type Defoe popularized in *Robinson Crusoe*. Quarll becomes a simple and uncomplicated embodiment of the religious values of passivity and submission, as Crusoe's great practical abilities and technological sophistication are strategically minimized and counteracted in various ways. The narrative tends to suggest by its rhetorical tone and emphases and its arrangement of events that Quarll achieves his efficient and bounteous Eden only with Providence's direct intervention. This English hermit's existence is designed to rehearse with numbing frequency the emotional commonplaces which surround the idea of providential deliverance, and his island is a natural opportunity for these clichés.

The effect of this carefully emphasized isolation (Friday is replaced by a trained monkey named Beaufidelle) is also to allow the hermit to act out gratifying fantasies of total self-control and self-sufficiency without their subversive secular implications. An independent establishment, the conquest of nature in an exotic locale, can easily turn into a daemonic enterprise without an elaborate and insistent religious frame of reference or network of motives. The difference between a great and sensitive work such as *Robinson Crusoe* and an inept publisher's machine such as *The English Hermit* is that the former communicates the vital dialectic process which is historical reality, combining in its narrative that religious constellation of motives with their partially secular origins and results. The latter merely rehearses and reiterates the inert conclusions of that process, distorting the authenticity of the original, as

[1] Quarll also dreams that his island is literally an Eden: 'These most agreeable Objects [various exotic flora and fauna], join'd with the delightful Noise of the Fountains falling into their Basins, and the purling Streams running their Course, together with the various harmonious Notes of diverse Kinds of Singing-Birds, did put him into an Ecstasie; sure, said he, this is the Garden of Eden, out of which unfortunate Adam was cast after his Fall, as being a Dwelling only for Innocence' (p. 243

most popular literature will, by producing a simplified reproduc-
tion. Crusoe in his various ordeals is an eighteenth-century saint
of flesh and blood, Quarll is clearly made of plaster.

The necessity of establishing this frame of reference, of qualify-
ing the ethos of self-determination by a religious orientation, is
especially urgent in narratives which exploit the rest of Crusoe's
roles. Crusoe, we remember, begins as a sailor and guilty wanderer
from the safety of a career in the middle station of life. After his
profitable first voyage to Africa (he returns home with £300),
he is captured by Moorish pirates and made a slave in Sallee. It is
a symbolic transformation, as Crusoe puts it, 'from a Merchant to
a miserable Slave', a compensation, in mythical terms, for the
triumphant secular enterprise of commercial travelling on the high
seas and into exotic places.

Captivity in Barbary had achieved by Crusoe's time a European
legend all its own, and was, as a recent summary of the English
literature concerned with it has put it, 'familiar to English readers
as a lively emblem of Hell'.[1] In *Robinson Crusoe* such captivity is
a purgatory, a temporary punishment for his disobedience: 'I look'd
back upon my Father's prophetick Discourse to me, that I should
be miserable, and have none to relieve me, which I thought was
now so effectually brought to pass, that it could not be worse; that
now the Hand of Heaven had overtaken me, and I was undone
without Redemption' (p. 20). Barbary, or any non-Christian, non-
European place, gains its appropriately religious horror as a suitable antidote to secular excess because of its specifically heathenish
associations. The 'punishment' need not be explicit and the traveller
may be easily presented as a Christian champion, converted into
such willy-nilly through the demands of his heathenish captors.
Slavery among the avowed enemies of Christianity and eventual
deliverance had obvious biblical echoes and heroic resonances
which served as ideological ballast to the high-flying implications
of travel.

For example, there appeared in 1714 an extremely coherent

---

[1] G. A. Starr, 'Escape from Barbary: A Seventeenth-Century Genre', *HLQ*,
xxix (November 1965), 35.

narrative whose title advertises the exotic miscellany in which it deals: *The Adventures of Five Englishmen from Pulo Condoro, A Factory of the New Company in the East-Indies, Who were Ship-wreckt upon the little Kingdom of Jehore, not far distant, and being seized on by the Inhabitants, were brought before the King, and detain'd for some Months; with the many Accidents that befel them during their Abode in that Island. Together with an Account of the Mannors* [sic] *and Customs of the Inhabitants, and of the Birds, Beasts, Fruits, etc. both of the Islands of Jehore, and Pulo Condore* [sic]. It is presented as a journal kept by one of the expedition, Walter Vaughan, and in a manner which from the beginning underlines the twin attractions of the story; for it carefully lists all the practical details and mysterious omens which mark the venture:

Now the same Prow [that is, their boat] had Four Guns put into her, each near a Thousand Weight, Seven Huddles Six Foot broad, and Fifteen Foot long, a Butt of Line, a Canister of Sugar, a Musket, Cartouch Box, Four Gun Cartridges, a Case Bottle of fresh Water, and about Fourteen Gallons of Rack, the She Cat, and her Two Young Ones, which belonged to the Two Women.

.   .   .   .   .

This Morning the Women told the Captain, that they had been troubled in the Night with strange and frightful Dreams, as did likewise Mr. Williams, the Clerk of the Factory; that their Hearts fail'd them; and that they had rather undergo the Fatigue of travelling o'er the Hills, and through the Woods, then venture about with the Prow. This Morn-ing as I was Smoaking a Pipe in the Larboard Gang-way my Nose dropp'd Six or Seven Drops of Blood on my Hand.[1]

The voyagers survive a storm which wrecks their ship, and they commit themselves 'to the immediate Protection of our most Merci-ful and Compassionate Creator without which it had been Stupidity to think of surviving those dismal impending Dangers in so crazy and leaky a Boat'.[2] They manage to come to land safely, and we hear about their difficulties in finding a large settlement from which they can find their way back to civilization. All along, various curious sights which the country affords are set down for

---

[1] pp. 4–5, 7–8.   [2] pp. 12–13.

our delight, along with pertinent economic sidelights: meeting a native trader who says that he will take them to Jehore, they are told 'that he Sold the People Arse-clouts, and took Canes for them. I ask'd how he would Sell Canes? He told me for 3 Dollars per Hundred. I have ask'd others the same Question, who would take 2 Dollars or an Arse-clout per Hundred.'[1]

Brought at last to the palace of the king of Jehore, they are there confronted with a choice between embracing the local religion and death. They stand firm, in spite of a Dutchman who has already apostatized and assures them that only formal renunciation is required.[2] Deliberate and sensible compromise such as this would only dilute the heroism which sustains the narrative, and they reject it as a possibility, even in the face of their reception at court the next day: 'They told us if we did not assent to their Propositions we must expect nothing but Death; for the more ready Execution of which they had placed Men by us with Naked Creeses in their Hands, who we expected (upon our Refusals) were to have obeyed their Bloody Commands.'[3]

At last, however, the narrator is the only one to remain faithful. But they have all been made to act out, the narrator to the point of heroism, a mythical pattern which insists that they have entered a sphere in which no resistance is possible, where submission and dependence upon Providence are the only possibilities. Once the stand has been made and the religious credentials of the heroic participants established, then the consequences of the situation can be mitigated by the practical skills and secular resources of the narrator and his comrades. Martyrdom is escaped indirectly through the narrator's skill in medicine, which makes him an indispensable person at the king of Jehore's court. After this muted heroism, the rest of the book is devoted to the various attractions of the travel account. A large part of this, as the title

---

[1] p. 47.
[2] Swift testifies at the end of the third book of *Gulliver's Travels* to the proverbial flexibility of Dutch traders in such matters. The Emperor of Japan is led to suspect Gulliver's pose as a Dutch merchant when he refuses to trample on the crucifix, a traditional ceremony used to demonstrate the good intentions of European visitors to Swift's Japan.   [3] p. 74.

announces, is simply a description of the techniques of trading in the East Indies. But the merchant has already proven himself as a Christian hero.

The pleasures and advantages to be gained from such a work in 1714 had not changed by 1739. They are all summarized neatly on the first page of *The History of the Long Captivity and Adventures of Thomas Pellow in South Barbary*:

> The Facts and Adventures it relates are of so extraordinary a Nature, afford so great a Variety of Entertainment, and have been so little mentioned by any other Writer, that it cannot fail of gratifying the Curiosity, and giving Pleasure to every Reader. Here he will find described the Manners, Customs, Temper and Genius of a People, all entirely different from his own. Here he will see the most Savage Wars, and the most violent Revolutions, that ever happened in any State or Kingdom: Here too his Eyes will be struck with the piteous Spectacle of his Fellow Countrymen enduring Hardships and Cruelties, which, but to think of, is dreadful Horror, and which may serve to raise in him a most tender Compassion for such unhappy Sufferers, and the most grateful Acknowledgments to the Almighty, that he himself has been exempted from such severe Trials.[1]

Pellow is a very young Crusoe, having gone to sea at eleven, when he is captured, made a servant to one of the emperor's sons, and continually urged to turn Mahometan. But 'I was thoroughly resolved not to renounce my Christian Faith, be the Consequence what it would' (p. 14). He is forced to yield after torture, but even this surrender is described in terms of providential arrangement: weak from torture and starvation, he expects death 'and happy, no Doubt, had I been, had it so happened: I should certainly then have dy'd a Martyr, and probably thereby gained a glorious Crown in the Kingdom of Heaven; but the Almighty did not then see it fit' (p. 15). The book ends with the same kind of declaration, as Pellow says with appropriate italics that his life has been so full of incredible dangers

that all must allow that nothing but the *Almighty Protection* of *a great, good, all-seeing, most-sufficient, and gracious GOD*, could have

---

[1] pp. 1–2. All further references are included in the text.

carried me through it, or delivered me out of it; therefore, to *HIM* be the *Glory, Honour,* and *Praise,* and may HE so order my Heart, as always to continue a *lively Remembrance* thereof, and so order my Ways, to live up to HIS *Divine Precepts,* during the Remainder of this *Mortal Life*; that after all these my Sufferings ended here, I may be crowned with a *glorious Immortality* in the Kingdom of *HEAVEN.* (p. 388)

These are set pieces, religious book-ends which support a shelf of fantastic and exotic trials through which the narrator passes with an equally fantastic equanimity. We are made conscious not so much of preservation as of survival through Pellow's great ability and agility, qualities which develop to match each crisis.

After his 'apostasy', he is made a servant of the queen's favourite son, a boy of eight; but he has still, as he makes clear, to depend upon his own discretion and circumspection: 'I was oblig'd to walk like one walking on the Brink of a dangerous Precipice; whence, should he happen to make but the least wry Step, he is sure to tumble down and break his Neck' (p. 24). Even his young master, for example, is so barbarously cruel and absolute a tyrant that Pellow sees him 'kill his favourite Black with his own Hand, by stabbing him into the Belly with a Knife, and only for coming very accidentally where he was feeding a Pair of Pidgeons, and their flying away for a few Minutes' (p. 26). He is forced to move gingerly in a society filled with menacing, gigantically cruel Moors, who are made to act out their legendary monstrosities with histrionic gestures. Thus, the emperor's normal ferocity is such that instead of issuing verbal commands for the execution of someone who has offended or displeased, he simply signals to his minions: 'when he would have any Person's Head cut off by drawing or shrinking his own as close as he could to his Shoulders, and then with a very quick or sudden Motion extending it; and when he would have any strangled, by the quick Turn of his Arm-wrist, his Eye being fixed on the Victims' (p. 27).

Pellow not only manages to survive the emperor's moods but rises in his service to a position of power in the army. He participates in many dangerous military expeditions and numerous pitched battles but escapes unscathed. The old emperor dies and

Pellow is arrested and almost executed as the vacant throne is jockeyed for amid intrigue and counter-intrigue. But again Pellow survives and serves the new emperor. He lives comfortably but sees the inevitable outcome of the unparalleled oppressions of the new emperor, and calculates action: 'as I found the Ruin of the Country every Day more apparently approaching and plainly foresaw that it could not be long e'er the tyrant was driven out, and then all would be in the utmost Confusion, I for the Time lived as contentedly as I could, and with Christian Patience awaited the Event' (p. 222). Christian patience sees the right moment, and Pellow makes definite plans for escape, but not without a meditation on his many deliverances:

how wonderfully I had been hitherto (through the Goodness of God) preserved from so many Perils and Dangers, how many Thousands I had slain in the Field of Battle, and why it might not have been my unhappy Fate as well as their's [*sic*]; then humbly offering up my most unfeign'd Thanks to God for all his Mercies thitherto received, and earnestly imploring his future Protection, got me up, and soon with an eager Resolution set myself in Order for my March: and as all my Transactions under any of their Emperors end here, I shall (and I think very properly) call the following Part of my History my *Wonderful Escape* and *Happy Return*. (pp. 243–4)

His escape is naturally a prodigious venture, full of horrendous obstacles and miraculous deliverances. Like other captives in Barbary (some historical figures), who had survived, escaped, and published, Pellow insists upon the necessity of God's assistance.[1] He describes himself and his trials at the very end of his narrative in biblical language which makes use of the religious analogies which come easily: 'And now is the so long lost Sheep again restored to his Owners after his long straying' (p. 388). And his captors owe their significant and peculiar dangers to their automatic religious classification as 'Monsters and ravenous Wolves of

---

[1] Speaking of the various seventeenth-century accounts of escape from North African slavery, G. A. Starr notes the following pattern: 'In these narratives, human effort is directly, not inversely proportional to divine assistance; man's stamina and ingenuity are complemented, not obviated, by supposed miracles.' See 'Escape from Barbary: A Seventeenth-Century Genre', *HLQ*, xxix (November 1965), 46.

Infidelity' (p. 388). Pellow's tremendous capacity for survival is accommodated and indeed enriched by the wealth of religious meanings and suggestions which his story contains. The normal suspenseful satisfactions of the adventure narrative are complemented, then, in a very full way by the combination of two mythical types: the intrepid traveller through exotic places bringing news of strange cultures back to a curious Europe, and the pilgrim-child of God being led from a land of Egyptian bondage.[1]

Hermits and slaves provoke fantasies of escape from worlds of paralysing corruption (even though one is trying to get back to the place that the other has left) as well as escape from the ordinary daily landscape to novel vistas. The traveller *per se* provides similar vicarious satisfactions, and he, too, is invariably a figure of legendary dexterity and adaptability in the face of disaster after disaster. But his enemy is neither primarily the heathen nor his own sins, although these may occasionally play a part. The ideological tension is supplied by the very nature of travel, not only its intrinsic dangers and huge commercial possibilities but the exhilarating sense of freedom and total possibility which the ethos of the travel-adventure book communicates.

[1] *Robert Drury's Journal* (1729), now attributed to Defoe, relies to a large extent on the same pattern. Drury survives as a slave among the heathen in Madagascar, but he refuses to kneel to his master and to participate in idolatrous ceremonies. Like Pellow, Drury is in constant danger among his captors, even though he manages to attain some status and acceptance within the native community. He, too, manages a long and arduous escape which takes him clear across Madagascar with the usual endurance and ingenuity. But this escape is punctuated with exclamations such as this: 'I lay down, thinking of the hard Fate which prosecuted me; but as Providence had conducted me hitherto, I did not doubt, in due Time, my Deliverance would be perfected; and with this Resignation I went to sleep' (p. 310). Throughout his long account of perilous survival, Drury is careful to use the religious frame of reference which exploits the extraordinary as a clear manifestation of the providential.
Captured again after his trek, he displeases the old and choleric king of the area and is taken out to be executed. He is saved by the pleas of the king's harem and taken back to his master. 'In my Journey, my Guards told me, I was the First that was ever brought back alive from the Place of Execution; which I could not but ascribe to a special Providence' (p. 421). There are, of course, many other aspects of the travel account present in *Robert Drury's Journal* such as social and political reflections, geographical and cultural descriptions, and even the Deistic speculations which have made some uneasy about the attribution to Defoe. But all of this is firmly placed within the key fable of the child of God helpless and alone among menacing heathen.

The traveller-adventurer is not confined to the limiting roles of hermit or slave, although he may play them both for a while in his story. He comes dangerously close at times to the secular independence of the pirate in his protean capacity for further travel and more adventures. His condition lacks the natural religious analogies of the hermit or slave, but his greater freedom demands as much if not more instinctive compensation by the religious motives and meanings which can be assigned to him and his story. What is convincingly integrated in *Robinson Crusoe* becomes obtrusively and crudely clear in popular repetitions of Defoe's successful formula. A popular work such as William Chetwood's *The Voyages, Dangerous Adventures, and imminent Escapes of Captain Richard Falconer* (1720),[1] like the *English Hermit*, shows again just how much the combination of the clichés of religious polemic and the attractions of travel literature were regarded as a profitable merger.

Chetwood is probably copying Defoe when he begins by quoting the advice of Falconer's father to stay home and take up a safe land trade. But circumstances rather than personal compulsion force Falconer to sea when his father is ruined and has to flee the country. His seafaring career begins when he is shipwrecked during his first voyage and stranded on an uninhabited island. He is later joined by others from another ship who have survived their wreck. They all merely subsist without establishing themselves as hermits and Falconer begins to despair. One of his companions, Randal, warns him:

Mr. Falconer, and my Fellow-Sufferers; but 'tis to you (pointing at me) [Falconer] that I chiefly address my Speech, being you seem to despair of a Redemption from this Place (as you call it) more than any other of the same Condition. Is not the Providence of a Power Supreme shewn in every Accident in the Life of Man; even you your self, how much better is your Condition now, than you cou'd have imagin'd it

---

[1] Chetwood was a bookseller, dramatist, and prompter at Drury Lane from 1722 to 1742. He wrote a number of plays, *A General History of the Stage* (1949), *The British Theatre* (1750), and several other novels, *Voyages of Captain Robert Boyle* (1726) and *Voyages of William Owen Gwin Vaughan* (1736). All references in the text are to the first edition.

would have been a Month ago? . . . Think you that the Divine Providence that cast Jonas from the Bowels of the Whale, has not that Retentive Power still left, to aid and fetch us from this Place. (Part ii, p. 2)

Captain Falconer is being reminded of the eternal efficiency of Providence in disposing human events. This is important and has to be stressed often in the course of the book, for the seemingly shapeless and improbable narrative can thus acquire a degree of pattern, and the extravagant misfortunes can be justified as dramatic opportunities to display the power of God. The succession of cliff-hanging near-disasters in which the book deals is thereby enriched by the sensational popular apologetics of the day. In the passage just quoted, the stilted elevation of style and the biblical allusion simplify matters for a moment and squeeze the religious implications out of the situation. It is a conventional and facile sort of gloss, for Falconer has hardly been running from God like the reluctant prophet. He lacks Crusoe's hard-won sense of beatitude, but the narrative makes him mechanically capable of the appropriate response to his escapes and deliverances.

He does, however, begin by almost despairing. Randal, who has noticed this spiritual impropriety, declares that he has first-hand knowledge of the workings of Providence and tells two long and pious stories of how he had escaped from North American Indians and then escaped after being shipwrecked alone on a rock about half a mile in circumference. In both instances he displays the same inventive resourcefulness we have noted in other stranded souls, but this independence, although much described, is not stressed. Randal concludes with an application of his case to their present extremity:

Now think with yourself, Mr. Falconer, whether we need doubt the Providence of God in helping us from this Island? There's nothing here like the Hardships I have undergone, and yet have been happily freed from; and therefore you need not despair. Despair is the Frenzy of the Mind, and ought to be avoided by having a true Notion of the Power we serve. (Part ii, p. 31)

Falconer happens to smile at this point and seems to question the real usefulness and relevance to their situation of Randal's piety. Randal's reply is tendentious; he sees in the doubting smile a rival ideology:

As to your own Belief, (Mr. Falconer, said he) I leave it to your self; but I don't like jesting with Sacred Things . . . . your Knowledge seems to be profane! I have known a great many airy young Fellows that have talk'd idly on such Things to make People have an Opinion of their Wit; but yet, I believe, even in the very Time of their Utterance, their Conscience told 'em, they were doing what was not pleasing to God or Man. (Part ii, p. 33)

Falconer is naturally convinced, for Randal has gone from exhortation to ideological mobilization. He has for the moment made quite explicit the nature of the struggle and the tactics of the enemy. That enemy seems especially near in a book such as this because of the dangerous symbolic possibilities of travel literature, and Falconer and his mates never quite lose this connection with the devil's party. The ideological strategy of the genre demands, however, that they do their best for the angels, and the rest of the narrative is an extended refutation of the secular independence they still helplessly embody.

After a number of trials, they begin their journey back to England. Their ship is taken over, however, by its mutinous crew, who are soon revealed as ex-pirates. About to be set adrift in a small boat by the pirates, Falconer and his men gain control by virtue of a lucky accident. A dying pirate recites the appropriate lesson:

I see you have overpower'd us, and I likewise see the Hand of Heav'n is in it. I now with Horror find (added he) that what you intimated to me about Heav'n to be true; I see it more in this one Accident, than in all the Preachings of the Fathers. . . . I forsook all Religion in general, and now too late, I find, that to dally with Heav'n is fooling ones self; but yet in this one Moment of my Life, that's left, I heartily repent of all my past Crimes, and rely upon the Saviour of the World, that dy'd for our Sins, to pardon mine. With that, he cross'd himself, and expir'd. (Part ii, pp. 77–8)

Such moments make it clear that the procedure of the book can be resolved into a series of broadly drawn melodramatic tableaux, opportunities to present standard moral-pathetic figures such as this ,repentant pirate, opportunities, specifically, to repeat the emotionally charged commonplaces of submission and deliverance. Scenes such as this, with their sensational demonstration of the poetic justice Providence always arranges, are ready-made from the popular iconography of the day. These static moments represent a very noticeable arresting of the onrushing action, the formless and plotless variety in which such a book deals, in order to allow the principals to strike attitudes and to recite set speeches.

What we participate in most of the time in reading Falconer's story is a succession of voyages, commercial transactions, wrecks, captivities, daring and ingenious escapes, and wide-ranging travelogues. But in its static moments the book insists that this sheer movement, which seems to provide its own justification by its very variety and intensity, possesses pattern and significance. The daemonic attractions of the careers of traveller-adventurers such as Falconer remain; his progress through strange sights and daring adventures invokes the secular world of total possibility and independence which is the mythical core of travel literature. But moments of arrested motion such as the ones we have examined do their best to establish a proper ideological balance, to make sure that we remember the older mythical associations of travel as an arduous pilgrimage directed from above.

Such a balance is maintained in a more integrated way by *The Four Years Voyages of Captain George Roberts* (1726), a work now attributed to Defoe.[1] The extravagant if attractive variety of Falconer's adventures is here exchanged for a fairly unified treatment of Roberts's long and difficult attempt to get back to English civilization after being set adrift in the middle of strange seas by pirates. All of the usual satisfactions and symbolic possibilities of travel-adventure are provided, but the concentration supplied by the novelistic limitation to one basic situation gives the narrative a pattern and religious coherence which is able to do without abrupt and artificial moral tableaux. The traveller is nicely and unobtrusively accommodated to the pilgrim.

---

[1] See McBurney, *A Checklist of English Prose Fiction 1700–1739*, p. 69. All references in the text are to the 1726 London edition.

The book begins with the customary doxology by referring to itself as a 'faithful Relation of the several Dispensations of Providence to me' (sig. A2ʳ). Roberts, a ship's surgeon, is captured by pirates, who treat him fairly enough. Recognizing Roberts's capabilities and admiring his moral rectitude, they ask him to join them and tell him that he will be given the first ship they take. Roberts refuses in a speech which reminds the pirates of their unregenerate state and, of course, implicitly increases his own righteousness:

> Yet I hope, said I, and God forbid that there should not be some of you, who have a Thought of a great and powerful God, and a Consciousness of his impartial Justice to punish, as well as of his unfathomable Mercy to pardon Offenders upon their unfeigned Repentance, which would not so far extend as to encourage us to run on in sinning, thereby presuming to impose on his Mercy. (p. 67)

The contrast which Roberts draws between the pirates and himself is deliberate; he is ever mindful of his dependence upon God, where some of the pirates, as they are quick to retort, have 'no God but their Money, nor Saviour but their Arms' (p. 67). The ideological antitheses meet here, and Roberts is in the subsequent journey to illustrate the possibilities of movement within full acknowledgement of divine influence; in fact, the narrative is really built upon the paradox of complete helplessness in the hands of God as the best guarantee of calm self-reliance. The great accomplishment of this compelling story from this point on is that it arranges a series of trials which makes such a combination (the surrender to Providence becoming from a modern point of view a perfectly plausible psychological serenity) not only convincing but coherent in its symbolism.

When he is at last sent off by the pirates, Roberts reminds them again of their limitations: 'you can do no more than God is pleas'd to permit you; and I own, for that Reason, I ought to take it patiently' (p. 92). His worst enemy among the pirates, one Russel, answers sarcastically that 'if it be done by God's Permission, you need not fear that he will permit any Thing hurtful to befall so good a Man as you are' (p. 92). This misses the point, for Roberts's survival will be due not to any direct and sensational intervention of Providence, but to the calm resourcefulness which can function unimpaired in a crisis because of the spiritual serenity provided by his active and unassailably logical resignation to Providence:

> . . . if I was permitted to perish, I knew the worst; and doubted not but he would graciously pardon my Sins, and receive me to his Everlasting Rest; and in this Respect, what they had intended for my Misfortune, would be the Beginning of my Happiness; and that in the mean Time, I had nothing to do but to resign myself to his blessed Will and Protection, and bear my Lot with Patience. (p. 96)

Roberts's coolness is presented as the result of this psychological and theological strategy, and he proceeds with utter equanimity about the business of surviving in a hopeless situation. He is set free in a sloop which lacks its main sail, given only two young boys to help him sail it, and no provisions. The ensuing journey is an ordeal which Roberts survives by calculation such as this:

> I came upon Deck, and ask'd Potter, my biggest Boy, if the Pumps were in order, or whether the Pirates had broke or put them out of order? He said, he thought not; so I went to work with them, being the only Way to know; I put the two Boys to one Pump, and I exercis'd the other; I bid them not strike with the Pump, but to draw a long drawing Stroke, which in a Manner delivers as much Water as striking, especially when there are not Hands to Spell (that is, to take Turns while the others recover Breath) besides, it doth not tire so soon, and consequently would not make them so drowthy as striking would. (p. 99)

We are hardly conscious, as we are in other accounts, of any 'signs' of providential intervention, but are instead fascinated by exact descriptions of the procedures of survival such as searching the ship for provisions, fashioning a fishing-line, catching a shark with it, cooking and salting it, and keeping careful track of time and place. To be sure, all of this is carefully balanced with the conventional religious rhetoric of dependence. When they come to land, for example, their boat is caught in a heavy sea and matters grow desperate. Some natives who have come aboard to help him bring his boat into port resolve to leave in their boat and offer to bring him along. Roberts judges his chances to be better in his boat, but his judgement is carefully encased in the correct pious commonplaces: 'Whereupon I told them, I was resolv'd to trust to Providence, and continue in the Sloop; and if they would do so too, I doubted not, with God's Blessing, but they would by far, stand the better Chance' (p. 128).

When he at last reaches land, his ship is wrecked on the island of St. John, one of the Cape Verde group. It becomes apparent that his deliverance is only partial, for he is stranded at the bottom of an almost sheer cliff. The friendly natives who cluster about him can climb this rock, but with difficulty; and Roberts, weak from his ordeal, is almost killed as they help him climb. He falls ill from exposure and improper food, defeated at last by his natural human limits. This defeat and subsequent illness under a huge and impassable natural obstacle restore that sense of human limitation and weakness which the triumphs of the travel-adventure narrative are liable to obscure. Roberts's almost fatal prostration under the mountain is, in terms of the ideological strategy of the travel account, a final compensation for the great secular energies which he possesses.

Taken, at length, to the village by canoe, he recovers and diligently observes the various industries of the island, recording them and their techniques in engrossing detail. With the help of the islanders, he sets out to build a boat to return home in and exhibits the characteristic ingenuity and resourcefulness of the Englishman alone. He sharpens, for example, a discarded saw to the great amazement of the natives:

> I sharpened it with the File, and set it as well as I could, so that I made it cut tolerably well, which they all much admired at, saying, That none of the People on the Island, could find the Way to make the Saw sharp; and that they believed, it exceeded the Ingenuity of Signore Carlos [a Welshman who has been stranded there for some years] though he was very ingenious, and, till I came among them, they thought no-body could go beyond him; but they saw, as they said, I could far outstrip him, as he outstripped them. (p. 277)

The barely suppressed pride of this passage shows us just how delicate is the balance between the rhetoric of dependence and the realities, in the literal sense, of the narrative. Alter the perspective slightly and the Providence which Roberts keeps thanking is really the main obstacle to his survival, the inscrutable power that arranges the succession of near-disasters. But for such heroes as Roberts this religious perspective is not a blueprint of the world but a set of motives with which to conquer it. Just as the elaborate deference paid to the older religious associations of travel allows the traveller-adventurer to be an impeccably moral culture hero, so too, Roberts's fatalism and pious acceptance of the inevitable make his self-creating genius an act of submission to Providence.

The traveller, then, whether primarily a hermit, slave, or merchant-adventurer, is a figure whose contradictory personality seems to express an otherwise unsuspected uncertainty in the expansive and energetic middle-class civilization of eighteenth-century England. Whatever his specific objectives, the traveller is inescapably involved in the modern secular enterprise of conquering nature, of asserting human control in a new and total fashion. It is this symbolic enterprise and the powerful daemonic personality it requires which give the diverse events he narrates their unity and significance. But this egoism of the traveller cannot be allowed its full implications, or he becomes like his anti-type, the pirate. These implications are instinctively checked and his story purified by a system of motives which denies that egoism and substitutes what I have called the religious definition of man and nature. This definition requires the traditional rhetoric of submission and petition to a supreme power and the older set of suggestions and associations connected with travel. All of these narrative strategies are qualifications of the 'scenic' properties involved; they effectively shift the field of the travellers' acts so that their enterprises acquire edifying and unsubversive ideological meaning.

IV

'AS LONG AS ATALANTIS SHALL BE READ': THE SCANDAL CHRONICLES OF MRS. MANLEY AND MRS. HAYWOOD

TRAVEL literature was and is easily justified as positive diversion, painless education. We can understand its appeal and celebrate its success as a fortunate and pleasing thing. But if we approach the enormously popular work of writers such as Mrs. Manley and Mrs. Haywood with the high-mindedness that literary history has traditionally required, our mood must change to dismay at the corruption of popular taste. Literary historians thus appalled at the undeniable vogue of the *chronique scandaleuse* and the scurrilous *roman à clef* have paused only to fit these works into the proper slot and to establish the necessary origins and genealogies. Thus, Bonamy Dobrée disposes of Mrs. Manley and Mrs. Haywood in a sentence by noting that they were 'largely influenced by French fiction' and 'merely worked out variants of the Portuguese Nun range of emotions, without achieving any individualization, or attempting even Mrs. Behn's timid realism'.[1] *Sub specie aeternitatis*, of course, Mrs. Manley and Mrs. Haywood deserve no more than this; to us they are absolutely irrelevant in either a moral or an aesthetic sense, and Professor Dobrée is being mildly ironic when he suggests that both ladies 'may well remain unread'.[2]

---

[1] *English Literature in the Early Eighteenth Century* (Oxford, 1959), pp. 409–10. The 'Portuguese Nun' refers to an enormously popular work published in France in 1669 called the *Lettres portugaises* which claimed to consist of five actual letters written by a Portuguese nun, Marianna Alcoforado, to her lover, the Comte de Chamilly, who had deserted her. These were first translated into English in 1678 by Sir Roger L'Estrange, and by 1740 had appeared ten times. They also appeared in a bilingual edition in 1702, and several versified versions were also published. See Robert A. Day, *Told in Letters* (Ann Arbor, Michigan, 1966), pp. 33–8, for a full description and analysis of this work.

[2] Dobrée, p. 409.

But what has been left out, what has gone without the necessary emphasis, is that their books were widely and continually read during the first four decades of the eighteenth century. We have not really disposed of them and their embarrassing popularity by drawing schematic diagrams which reveal the components out of which their popular entertainment machines were built. It is perfectly true that the genre began in France, that translations of French *chroniques scandaleuses* were frequent and popular in the early eighteenth century, and that English versions merely represent an adaptation and localization of these French techniques.[1] The question still remains: why were these *romans à clef* so successfully naturalized in England? and what does their popularity, since they are grossly deficient as 'realistic' novels, tell us about the taste and ideological requirements of their wide audience? We might take refuge in the pessimistic speculation that scandalous

[1] A. J. Tieje pointed out long ago that the *chronique scandaleuse* emerged as a formal type in 1660 with Bussy-Rabutin's *Histoire amoureuse des Gaules*. See *The Theory of Characterization in Prose Fiction Prior to 1740*, University of Minnesota Studies in Language and Literature, no. 5 (1916), p. 54. Ernest A. Baker, in describing what he calls the 'school' of Mrs. Behn, says that Mrs. Manley and Mrs. Haywood differed from Mrs. Behn in that they 'were more under the sway of foreign fashions, however, than she was; they revelled in the scandal-mongering chronicle now enormously popular in France'. See *The History of the English Novel*, iii. 107.

Mrs. Manley's 1705 *Secret History of Queen Zarah*, for example, resembles in lubricious and malicious technique a 1704 translation of the *Histoire politique et amoureuse du fameux Cardinal Portocarrero, archevêque de Tolède*. Her *New Atalantis* was doubtless influenced by such translations as the Countess d'Aulnoy's *Memoirs of the Court of England* (1707), *The History of the Earl of Warwick* (1707), *Hypolitus Earl of Douglas. Containing some Memoirs of the Court of Scotland; with the Secret History of Mack-Beth King of Scotland* (1708), *Secret Memoirs of the Duke and Dutchess of O[rleans] Intermix'd with the Amorous Intrigues and Adventures of the Most Eminent Princes of the Court of France* (1708), and *The Memoirs of the Marquis de Langallerie: Containing an Account of the most Secret Intrigues of the French, Spanish, and Bavarian Courts* (1708).

A translation of Bussy-Rabutin's book was published the year of Mrs. Haywood's *Memoirs of a Certain Island* (1725), and other similar works had appeared in translation in the preceding few years: Charlotte de la Force's *The Secret History of Burgundy . . . Faithfully Collected by a Person of Quality of the French Court* (1723), Jacques Roergas de Serviez's *The Lives and Amours of the Empresses, Consorts to the first Twelve Caesars of Rome* (1723), and Mrs. Haywood's own translation of Madame de Gomez's *La Belle Assemblée . . . A Curious Collection of Remarkable Incidents which happen'd to some of the First Quality in France* (1724).

lubricity will always command a wide and eager audience, but this seems a useless, Olympian kind of moralism which neglects some salient historical facts. An effort must be made to account in a fairly specific manner for the popularity of the early eighteenth-century scandal novel, an effort which requires analysis of the sort suggested in Chapter I.

If we attempt, that is, to judge the scandal novel by any of the criteria used to analyse and evaluate what is usually called the emerging realistic novel, we will not get very far beyond a patronizing or bemused scorn. Works such as the *New Atalantis* or Mrs. Haywood's *Memoirs of a Certain Island* possess none of the unity of theme or characterization that makes a narrative meaningful to us. There is in them no attempt to render that sense of a conditioning milieu, that biographical density and verisimilitude which make characterization possible and relevant. Moreover, the plain style which reinforces the necessary illusion that we are in a world of things and events rather than participating in an order of words is the last thing we will find in these works. There is, rather, a deliberate and awkward artificiality, a mannered and debased conventionality about the prose, characters, and events in which that prose deals which strikes us as dull, tedious, and repetitive. In fact, all these critical terms and distinctions are ludicrously inappropriate in any discussion of the scandal novels, for they are formally nothing more than a series of anecdotes, some swollen to novella length and complexity, unified only by a narrative occasion similar to that which unifies such well-known framework collections of stories as the *Decameron* and the *Canterbury Tales*.

To be sure, the last comparison is blasphemous and the resemblance superficial, for these works were obviously written carelessly and assembled at top speed, as E. A. Baker put it, 'for readers eagerly awaiting the next number, and demanding edition after edition'.[1] The most famous and popular example of the genre, Mrs. Manley's *New Atalantis*, has a construction which is, as one outraged commentator has put it, 'execrable'. There is no denying that it 'consists of endless conversations between vague individuals,

---

[1] Baker, iii. 111.

or rather monologues so long and so involved that we forget the speaker, and are surprised when a question or a reply reminds us of their existence'.[1] But it is equally undeniable that all London read it when it first appeared,[2] that someone like the young Lady Mary Wortley Montagu could write to a friend and ask enthusiastically for the second part. Her brief defence of the work and its authoress is revealing:

I am very glad you have the second part of the New Atalantis; if you have read it, will you be so good as to send it me, and in return I promise to get you the key to it. I know I can. But do you know what has happened to the unfortunate authoress? People are offended at the liberty she uses in her memoirs, and she is taken into custody. Miserable is the fate of writers; if they are agreeable, they are offensive; and if dull, they starve. I lament the loss of the other parts which we should have had; and have five hundred arguments at my fingers' ends to prove the ridiculousness of those creatures that think it worthwhile to take notice of what is only designed for diversion. After this, who will dare to give the history of Angella? I was in hopes her faint essay would have provoked some better pen to give more elegant and secret memoirs; but now she will serve as a scarecrow to frighten people from attempting anything but heavy panegyric; and we shall be teized with nothing but heroic poems, with names at length, and false characters, so daubed with flattery, that they are the severest kind of lampoons, for they both scandalize the writer and the subject, like that vile paper the Tatler.[3]

[1] B. G. MacCarthy, *Women Writers: Their Contribution to the English Novel 1621–1744* (Cork, 1944), p. 218.

[2] The great popularity of the *New Atalantis* can be gathered from the number of casual references to it which abound in the literature of the period, the most famous of which is Pope's line in 'The Rape of the Lock' which serves as the title of this chapter. See P. B. Anderson, 'Delarivière Manley's Prose Fiction', *PQ*, xii (April 1934), 170; and G. B. Needham, 'Mrs. Manley: An Eighteenth-Century Wife of Bath', *HLQ*, xiv (May 1951), 268. A convenient gathering of the many contemporary references to the book is to be found in Joyce M. Horner, *The English Women Novelists and their Connection With the Feminist Movement (1688–1787)*, Smith College Studies in Modern Languages, no. 11 (1929–30), pp. 11–12.

[3] *The Complete Letters of Lady Mary Wortley Montagu*, ed. Robert Halsband (Oxford, 1965), i. 18–19. Mrs. Manley and her publishers were indeed taken into custody on 29 Oct. 1709. She was released a week later, tried the following February and dismissed. See Narcissus Luttrell, *A Brief Historical Relation of State Affairs from September 1678 to April 1714* (London, 1857), vi. 505, 508, 546.

The *New Atalantis* was indeed designed for diversion, but we might qualify Lady Mary's judgement by reminding her that the book was specifically intended to serve definite political ends, to attack prominent persons attached to the Whig side and to praise the Tories to the heights of panegyric. Mrs. Manley's importance as a political writer, as a strategic weapon in the Tory propaganda of Queen Anne's reign, cannot be underestimated.[1] But at the same time, Lady Mary's enthusiasm makes it quite clear that the great success which the *New Atalantis* enjoyed cannot simply be explained by its political purpose. Its continuing popularity,[2] long after the scandal had cooled down, indicates that Mrs. Manley's particular success and the popularity of her various imitators arose, as a close student of her exact political purpose notes, 'more from the allurement that her fiction gave to the recital of amours than from the scandal itself'.[3]

The point is that Mrs. Manley's scandalous 'revelations' appealed immediately to the prurient curiosity of her first audience; but they continued to be read because they succeeded in providing certain satisfactions fundamental to fiction itself. In other words, the scandal novel or 'chronicle' of Mrs. Manley and Mrs. Haywood was a successful popular form, a tested commercial pattern, because it presented an opportunity for its readers to participate vicariously in an erotically exciting and glittering fantasy world of aristocratic corruption and promiscuity. That fantasy world was,

[1] G. B. Needham, in 'Mary de la Rivière Manley, Tory Defender', *HLQ*, xii (May 1949), 253–88, presents a very convincing account of Mrs. Manley's political importance and concludes that the *New Atalantis* that 'Its help in undermining public confidence in the Whigs came at the psychologically right time for the Tories, who were striving to overthrow the ministry' (p. 263).

G. M. Trevelyan calls it 'the publication that did most harm to the Ministry that year . . . a book of the lowest order, the *New Atlantis* [*sic*], wherein Mrs. Manley, a woman of no character, regaled the public with brutal stories, for the most part entirely false, about public men and their wives, especially Whigs and above all the Marlboroughs'. See *England under Queen Anne: The Peace and the Protestant Succession* (London, 1965), iii. 62.

[2] In 1736 a 'Seventh Edition' was printed in four 12mo volumes. Significantly, this edition appeared in weekly instalments, fifteen numbers at 4*d*. a sheet, as *The Weekly Novelist* during this same year. See Roy McKeen Wiles, *Serial Publication in England before 1750* (Cambridge, 1957), p. 300.

[3] Needham, 'Mary de la Rivière Manley, Tory Defender', p. 287.

in the long run, more important in making the book popular than the specific scandals and libels in which Mrs. Manley dealt.

Now fantasy is, of course, a personal mental reflex of individual readers, and may vary tremendously depending upon the reader's attitude and personal background. What I wish to emphasize is that a popular work, deliberately aimed at a relatively naïve and impressionable mental norm, is an opportunity for a fairly limited and predictable vicarious experience, especially given the limitations supplied by the social and economic factors of the age.

Broadly speaking, the scandal novel's chief source of fantasy experience lay in two basic conflicts which it dramatized over and over again: latent social antagonism—the values of corrupt aristocracy condemned by a sobriety and rectitude implicitly classless— and sexual antagonism—helpless and virtuous females destroyed by a malign masculine ethos; or, less frequently, innocent masculine youth seduced by ageing and lascivious courtesans. These conflicts contain basic fantasies of power and sex, but they are here grounded in a popular mythology appropriate to the social realities of the age. The two key figures of that mythology, the persecuted and innocent maiden and the aristocratic *libertin*-seducer, and the backdrop against which they appear, a world of universal and controlling lechery and avarice, have some basis in reality, just as the specific characters and events have some historical foundation under the libellous exaggerations.[1] But such works

---

[1] Mrs. Manley often began her slanderous exaggerations from certain more or less well-known aspects of a public figure's personality. Needham makes the point that Godolphin's constitutional timidity, Lord Somers's weakness for women, the Earl of Halifax's vanity, and the Duke of Ormond's foolish generosity are all traits which Mrs. Manley emphasized in her book and all are more or less verifiable from contemporary testimony ('Tory Defender', p. 260). Mrs. Manley had lived for a time as a young girl in the household of the Duchess of Cleveland and had doubtless picked up a great deal of gossip. Needham realizes the extravagant nature of Mrs. Manley's fabrications, but claims that they usually 'contained a substructure of truth' (p. 261). She cites a letter from the Duchess of Marlborough to Queen Anne which admits this about one of the stories in the *New Atalantis*: ' "It is a dialogue between Madame Maintenon and Madam Masham, in which she thanks her for her good endeavours to serve the King of France here, and seems to have great hopes of her, from her promising beginnings and her friendship for Mr. Harley; and is stuff not fit to be mentioned of passions between women, and a long account of that lady's famous amour with

as Mrs. Manley's and Mrs. Haywood's, I wish to argue, had their basic effect and impact as narratives at that same level of ideological simplification that I have already discussed in connection with criminals, pirates, and travellers.

Scandal novels owed a significant part of their popularity, that is, to their ability to evoke an essentially fictional world whose inhabitants were not so much real persons as they were embodiments of popular concepts, capable of provoking personal fantasy and projection precisely because they appealed to an immediately available and more or less communal mythology. That myth, the destruction of female innocence by a representative of an aristocratic world of male corruption, is a well-known eighteenth-century preoccupation, from its prominence in the drama to the prose fiction which begins with Richardson and expands all over Europe.[1]

The popular scandal novel or 'chronicle' is of great historical importance because it shows us this fable in the process of being widely disseminated in prose narrative form, being transmitted, in a sense, as an effective erotic-pathetic cliché to the audience for which Richardson is to write, creating an emotional convention as it were. I will attempt in the following discussion to describe and to illustrate the permutations and combinations of this key fable in the scandal chronicles of Mrs. Manley and Mrs. Haywood, and to suggest the range of social and moral meanings which this fable expressed in a dramatic and compelling manner.

It is probably no accident that the most considerable writers of scandalous memoirs during the early eighteenth century were

Mr. Chudd, managed by Lady Newport. Some part of that I know to be true, but I will not trouble you longer upon so disagreeable [a] subject"', *Private Correspondence of Sarah, Duchess of Marlborough* (London, 1838), i. 235, cited by Needham, 'Tory Defender', p. 261.

[1] In itself, of course, the idea of the persecuted maiden is, as Mario Praz pointed out, 'as old as the world, but was refurbished in the eighteenth century by Richardson'. See *The Romantic Agony* (London, 1960), p. 114. Praz discusses in his chapter called 'The Shadow of the "Divine Marquis"' the various appearances of the figure in that strain of Romanticism which is made explicit in the works of de Sade; but he tends to assume that Richardson was the first to exploit the idea and bring out its erotic-sadistic-pathetic implications. In fact, Richardson was handling, perhaps more effectively than anyone had before, a well-known social mythology.

women, and it is certainly likely that their most eager readers were largely women as well. It is important to say this without lapsing into that condescension with which the Augustans regarded female literature and scribbling women, for the changes which take place in prose narrative are partly the result of the changes in the market brought about by the needs of an expanding female audience. Given the increased leisure time of many middle-class women and the widespread literacy among the female upper-servant class,[1] as well as the severe legal and social limitations upon female action, it is not surprising that novel reading, with its great possibilities for vicarious experience and liberating fantasy, formed an important part of their lives. Neither should we underestimate the importance of that 'social learning' and extension of emotional capacity which novel reading made possible for many eighteenth-century women. As the market for prose narrative expanded under these conditions, the changes which it underwent represent an adaptation to those conditions: the short novella replaced the elaborate and sophisticated heroic romance, the vulgarized fustian style and broadly drawn stereotypes of the former driving out the complex rhetorical and psychological constructions of the latter.

The preface to Mrs. Manley's first *chronique scandaleuse, The Secret History of Queen Zarah and the Zarazians*, testifies to this shift in the market. Mrs. Manley explains that French romances are out of vogue now and 'little Histories' of the sort to be offered are in. The preface itself is a fairly cogent plea for what strikes us as realism and common sense in the devising of narratives, the sort of statement which students of the novel are perhaps too ready to seize and brandish high as a sign of incipient and emerging modern realism.[2] The preface is, in fact, not so much literary criticism as market analysis:

These little Pieces which have banish'd Romances are much more agreeable to the Brisk and Impetuous Humour of the English, who have

[1] See on this point Ian Watt, *The Rise of the Novel*, pp. 48–9.

[2] Robert A. Day, *Told in Letters*, p. 99, calls it 'the most interesting and detailed piece of early theorizing on the qualities of the new "novel",' and claims that 'in contrast to the absurdly vague remarks of Mrs. Manley's contemporaries its attention to detail is remarkable'.

naturally no Taste for long-winded Performances, for they have no sooner begun a Book but they desire to see the end of it: The Prodigious Length of the Ancient Romances, the Mixture of so many Extraordinary Adventures, and the great Number of Actors that appear on the Stage, and the Likeness which is so little managed, all of which has given a Distaste to Persons of good Sense, and has made Romances so much cry'd down, as we find 'em at present. (i, sig. A2ʳ)[1]

This shift in taste which the preface comments upon, and the narrative ideals of plainness of style and verisimilitude which it goes on to recommend, cannot simply be greeted approvingly as the destruction of an older decadent set of narrative ideals. It must be emphasized that the 'shift' begins as an attempt to serve the needs of an expanding literate public possessed of severely limited capacities, a public which required the plain style and simple event because ornate style, intricate plot, and psychological complication were beyond its comprehension and appreciation.

The narrative itself is simply an attack on the Duchess of Marlborough (Zarah), but so successful and effective a slander that 'Zarah' and 'Zarazians' became popular epithets for the Duchess and her political associates.[2] Unlike Mrs. Manley's later works, this is a concise, unified, and fairly straightforward account of the Duchess's rise to power and influence. Like them, however, it depends for its effects upon a carefully established and almost stylized 'scene' of aristocratic elegance, gallantry, intrigue, and corruption.

The first two are supplied by the historical period carefully evoked in the opening pages, the court of Charles II. Lady Zarah, we are told, was born 'in the Reign of Rolando, King of Albigion,

---

[1] *The Secret History of Queen Zarah, and the Zarazians; being a Looking-glass for In the Kingdom of Albigion. Faithfully Translated from the Italian Copy now lodg'd in the Vatican at Rome, and never before Printed in any Language* was published in two separate parts in 1705. It was reissued in two parts in one volume in 1711, 'By Way of Appendix to the New Atalantis'. All of the citations in the text are to this edition, the Roman numerals referring to the separately paginated parts.

[2] Needham, 'Tory Defender', p. 258. Trevelyan, *England under Queen Anne*, iii. 62, notes that Sacheverell was thought to refer in his notorious sermon to Godolphin by the name Volpone, his name, as Trevelyan was not aware, in *Queen Zarah*.

one of the most Gallant Princes the World ever had, when Gallantry was so much in Vogue, that it was almost as Natural to be a Gallant as to Live' (i. 3). This is a land of instant fires and unbridled heats, as we see when Hippolito (Marlborough) finds Zarah in his mistress's bed and begins to declare and make love almost immediately. Mrs. Manley is certainly being partly ironic here but also continuing her depiction of an exotic fantasy world where all desires are gratified:

It may be admired perhaps that Two Persons so little acquainted shou'd in so few Minutes become so familiar; but we must know Love in those Countries makes far quicker Progress than in ours where the Winds, and the Snow, and the Rain, spoil his Wings, and hinder his Flight; for it is the Custom of the Grandees of that Country, when they have not a particular Inclination for any Woman, to take this to Day, and another to-Morrow: And having lost the Taste to Love, to Search for Pleasure in Change and Variety. (i. 15)

Hippolito is engaged in a profitable love affair with Clelia (the Duchess of Cleveland), who is officially the king's mistress. He is tricked into marrying Zarah, and the king is made to hear of his dalliance with his mistress. Elegant hedonistic banter is the king's only reaction:

What would become of Men and Women of Gallantry, says he, if when they engage in Kindness with one another, they should absolutely sell themselves, and not be allow'd to change when they grow weary, or have a greater Inclination for another: 'Tis a natural Right to bestow our Affections where we please: They are wretched who enjoy not that Liberty. And you know, Hippolito, continued the King, I glory in those Maxims; for if Clelia had not been of my Humour, I fancy I should not have loved her so well; and perhaps I love her for nothing more than that she loves Inconstancy. I once endeavour'd to engage her to be false to me, insomuch that I told her one Day I dream'd I had seen her in your Arms, and it was not long ere I found it true: Now, Hippolito, wou'd you take it ill the King shou'd do as much for you as you did then for him? Yes, without Doubt, says he, Sir, for I did it not for that Purpose that you shou'd do as much for me. Well, answers the King prophetically, if I do not, another may. (i. 32–4)

It is within this atmosphere of casual adultery and sexual intrigue that the political machinations which it is Mrs. Manley's main task to expose and denounce take place. But all of this sexuality is presented with a kind of admiring nostalgia, or often a tolerant and witty sympathy; passion is a weakness, it is implied, which can easily be understood and forgiven. In fact, the sympathetic light and glittering colours in which this aristocratic hedonism is presented fade only when pleasure is made ancillary to power. Zarah herself, for example, begins as a victim of her mother's ambitions (it is her mother who arranges that Zarah shall be in Clelia's bed when Hippolito arrives), Hippolito's male aggression, and Clelia's jealous fury.

Political malice will come later in the book. Here, Mrs. Manley is concerned to work out the erotic-pathetic possibilities of the young and still-innocent Zarah as she forms the centre of an extravagant scene. Finding Hippolito dazed and desperate after his forced marriage to her, Zarah

fell at his Feet with all the Agonies of a despairing Lover; Am I then despis'd already? said she; and with Tears in her Eyes continued, Do you insult o'er your Conquest, because it was so easily gain'd? You have already too cruelly wounded me, not to pity me a little. More she would have said, but the Excess of her Passion stifled all her Endeavours to proceed, and she sunk down under the Conflict between her Love and Resentment. Hippolito snatch'd her from the Ground, rais'd her up into his Arms, and claspt her round with all the Tenderness possible; for the Transports of his Love had banish'd the Extravagance of his Fury, and he melted into all the Softness of a happy Lover. It is beyond Imagination to conceive the Joy Zarah was in at this sudden change of Hippolito; and being about to return his Passion an equal Fire, after having given him some Looks that discovered her Inclination, she had Time to say no more, than Heaven and my Hippolito support me, for I'm ravish'd with Excess of Pleasure. (i. 25–6)

Clelia enters at this point, and enraged by what she sees and by Hippolito's cool rebuff, goes to stab Zarah but wounds Hippolito slightly when he interposes himself. The pathetic heroine becomes the calculating female politician abruptly a few pages later as we learn that 'Fortune' had made Zarah 'purely for the Service

of her own Interest, without any Regard to the strict Rules of
Honour or Virtue' (i. 40). Consistency and plausible character
development are not problems here, and we pass easily from one
stereotype to another.

Slander can now be served, for the attractive eroticism of Mrs.
Manley's version of the Restoration court has gained her readers'
attention and established in a scene such as the one above a female
norm of passive submission to love as the core of virtue. Heroines
are by definition helpless, in need of manly support when they
are, like Zarah, 'ravish'd with Excess of Pleasure'. The personality
which the Duchess of Marlborough is given (not quite gratuitously
of course) is the deliberate antithesis of this heroic character, and
in terms of the narrative mechanism at work her villainy requires
this moral norm in order to attain the proper evil proportions.

Zarah is made an attendant of the Princess Albania (Princess,
later Queen, Anne), and learns that Albania has a secret inclination
for Mulgarvius.[1] She resolves to exploit both of them

> to the Satisfaction of her Ambition, in having the Opportunity of
> communicating an Affair of this Consequence, both to the King and
> Albanio [the Duke of York, later James II]; and next in gratifying her
> Pleasure with Mulgarvius, who was one she greatly admired. . . .
>
> This was a treacherous Part, as was ever acted by Woman fill'd with
> Love and Ambition; for though she was resolved to gain the Last,
> she was one who left no Stone unturn'd to secure to her self the First,
> which has always made her Life one continued Scene of politick
> Intrigue. (i. 40–1)

Courtly cunning debases the spirit of love, and gay promiscuity
becomes predatory lust. Zarah is, in terms of the system of values
implied by Mrs. Manley's invective, worse than the male conspirators who surround her. The moral burden of the attack on
her is that she has surrendered the blessed passivity before passion
natural to women, and betrayed her femininity by giving up love
and the heroically selfless and even self-destructive spontaneity it

---

[1] This part of the libel is true enough. Mulgarvius is John Sheffield (1648–
1721), third Earl of Mulgrave, later first Duke of Buckingham and Normanby,
who was banished from the court and stripped of his places by Charles II for
courting Princess Anne. See *DNB*, lii.

involves for the masculine virtues of self-aggrandizement and ambition. Mrs. Manley has already made this quite explicit. At the very beginning of the book she has declared that, 'No Passion, but that of extraordinary Love, can fix a Woman's Heart. Ambition alone is too weak a Gage for their Fidelity' (i. 9).

When Solano (probably Robert Spencer, 2nd Earl of Sunderland) proves a traitor to Albanio and declares himself a supporter of Aurantio (William III), Zarah rants to herself and describes her effort as a deliberate attempt to renounce love for ambition and to compete in this world of masculine treachery:

Weak Woman, cry'd she, and unfit for those Designs thou are surely Born for, that could not penetrate into Solano's Treachery. I might have known a Man like him, Bred up in all State-Craft, could never design what he pretended, or was so shallow as to make Pretentions of any thing that he design'd. Poor Fool, is it for this Hippolito betray'd his Benefactor? [i.e. James II] Is it for this Volpone has lost his Royal Bubble? Is it for this I have Rul'd Albania? And is it for this at last I must repent? I hate my self for such a Thought, but worst of all I hate Aurantio who occasions it; in this Way she spent the remaining Part of the Day. (i. 72–3)

Zarah does succeed eventually in her ambitions, her male aggressiveness and courtly duplicity dominating the now Queen Albania so that she becomes 'Queen Zarah': 'for it may be said without Exaggerating upon the Subject too much, Albania took the Crown from her own Head to put it on Zarah's' (i. 99).

In Part II of the *Secret History of Queen Zarah*, published in the same year, Zarah is shown solidifying her power, and the inhabitants of Albigion see 'to their Sorrow Men of Vicious and Corrupt Lives and Conversations, without one good Action to recommend them, rais'd in a Trice from Slaves, to be Governours of Provinces, from Poor, to be Rich and Powerful, from Base and Unknown, to be Noble, and Chief of the State' (ii. 94). This is Tory rhetoric, appealing to a conservative ideal of moral and social hierarchy which is beyond the issues of the day. The perversion of society just described is the result, we have been shown, of Zarah's perversion of normal male–female relationships. Constantly avaracious and ambitious, she debases her natural powers as a female by using them to control men for political ends. Having been resisted politically by Devonius, 'Principal Staff-Officer of the Household', she resolves to oust him and put Canutius in his place. Canutius is her political ally and sexual partner, having 'lost more than a Talent of Gold to her':

> not at Cards or Dice, which were not known in those Days, but at a certain Game they call in Albigion Loose-all. And this Lady, who was always fam'd for Gratitude, finding she had so great an Obligation laid upon her, and he the only Person in the World she would have had that Place, without further Delay put him in Possession of his Desires: of which some Malicious People said he Purchas'd at too Dear a Rate: But howsoever it was, he was gratified, and Zarah pleas'd she had got a Gamester that understood Loose-all so well. (ii. 13–14)

In the same vein, we also hear at length later on how Zarah and Volpone are political intimates whom the world rightly suspects of other intimacies. For Zarah, Mrs. Manley demonstrates again and again, sexual experience is a desirable result as well as a method of political power. Her careful manipulation and exploitation of sexuality profanes what should be a 'mystery', converting the tragic knowledge and ruin which sexual experience brings (in the ethos of popular amatory narrative) to the virtuous into triumphant and unparalleled success.

The relative coherence of this compact and sometimes witty narrative is, of course, provided by its single-minded attack on the Duchess of Marlborough. This unity is lost in the *New Atalantis*, where the Marlboroughs are only one of many targets of the slander and invective. But another kind of unity or completeness is gained by the expansion. The widening of the attack to include a huge circle of victims allows all of the stock characters in the fable of woman's ruin to appear fully delineated. In addition, the moral claims of the book are much more strenuous and elaborate, the style and rhetoric much more extravagant and calculated to bring out the simple moral antitheses upon which the slander is founded. These moral antitheses require illustration and personification; contemporary political figures provide the names and, indeed, some of the moral details: but the characters themselves and the patterns formed by their relationships are parts of a social myth to which, if the popularity of the *Atalantis* is any indication, many eighteenth-century readers responded eagerly.

The great ostensible theme and provocation of the *New Atalantis* is much wider than Zarah's female conspiracy. It is nothing less than the decay of love and the domination of Atalantis by a masculine spirit of lust and selfish possession, both in an economic and a sexual sense. The easy-going Restoration promiscuity which is presented in so nostalgic a way in *Queen Zarah* is exchanged here for a fantastically sordid degeneracy which is the main tool for achieving and maintaining power. All of this is announced in pompous fashion by Virtue, one of the three allegorical personages by whom the story of the first two volumes of the *New Atalantis* is told.[1]

I have no Sanctuary among the Lovers of this Age; the youngest Virgin, and the most ardent Youth, are contented to quote me only as a Name, something Fine, that their Histories indeed make mention of; a thing long since departed, and which at this Day is not to be found among them. Innocence is banish'd by the first dawn of early Knowledge. Sensual Corruptions and hasty Enjoyments affright me from their Habitation. They imbellish not the Heart to make it worthy of the God: their whole Care is outward, and transferr'd to a Person. By a Diabolical way of Argument they prove the Body is only necessary to the Pleasures of Enjoyment; that Love resides not in the Heart, but in the Face. . . . Hymen no more officiates at their Marriages, the Saffron Robe hangs neglected in the Ward-robe, the Genuine Torch is long since extinguish'd; the Glare only of a false Light appears: Interest is deputed in his room, he presides over the Feast, he joyns their Hands,

---

[1] The various scandals are related by Lady Intelligence to Astrea, who has returned to earth to see if men have improved, and to Virtue. The three tour Atalantis and Astrea and Virtue interrupt the narrative to make moral comments. Mrs. Manley produced her own sequel in 1710, *Memoirs of Europe, Towards the Close of the Eighth Century. Written by Eginardus, Secretary and Favourite to Charlemagne; And done into English by the Translator of the New Atalantis.* Here, as the title makes clear, another narrative pretext was employed. This work was printed in 1720 and 1736 as volumes iii and iv of a four-volume work titled simply the *New Atalantis*. All references in the text are to the 'Second edition' of 1709 in two volumes.

and brings them to the sacred Ceremony of the Bed, with so much indifference, that were not Consummation a necessary Article, the unloving Pair could with the utmost indifferency repair to their several Chambers. (i. 3–4)

Volume i is really an illustration of these conditions, and Astrea is thus provoked at the beginning of volume ii to question Jupiter's wisdom in creating love as he did: 'permit Astrea to expostulate, why thou hast given this soft Passion strength to triumph over the Endeavours of the most accomplish'd Mortals?' (ii. 1). Virtue's immediate defence of love defines it as the triumph of divine inclinations and locates its greatest enemy:

Is it then nothing to animate wretched Clay to the Degree of Godhead? To make it their Choice! go give 'em Power and Capacity to share with Angelick Natures; Immortality, and immortal Bliss? And by a Method so enviting and so easy; that all who have their Reason about 'em, wou'd prefer the Law to Liberty; the Precepts of Jupiter to those of Nature; the easy, happy Possession of his own Wife to the turbulent guilty pursuit of anothers [sic]. Were Marriages not the Result of Interest, but Inclination! were nothing but generous Love! the Fire of Virtue! the warmth of Beauty! and the Shine of Merit! consulted in that Divine Union, guilty Pleasures wou'd be no more. But Avarice! contemptible Covetousness! sordid Desire of Gain! not only mingles with the more Generous Native Sentiments, but have quite extinguish'd the very Glimmerings of that informing Light. (ii. 2–3)

The casual beatific analogies are part of traditional amatory hyperbole, but they are carefully contained within the heavy panegyric or marriage, a bourgeois protest against the quasi-blasphemy of the comparisons. Love is redeemed by this rhetoric without any blasphemous wit, for the analogies are now supported by the sacramental implications of marriage. The spirituality and sanctity of marriage thus established, we are free to enjoy a series of stories in which love is never a part of marriage and, indeed, always leads to pre- or extra-marital tragedy. The reason for this tragedy is that the destruction of marriage as love's great sacrament has been accomplished by that material calculation which, in the popular mythology I am trying to isolate, is attached to the unregenerate

male who dominates the world of which Virtue complains so loud
and long.

As we have seen in *Queen Zarah*, it is Zarah's adaptation to and
domination of this corrupt masculine world that has made her a
moral monster; here it is Fortunatus (Marlborough) who is made
to embody in an absolutely thorough way all of the negative values
of this world. We are told that he is incapable of any excess, *except
avarice*. He is given virtues such as self-control, restraint, contin-
ence, and discretion, but these are explained as merely means to
serve the ends of avarice and ambition. There is a method in Mrs.
Manley's flow of vituperation that instinctively condemns Marlborough as *the* enemy of the female ethos with which the reader is
impelled to identify.

He begins as the lover of the Duchess of Cleveland, but 'not
born a Slave to Love, so as to reckon the possession of the charming'st Woman of the Court, as the Zenith of his Fortune, but
rather the first auspicious, ruddy Streaks of an early Morning, an
earnest to the Meridian of the brightest Day' (i. 22), he keeps himself emotionally aloof and uses this liaison to begin his conquest of
the world. His incredible phlegm makes him, we are told at
length, an absolutely inscrutable courtier, incapable of passion,
unable to forget personal ambition, which 'lies smothered beneath'
his smooth surface like 'some distant Views, a depth of Design,
which none has yet had Line enough to fathom' (i. 27). Even his
bravery is disposed of in this context by being related to his conscious designs for money and power:

His Flatterers cry up his Courage, but it seems to me not to be inborn to him, but acquir'd; for certainly he may as well learn to be
Valiant as Judicious. A proof of what I advance, may be taken from
always ducking his Head at the Noise of a Bullet; the first apprehension
is in his Nature, and only to be controul'd, not prevented by Reason:
That immediately comes in for a Second, and carries him safely through
to Glory, which all Hero's should chiefly aim at. (i. 26)

Certain moral polarities become increasingly obvious. Control
and manipulation, restraint and reason, are opposed to passionate
spontaneity and irrationality. The acquired and the artificial are

despised as shallow and insincere next to the inborn and the natural. Marlborough's rumoured 'thrift' and obvious ambition are capitalized upon by drawing his character in huge and grotesque lines so that it embodies the negative poles of these antitheses.[1] Even in the presentation of what is perhaps the most notorious and lusciously erotic scene in the *New Atalantis*, Mrs. Manley can be observed exploiting these moral antitheses which make Marlborough a symbol of a malign masculine ethos as much as a specific target of personal abuse.

In the *Secret History of Queen Zarah*, Mrs. Manley had related how Jenisa (the Duchess's mother, Mrs. Jennings) had tricked Hippolito into marrying Zarah by arranging to find them together in a compromising position.[2] After the marriage, they are again surprised in their embraces by Hippolito's mistress, Clelia. The scene was set there in a brief but erotic way:

. . . it [Clelia's bedroom] was very spacious, and made on purpose for a Cooling Room in the Heats of Summer, and had in it several Beds of Turf very prettily made, with Pots of Jessamine Flowers, and other Sweets all about; in a Word, it was a Place picked out for the King's Pleasure: Here Zarah was in Bed; and as there is nothing so handsome as a Beautiful Woman in Bed, he was so much disorder'd as she, and knew not what he did.[3]

In the *New Atalantis* the story is retold but with the main characters cast in different roles. Here, significantly, it is Marlborough who devises the stratagem in order to have an excuse to be rid of his mistress and marry Zarah. Shrewdly consistent with the personality he has been given, 'Fortunatus' is here made the cunning aggressor. His mistress changes from a possessive virago into a partially sympathetic victim of compulsive desires. Zarah

---

[1] Trevelyan, *England under Queen Anne*, i. 191, notes that Marlborough had 'thrifty personal habits . . . he had acquired in his penurious youth, when he was living at Charles II's Court on his ensign's pay, and they clung to him when he grew rich'.

[2] Mrs. Manley used different names for the same people in her various works. To avoid confusion I have only identified the most important and obvious characters. It is quite likely that as time passed the names of the minor actors became very obscure indeed for most of Mrs. Manley's readers.

[3] *Secret History of Queen Zarah*, i. 12–13.

does not appear; she is not even granted (as in *Queen Zarah*) a temporary innocence as the passive tool of her scheming mother. The scene itself is much longer, the erotic details expanded and heightened as Mrs. Manley grew more practised and confident.

Fortunatus's mistress is to meet him at his house, the king having gone hunting in the country. But Germanicus (Lord Davers, says the Key) has agreed to take Fortunatus's place. Told by the servants that 'his Lord was lain down upon a Day-bed that join'd the Bathing-Room . . . fallen asleep, since he came out of the Bath':

The Dutchess softly enter'd that little Chamber of Repose. The Weather violently hot, the Umbrelloes were let down from behind the Windows, the Sashes open, and the Jessimine, that cover'd 'em, blew in with a gentle Fragrancy. Tuberoses set in pretty Gilt and China Pots, were plac'd advantageously upon Stands; the Curtains of the Bed drawn back to the Canopy, made of yellow Velvet, embroider'd with white Bugles, the Panels of the Chamber Looking-glass. Upon the Bed were strew'd, with a lavish Profuseness, plenty of Orange and Lemon Flowers: And to complete the Scene, the young Germanicus in a Dress and posture not very decent to describe. It was he that was newly-risen from the Bath, and in a loose Gown of Carnation-Taffety, stain'd with Indian Figures. . . . he had thrown himself upon the Bed, pretending to sleep, with nothing on but his Shirt and Night-Gown, which he had so indecently dispos'd, that slumbering as he appear'd, his whole Person stood confess'd to the Eyes of the Amorous Dutchess; his Limbs exactly form'd, his Skin shiningly white, and the Pleasure the Ladies graceful Entrance gave him, diffus'd Joy and Desire through-out all his Form. . . . giving her Eyes time to wander over Beauties so inviting, and which encreased her Flame; with an amorous Sigh, she gently threw herself on the Bed, close to the desiring Youth. . . . The burning Lover thought it was now time to put an end to his pretended Sleep; he clasped her in his Arms, grasp'd her to his Bosom, her own Desires help'd the Deceit; she shut her Eyes with a languishing Sweet-ness, calling him by Intervals, her dear Count, her only Lover, taking and giving a thousand Kisses. He got the Possession of her Person with so much transport, that she own'd all her former Enjoyments were imperfect to the Pleasure of this. (i. 33–4)

The Duchess is startled when she discovers her lover's identity, but pleased with the replacement, 'bestow'd upon Germanicus, what she before in her own Opinion had bestow'd upon the Count' (i. 35). Fortunatus bursts in and 'finds the happy Pair at the ultimate of all their Joys' (i. 35). He counterfeits anger and announces to the Duchess that he will marry Jeanatine (Sarah Jennings) to avenge this infidelity.

'Warm' scenes such as this one made a large part of Mrs. Manley's eighteenth-century reputation. She could still in 1752, for example, be complimented in a popular biography for the 'peculiar vivacity' with which she treated 'the passion of love'.[1] There is certainly a great deal of vulgar energy and erotic bluntness in the only barely oblique sexual description. But this pornographic facility which made her famous could not have existed without the moral antitheses mentioned above; they provide, for one thing, the necessary motives for all of the participants in the scene. All three are motivated to some extent by that aggressive economic and sexual self-seeking which is the sign of sin in Mrs. Manley's frame of reference.

Fortunatus is, of course, the most unregenerate; he has denied the rumours of his marriage and pledged himself anew to the Duchess in order to get more money from her. His exploitation of her and his deliberate arrangement of the scene to serve his ends violate the easy, yielding Restoration promiscuity which the Duchess represents. She has encouraged this particular assignation by urging Fortunatus to '*live* whilst *Life* is pleasing, whilst there's a *poinancy* in the Taste, desire at heighth, the Blood in perfection, and all our Senses fitted for those Raptures you know so well how to receive and give' (i. 31–2). The narrative leaves this passionately expressed hedonism without the explicit condemnation that Fortunatus's avarice and ambition receive.

Moreover, in so far as the Duchess remains faithful to Fortunatus, faithful that is to 'love' at the risk of her position as royal mistress, she is a victim and therefore a sympathetic figure. She lacks, to be sure, the innocence and selfless joy that an authentic heroine

---

[1] *The Lives of the Poets of Great Britain and Ireland. By Mr. Cibber, and other Hands* (London, 1753), iv. 18.

requires, but in this scene the first rush of passion and the first fervid encounter with the lovely youth she thinks is Fortunatus are rendered as irresistible and therefore excusable effusions of passion. The reader is carried along by the erotic details and invited to participate. Fortunatus, we notice, is not allowed to enter when the Duchess has only made an 'honest' mistake. It is only when she realizes her mistake and coolly exploits the situation for her own pleasure that she is condemned, only then, in other words, that she dilutes her spontaneity and compromises her position as the sympathetic victim of passion.

She becomes, indeed, what Fortunatus calls her a few minutes later, 'the most immoderate of her Sex' (i. 38); for the scene when he enters is suddenly and decidedly lewd. The atmosphere changes from a dream-like haze (except for two slight concessions to moral comment in the word 'decent') to the sharpness of conventional euphemism: 'the happy Pair at the ultimate of all their Joys'. This context makes us aware just how broadly hypocritical Fortunatus is being as he mouths the moral platitudes of fidelity: 'I am undone by your killing Perfidy, I can never forgive it, neither can I cease to love you' (i. 39).

The destruction of the Duchess is necessary for the moral balance of the scene; she has served as the basis of an erotic fantasy and must now be eliminated. Mrs. Manley's instinctive strategy is to allow one mythical monster—here the ruthless male— to punish another—the insatiable adulteress. Fortunatus's counterfeit indignation accomplishes this and also completes his portrayal as the ravening masculine ego. The hypothetical reader has had erotic fantasy, even while exercising self-righteousness at the faithlessness of the Duchess and the cruel duplicity of Fortunatus. This, at any rate, is the ideological structure of the scene.

It is apparent from scenes such as this one that in its narrative context Mrs. Manley's notorious 'warmth' clearly depends for its total effect as satisfying fantasy upon the evocation of a fictional world peopled by characters who enact an almost ritualized conflict of male and female values. The moral antitheses we have observed thus provide much more than a superficial moral gloss; they not only give the characters their personalities and motives but relate them to that controlling ideology upon which the *New Atalantis* rests.

Just how effectively Mrs. Manley's attacks on the Marlboroughs accommodated this popular ideology and thereby survived their immediate political function can be seen by turning briefly to another contemporary *roman à clef* which dealt with the same subjects. *The History of Prince Mirabel's Infancy, Rise and Disgrace*, which had two editions in 1712, is a political defence of Marlborough and an attack on Harley (Novicius). The book is nothing less than a heroic biography, written in a style so extravagantly panegyrical that one almost suspects irony. The 'Introduction' prepares us for what is to come:

> . . . you will discover a promising Bloom, a bold disclosure of Greatness, a vigour of Soul not to be match'd, an Address irresistible with the Fair; a dexterity in Business surpassing all Mankind. . . . The Second Part . . . briefly Descants upon Mirabel's God-like Labours, his uninterrupted Successes and Triumphs; sets the first Attempt of Novicius's Treachery upon Mirabel and his friends in a true Light; Vindicates the Resentment of Mirabel. . . . Here you will find him Terrible in Arms, Humbling Tyrants, Thundring on the Plain, Routing Millions of Opposers, forcing Passes almost inaccessible, extending his Glorious Arms to the Cliffs of Alpino, and leaving a Monument of Immortality behind him. In this Mirrour you will see the liveliest Image of Ingratitude, Novicius rais'd by Mirabel's peculiar Care, and cherish'd by his Beams, basely Supplanting him.[1]

But like Mrs. Manley's books, this work relies heavily upon the erotic world provided by an evocation of the Restoration court. The author outdoes her in the 'warmness' of these scenes. We are given, for example, a detailed description of the sort of orgy that Charles II (the Emperor Salax) delighted in: after a banquet the assembled company undresses, the ladies bathing 'in Waters deep

---

[1] *History of Prince Mirabel's Infancy, Rise and Disgrace: With the Sudden Promotion of Novicius. In Which Are Intermix'd all the Intrigues both Amorous and Political relating to those Memorable Adventures: As also the Characters of the Old and New Favourites of both Sexes of the Court of Britomartia. Collected from the Memoirs of a Courtier lately Deceas'd*, 2nd edition, sig. A3. All the following references are to this edition.

scented with Orange Flowers and Jessamine'. This is followed by
flagellation with 'Rods of Myrtle', everyone 'mutually stroking
each other with these Myrtle Rods, 'til the Blood was put into a
violent motion, they fell, upon a signal given, into a regular Dance,
and having perform'd their Parts, turn'd off in Pairs into the Apart-
ments provided'.[1] Mirabel himself engages in various closely described amours. Acteon-like, he observes his desired Libissa about
to bathe, and the allegorical description the author indulges himself in here is more explicitly lewd than anything Mrs. Manley ever
allowed herself:

> He saw a small Enclosure in that vast Field of exquisite Beauty,
> beyond Expression Fair, and as if it was set thick with Tuberoses, with
> a Gentle Declivity that terminated in a Bed of Silky Moss; At the Foot
> of the Vail, an Oval Space that bespoke a Fountain, supported with two
> Pillars finer than any Parian Marble: In that beatified Minute what
> Trilling Agonies did young Mirabel sustain, to be within sight of
> Heaven, and yet confin'd by slavish Rites from entring there?[2]

Mirabel is called away from joys such as these to war, as 'the
Season favour'd his Inclination, and the shrill Trumpet sounded
to Action'.[3] He is also drawn away from the sinful caresses of the
Duchess of Cleveland, and his marriage to Sarah is described as
a conversion to purity:

> Then Mirabel first knew the Sweets of Hallow'd Love, the boundless
> Range his Fancy took before, had been but a sort of Riding Post in
> Pleasure; he was a Stranger to the Peaceful Joys of Settled Love, but
> now brought home and Circumscrib'd by Reason's Laws, he found
> more pleasing Warmth from Vestal Flames, then all the lawless Fires
> he had Indulg'd before, and possess'd more substantial Bliss in the
> narrow Circle of those lovely Arms of Mirabella, then in the wide
> Purlieus of rambling Love.[4]

From here on, the eroticism stops abruptly, and the book becomes a straightforward if extravagantly phrased account of
Marlborough's various military and political triumphs. But in
place of the male–female antithesis of the *New Atalantis*, we have

---

[1] Part i, p. 9.   [2] Part i, p. 18.   [3] Part i, p. 23.   [4] Part i, p. 52.

only Marlborough versus his political opponents. The panegyric and invective expended on both sides is as unrestrained as that of Mrs. Manley, and the narrative line is much clearer. The difference between the two works and the reason why one continued to be read is that the author of the *History of Prince Mirabel* failed to exploit, as Mrs. Manley did, the mythology of persecuted innocence to which the predominantly female audience for novels responded most eagerly. Pornography, even the rather witty sort found in *Prince Mirabel*, and colourful political slander were not enough.

So far, however, we have only observed the negative poles of the moral antitheses, and it might be objected that the positive values have been arrived at arbitrarily. But in the *New Atalantis*, the positive side of our circuit is usually fully present. After the initial onslaught on the Marlboroughs, Mrs. Manley recounts from her partisan point of view the events of 1688 and after, and interrupts this historical account with a long novella-like narrative. This is essentially a repetition of the same stereotyped characters we have met in the story of Fortunatus's early amours. Of course, Mrs. Manley is to tell this story over and over again before the end of the book; it is the amorous fable to which all her scandal is bent and which forms, curiously enough, the pattern of her own rather tragic life.[1]

---

[1] She had been born in 1672, the daughter of Sir Roger Manley, who fought for Charles I and had been made governor of the isle of Jersey under Charles II. When he died she was left an orphan and seduced into a bigamous marriage by her cousin, John Manley, by whom she had a child. When he left her, she went to live for a time in the household of the Duchess of Cleveland. She began as an authoress with several plays, producing her first work of fiction in 1696, *Letters Written by Mrs. Manley*, a series of letters describing a stagecoach journey to Exeter. The facts of her career and her subsequent service as a political hack for the Tories are given in authoritative fashion in P. B. Anderson's 'Mistress Delarivière Manley's biography', *MP*, xxxiii (1936), 261–78. Mrs. Manley herself wrote a fictionalized autobiography called *The Adventures of Rivella; or, the History Of the Author of the Atalantis* (1714) which is the only source for many of the details of her life.

She died in 1724 in the office of the printer, 'Alderman' Barber, whose mistress she had been for the last years of her life. Swift had met Mrs. Manley there and wrote to Stella in January 1711–12 that she was very ill. 'I am heartily sorry for her; she has very generous principles for one of her sort; and a great deal of good sense and invention: she is about forty, very homely and very fat' See *Journal to Stella*, ed. Harold Williams (Oxford, 1948), ii. 474.

In this case, the novella is first an incredible slander on William's Dutch adviser, William Bentinck, first Earl of Portland.[1] Called simply the 'Duke' in the narrative, he is at once established as a practicer of 'the wise Maxims of Machiavel', and Mrs. Manley provides a list of his qualities to enforce the allusion: 'cunning to conceal, crafty to foresee, wise to Project, and valiant to undertake' (i. 49–50).

The last two phrases are ambiguous. The Duke is an attractive figure. Were he less so, he would not be the sort of villain required. But a formal protest is needed; his qualities, though convincing, must be revealed to us as superficial. So Mrs. Manley makes the point blunter a page or two later, describing the Duke as a symptom of the age in an *O tempora! O mores!* passage which acts as a sort of refrain throughout these first two volumes of the *New Atalantis*:

> The Duke had a seeming Admiration for Virtue where ever he found it, but he was a Statesman, and held it incompatable [*sic*] (in an Age like this) with a Man's making his Fortune. *Ambition, Desire of Gain, Dissimulation, Cunning*, all these were meritoriously Serviceable to him. 'Twas enough he always applauded Virtue, and in his Discourses decry'd Vice. As long as he stuck close in his Practice, no matter what became of his Words; these are not times where the Heart and the Tongue do agree. (i. 52–3)

A great friend of his dies and leaves his young daughter in the Duke's care. Charlot is brought up with exaggerated caution as a creature apart from the follies and vices of 'this entirely corrupted Age' (i. 56). But one night as she participates in a poetic recital before the Duke in which she takes the part of the goddess Diana, he feels a 'cleaving sweetness' which 'thrill'd swiftly to his Heart, thence tinged in his Blood, and cast Fire throughout his whole Person' (i. 57). He resists mightily and seeks distraction in business but is unable to forget his new feeling for Charlot. He seeks

---

[1] Bentinck (1649–1709) was apparently William's closest associate, and served him very well, according to Sir William Temple, 'the best Servant I have ever known in Prince's or private Family'. See Temple's *Works* (London, 1720), i. 401. He was, however, disliked in England as a foreigner; as Burnet noted, 'he could never bring himself to be acceptable to the English Nation'. See *History of his Own Time* (London, 1734), ii. 5.

guidance in 'Michiavel', where he reads 'a Maxim, That none but great Souls can be compleatly Wicked' (i. 61) and decides that

> . . . neither Religion, Honour, Gratitude, nor Friendship, were Ties sufficient to deprive us of an essential Good! Charlot was necessary to his very Being! all his Pleasure faded without her! and, which was worse, he was in Torture! in actual Pain as well as want of Pleasure! therefore Charlot he would have. He had struggled more than sufficient; Virtue ought to be satisfied with the terrible Conflict he had suffered! but Love was become Master, and 'twas time for her to abscond. After he had settled his Thoughts, he grew more calm and quiet; nothing should now disturb him, but the manner how to corrupt her. He was resolv'd to change her whole Form of Living, to bring her to Court, to show her the World; Balls, Assemblies, Operas, Comedies, Cards, and Visits, every thing that might enervate the Mind, and fit it for the soft Play and impression of Love. (i. 61)

The mythical types have been clearly established, and what follows is, the reader now knows, the inevitable but still tragic losing battle of innocence against experience. The social convention of male sexual dominance has been complicated by the Duke's absolute control over Charlot. She has been deliberately fashioned by him as a paragon of innocence; but having made her what she is, he can easily shape her again to his own purposes. His masculine capabilities, his capacity to manipulate and control with such selfish and utter efficiency, are the unmistakable signs of the unregenerate. Charlot's absolute passivity and utter defencelessness are equally clear marks of blessedness. She will, in time, 'surrender' to love. His surrender to the same passion involves commitment to an elaborate plan of action, one which carefully preserves himself and his social status. She, on the other hand, will submit to the love which he carefully provokes, and will give herself totally to him without thought of present status or future calamity.

He begins his seduction by letting her read more poetry, giving her a poem by Ovid, open at the story of Myrra's love for her father. We are thus bluntly reminded of the incestuous implications of the Duke's seduction of his young ward. She is immediately affected, and the conflict is set down with that melodramatic directness (crudity if you will) that made Mrs. Manley so popular: 'The Duke, who was Master of Mankind, could trace 'em through all the Meanders of Dissimulation and Cunning, was not at a loss how to interpret the Agitation of a Girl who knew no Hypocrisy; all was Artless, the beautiful Product of Innocence and Nature' (i. 64). He kisses her and she feels, in Mrs. Manley's semi-physiological rendering, 'that new and lazy Poison stealing to her Heart, and spreading swiftly and imperceptibly thro' all her Veins' (i. 64). He does not press matters but gives her jewels and 'dangerous Books of Love . . . Books dangerous to the Community of Mankind; abominable for Virgins, and destructive to Youth; such as explain the Mysteries of Nature, the congregated Pleasures of Venus, the full Delights of mutual Lovers, and which rather ought to pass the Fire than the Press' (i. 67–8). Through his influence, she is brought to court and made a lady in attendance upon the Queen. He then carefully plants rumours of his marriage to a princess dowager. She retires to his villa with grief upon hearing this rumour, and the stage is at last set for another warm scene, here a rape succeeded by Charlot's submission to her own awakened 'guilty Transports' (i. 72).

The details of the scene are precise, fitted carefully to the erotic-pathetic fantasy being provoked. She is surprised in her night clothes, 'uncovered in a melancholy careless Posture' and holding a handkerchief 'that she employ'd to dry those Tears that sometimes fell from her Eyes' (i. 71). The Duke enters, and her first joyous reaction changes to fear as she realizes that 'he was not come there for nothing' (i. 71). His attack is wordless and brutal; he becomes the implacable ravisher as Mrs. Manley's vocabulary is ransacked for euphemisms which can convey the thrusting physical aggression he now embodies:

> She was going to rise; but he prevented her, by flying to her Arms, where, as we may call it, he nail'd her down to the Bed with Kisses; his Love and Resolution gave him double Vigour, he would not stay a moment to capitulate with her; whilst yet her Surprise made her doubtful of his Designs he took Advantage of her Confusion to accomplish 'em; neither her Prayers, Tears, nor Strugglings, could prevent him,

but in her Arms he made himself a full Amends for all those Pains he had suffered for her. (i. 71)

The rape is absolutely necessary to preserve Charlot's innocence. In terms of the implicit moral code of the story, she has been taken unawares, and the love which follows is merely the irresistible result of that rape. Her desires have been triggered, as it were, by the assault, and she is no more to blame for them than for the rape itself. The female myth, of which Charlot's story is a crudely explicit version, is an opportunity for extended erotic fantasy, even while it guarantees the moral innocence of the heroine and the readers who are invited to identify with her. The male villain, the archetypal aristocratic seducer, is made grotesquely evil so that he can be despised on the conscious and explicit level of moral praise and blame, even while he is desired and enjoyed at the deeper level of fantasy and vicarious experience to which the myth appeals.

Soon after this the Duke goes off to the wars and Charlot goes back to court. Violated but not corrupted, her innocence is asserted by contrasting her with a young widowed Countess in whom she confides and who reacts to her love-misery by expounding the worldly selfishness necessary for survival in the 'fashionable World' which she exemplifies:

. . . that never-dying Fire! those racking Uneasinesses! Languors! Expectations! Impatiencies! that the two Lovers express'd were all Greek and Hebrew to the Countess, who was bred up in the fashionable way of making Love, wherein the Heart has little or no part, quite another turn of Amour. She would often tell Charlot, That no Lady ever suffer'd herself to be truly touch'd, but from that moment she was blinded and undone. The first thing a Woman ought to consult was her Interest, and Establishment in the World; that Love should only be a handle towards it; when she left the Pursuit of that to give up herself to her Pleasures, Contempt and Sorrow were sure to be her Companions. No Lover was yet ever known so ardent, but time abated of his Transport; no Beauty so ravishing, but that her Sweetness would cloy; nor did Men any longer endeavour to please, when nothing was wanting to their Wishes. Love, the most generous, and yet the most mercenary of all the Passions, does not care what he lavishes, provided there be something still in view to repay his Expence; but that once over, the Lover possess'd of whatever his Mistress can bestow, he hangs his Head, the Cupid drops his Wings, and seldom feels their native Energy return, but to carry him to new Conquests. (i. 73–4)

Now this obviously exceeds the ideological requirements of political slander. It is the now familiar conventional indictment of the wicked and absolutely corrupt masculine world which Mrs. Manley needs not so much to convince her readers that the Whigs are evil men as to create a world where everyone is evil except isolated heroic (and doomed) individuals. The Countess expresses a cynicism about love which is never part of Mrs. Manley's proper narrative voices but is always given to the targets of her abuse.

What the Countess advises is, if we examine her vocabulary carefully, an almost ascetic reserve which recognizes the hair-trigger sensitivity of the female mechanism. Once a woman allows herself 'to be truly touched', that is, once she allows her infinite and natural capacity for passiveness and submission to assert itself, she is doomed to a kind of emotional self-immolation. Male love is in the 'natural' order of things a destructive consuming instinct, a psychological generalization about the nature of the male beast which the Countess expresses in five different ways, the last approaching the sort of pornographic allegory of the physical act itself which Mrs. Manley's rhetoric delights in. Since male disgust is physically and psychologically inevitable, a woman must insist upon insurance for the future, not only by refusing to respond to love, but by using the intellectual clarity which this lack of involvement maintains to extract a settlement. All this is, of course, the wisdom of the world and proper only for children of darkness like the Countess.

The Duke returns from the wars and grows sated with Charlot, as the Countess has warned her. He sends her away and proposes to the Countess in level, business-like terms:

I have took time to weigh the Design, all things plead for you, Beauty, Merit, Sense, and every thing that can render a Woman charming; whilst I pretend nothing to plead for me, but making it your own

Interest to make me happy. As I have avoided the tedious Forms, by which our Sex think they must engage yours, so I beg that you will use none to me. (i. 81)

The Duke and the cunning Countess live happily in a world of contracts and mercantile logic where gratification and security are the only personal values. Charlot ends her days in 'Horror, Sorrow, and Repentance' (i. 83), still a victim of inner compulsions but still heroically exemplifying a valid inner life which is intended to stand as the positive moral centre of the story.

Her specific actions must, of course, be disavowed and the story closes with the appropriate exemplary dying fall: 'She dy'd a true Landmark, to warn all believing Virgins from Shipwrecking their Honour upon (that dangerous Coast of Rocks) the Vows and pretended Passion of Mankind' (i. 83). An ending such as this might tempt one to argue here that Mrs. Manley's popularity was due to the imagined didactic value of her stories, that the *New Atalantis* was indeed a treasury of monitory fables wherein young ladies could learn useful lessons about the world of arranged and loveless marriages where predatory males prowled about relentlessly looking for victims.

But fiction, needless to say, never deals with life in so direct a manner. The relevance of Mrs. Manley's extravagant fables of blasted innocence to eighteenth-century life lies, as we have seen, in their ability to handle mythological simplicities with convincing energy. These myths reflect, in the oblique and distorted way that popular myths do, the moral and intellectual concerns of the age rather than the specific details of everyday life. For if the crude moral antitheses they deal in exploit certain truisms of sexual relationships, they also reflect that basic ideological split between what I have chosen to call the secular and religious views of experience which characterizes the early eighteenth century. Just as the seducer's sexual rapacity is naturally complemented by the formal religious and moral libertinism he is frequently made to profess, the persecuted maiden herself easily becomes a partisan in the struggle against infidelity and irreligion, the rhetoric by which she exists exploiting the emotive phrases and slogans of the polemic against unbelief. In Mrs. Manley's case, these ideological resonances are further complemented by the conservative rhetoric natural to a Tory propagandist.[1]

Just after the story of Charlot has been told, a pompous funeral procession files by the three observing deities. Intelligence comments on the vanity of all this, condemning it in the language of that agrarian utopianism that appealed to the age:

> Did Mankind confine themselves only to what was necessary, reasonable, or proper, there would indeed be no occasion for most part of the great Expence they are at; the Oar might lie at rest in its native Bed; Navigation would be useless; Diamonds, and other precious Stones, secure in their Quarry; the sea not ransack'd for Pearl, since, in the equal Distribution of the Creation, every Country is sufficient to it self for sustaining Life with Temperance, tho' not with Luxury. (i. 89)

Such sentiments are not at all irrelevant to the mythological simplifications of the narrative parts of the *New Atalantis*. This ideology, with its distrust of the complex world of financial power and aggressive economic manipulation, reinforces the female distrust of a masculine world where a woman is either only another pawn in the struggle for power and influence or a commodity to be possessed and devoured by the same ruthless individualism of a society whose highest values are economic laws. Mrs. Manley's Tory nostalgia helps to sustain the opposing values implied by the novellas, which in spite of their stylized and extravagant characters and situations are firmly rooted in certain basic if distorted economic realities.

[1] Frequently, Mrs. Manley pauses to denounce not simply the immorality of the age but the cause of that immorality in vicious first principles. The rhetoric is that of the polemic against infidelity: 'The Sect of Epicurus is revived in a more dangerous manner; he allows you Gods, almighty in their Indolence! in ever lasting Ease: undisturb'd by the Affairs of Mortals, who are govern'd only by that fortuitous Chance to which his World ow'd its Original. These Moderns destroy not only the Effects (like him) of their Attributes, but disown the very being of a Deity. Whilst others no less impious (under other Pretences) advance a System no less dangerous: And by their human Inventions, and diabolical Arguments, they endeavour to prove Man (as they call it) wholly Mortal; the rolling Stone and Vulters! [*sic*] with the whole Regiment of Rewards and Punishments! Radamantus: and the Elysian Fields: the Invention of Poets, the Dreams of Enthusiasticks, and the Craft of Priesthood' (ii. 3–4).

In these novellas it is always clear how over-dramatized economic realities determine status and influence character in a decisive way. A good example is provided by the story of Elonora, 'the Beautiful and the Innocent', where what Mrs. Manley's deliberate exaggeration sees as the automatic vulnerability of younger daughters and the necessary rapacity of younger sons under primogeniture help not only to establish but to make plausible and relevant the myth of female innocence and masculine evil which the story is to dramatize. Elonora meets the strolling deities and tells her story. She is a younger daughter with a portion too small to attract an eldest son. She is therefore courted secretly by one Don Antonio, a younger son with no patrimony in his future, whose disenfranchised economic status is made the cause of his sinister character:

> His Mind a Complication of seeming Good and real Evil is impenitrable! [*sic*] He lends the Clew to none; there is no searching the Recesses of his Breast! 'Tis all dark and benighted to the attempting invader. This one Inclination, the Love of Money being alone conspicuous in him.
>
> .   .   .   .
>
> He does not love Reading, unless it be the Opinions of those Philosophers and Atheists, that concludes [*sic*] this World to be the All of Life we ever are to taste. From their Doctrine he fortifies himself in Mischief, and thinks he may fearlessly pursue the Dictates of his Nature, since he is never like to be summon'd to give an after-Account of his Actions. (ii. 62–4)

There is a moral dialectic at work in Mrs. Manley's stories which pairs the evil 'masculine' vice of avarice with the atheistic nihilism that effective avarice requires. Don Antonio's subsequent career is pictured as a totally unscrupulous series of manœuvres to improve his status. So conscious is he of his economic position that he attempts to seduce Elonora by urging her to marry a rich old baron who has proposed to her. He plies her with love casuistry and tells her plainly 'to make the Baron happy in your Person, and let me be Master of your Heart' (ii. 69). When she tells her brother, Don Juan, of this, he sends her away to an aunt and takes her place at an assignation. Antonio is furious and kills Don Juan in a duel.

He escapes undetected; the estate passes to Elonora's younger brother, who, with the ruthlessness apparently natural to younger brothers, turns her out. She goes back to her aunt, but Antonio appears and manages to marry the aunt, thereby acquiring Elonora without compromising his status in the least.

But she refuses him, confessing, however, that she loves him in spite of the moral abhorrence he inspires in her. Her attitude seems curiously hypocritical, but is actually the invariable predicament of the embattled heroine, here punctiliously correct, if a bit too articulate to be quite convincing: 'Don Antonio had still the Assurance to sollicite me; I yet lov'd him, tho' I hated him; a Paradox that may easily be reconcil'd by those that know our Passions are involuntary, and the Opposition of Reason and Inclination' (ii. 102).

There is an appeal being made here to the sensitive, 'those that know' the proper and virtuous workings of the heart. Elonora stops short of compulsive action, but she recognizes the irresistibility of the emotion itself. Antonio has declared that his love is of the same compulsive kind; but this, we suspect, can hardly be true, for one cannot in these novellas serve both Mammon and Cupid. As it turns out, Antonio's fiendish equilibrium (his 'passion' for money results in total 'dispassion' towards everything else) and ascetic devotion to his financial goals can lead him to renounce love with appalling ease.

Elonora thus finds herself suddenly left alone in a secluded spot with one of her suitors, a Count ——, who begins to rape her and discloses that the assault has been engineered by Antonio in order to discharge himself of a debt of 4,000 crowns. The confrontation of moral polarities is deliberate and complete. Elonora and Antonio face each other like good and bad angels with all their attributes clearly rendered, but the lurid colours and poses of this popular iconography require the drab background of eighteenth-century economic realities. Elonora's set speech after she has been rescued from the violent Count by our three deities rehearses the usual topics of pathetic and defenceless innocence, but the circumstances which have led to this isolation are rooted in economic necessity.

To be truly defenceless, innocence in this fictional world must be poor in the literal sense; the persecuted maiden's story is an oblique comment on the absolute economic dependence of eighteenth-century women. The story is not, of course, a revolutionary fable or a socially conscious revolutionary document, but rather an emotional exploitation of certain social facts which presents an exaggerated and stylized version of them in order to obtain pathetic effects.

Base Antonio! ingrateful Emilia! [her maid] brutish Count! they've all conspired to my Ruin. Ah! what Retreat have I? Where in this bad World shall I find a Protection for my unwary Innocence? My Brother's Family averse! my Aunt's House Dangerous! Don Antonio is implac-able and resolute! I will never again return to a Place which he dis-honours. Oh Advise! assist me! tell me of a Sanctuary! Is there any such a Receptacle, for the Poor, the Innocent, the much unhappy Elonora? (ii. 108–9)

Now to be sure, Mrs. Manley's tireless flow of libel exploits other conventional patterns, those provided by highly traditional moral characters such as the virtuous hypocrite and the *senex amans*, and eighteenth-century satirical stereotypes such as the fop, the female rake, and even the female wit.[1] But the dominant fable, the one which asserts itself over and over again and which is the basis of Mrs. Manley's moral pose, is the tragic destruction of female innocence by a masculine world of rigid economic forces, summed up in her vituperative rhetoric by 'avarice' and by lust, which is simply avarice transferred to the world of the emotions. All of Mrs. Manley's political and pornographic effects depend, as we have seen, on her evocation of this imaginary world of over-powering corruption.

The great appeal of this image of society can be assumed not only from the popularity of the *New Atalantis* but from the slavish

---

[1] There is a rough comic scene (i. 157–63) in which a clergyman describes his shrewish wife, who has just thrown a hot apple pie on his head, as a woman whose disposition has become unbalanced by her poetic efforts. He warns us never to marry a woman of wit: 'I marry'd for Love. Lord bless us: Love of what? not her good Conditions; I'm sure. But I am an old Man, as you see, and she's a Wit, that took me, tho' I understood never a Word of what she writes or says. Deliver me from a poetical Wife, and all honest Men for my sake' (i. 162).

imitation of it which Mrs. Eliza Haywood produced fifteen years later in her *Memoirs of a Certain Island Adjacent to the Kingdom of Utopia.*

Mrs. Manley had provoked other imitators and there had been several works which attempted to associate themselves with the now magic name of Atalantis, promising by their titles to be sequels or continuations.[1] None achieved anything like the success of the *New Atalantis* until Mrs. Haywood's scandal novels appeared in the 1720s.[2]

---

[1] Defoe, for example, published in 1711 a pamphlet called *Atalantis Major. Printed in Olreeky, the Chief City of the North Part of Atalantis Major.* In 1714 appeared *The Court of Atalantis. Containing, A Four Years History of that Famous Island, Political and Gallant.* Each of these illustrates the usual limitations of the native secret histories and scandal chronicles which followed Mrs. Manley's great success. The former is, like *The Secret History of the October Club* published the same year, simply a brief political tract, free of Mrs. Manley's lubricious verve and given to dry rehearsals of current political rivalries: 'My present Relation refers more especially to the Affair of the Election of those representing Nobles, which, as before, the Northern Part of the Island, by a late Treaty of Coalition, were obliged to send up as often as the Soveraign of the Country thought fit to Summon her Hereditary Council to meet, which Summons was generally once in Three Years' (p. 9). Such a plain and matter-of-fact style makes the pamphlet of political interest only; the audience which bought *The New Atalantis* would have found it unbearably dry and reticent. Other political tracts attempted some kind of rudimentary narrative, some like *The Devil of a Whigg: or, Zarazian Subtility Detected* (1708) referring in their titles to Mrs. Manley's successful attack, others like *The Impartial Secret History of Arlus, Fortunatus, and Odolphus, Ministers of State to the Empress of Grand-Insula* (1710) dealing with Mrs. Manley's subject matter but not attempting her scandalous amplitude. John Oldmixion's *The Secret History of Europe . . . The whole Collected from Authentick Memoirs, as well Manuscript as Printed* (1712) was an ambitious work, reaching a fourth part in 1715, but was concerned with purely political rather than amorous-political machinations. Instead of accommodating their political victims to the stereotypes of the novella, such works were only able to rail at their villains; Mrs. Manley's invective was justified, on the other hand, by her lurid narrative flair.

The Court of Atalantis has very little to do with politics and is really a series of character sketches, some of them, as the 1717 Key claims, describing eminent persons. Here Mrs. Manley's racy scandals and libels are the sole concern, but the result is merely a collection of sketches lacking the bogus but effective unity provided by Mrs. Manley's political designs. This inconsequentiality is the chief weakness of other works in Mrs. Manley's vein such as *The Ladies Tale: Exemplified in the Virtues and Vices of the Quality, with Reflections* (1714) and *The German Atalantis: Being, a Secret History of Many Surprizing Intrigues, and Adventures transacted in several Foreign Courts* (1715).

[2] The only biographical and bibliographical study of Mrs. Haywood is G. F. Whicher, *The Life and Romances of Mrs. Eliza Haywood* (New York, 1915).

Less attached to party and more prolific and versatile a writer of narrative than Mrs. Manley, she began to use the sub-title 'secret history' in 1724, when it was attached to *The Arragonian Queen: A Secret History*, and to *The Masqueraders, or, Fatal Curiosity; Being the Secret History of a Late Amour*. She (or her publisher) had previously used only the word 'novel' as a sub-title, and here it was doubtless used, as G. F. Whicher, Mrs. Haywood's biographer, put it very gravely, 'as a means of stimulating a meretricious interest in her stories'.[1]

These are, however, still individual novellas and not really imitations of the *New Atalantis*'s elaborate presentational apparatus. It was not until the 1725 *Memoirs of a Certain Island* that Mrs. Haywood attempted to achieve the social panorama of scandal and libel which had made Mrs. Manley's name. She seems to have succeeded fairly well, for it became one of her most popular works, still familiar enough to be included in 1760 in a list of novels prefixed to Colman's 'Polly Honeycombe'.[2]

She seems to have left her husband, the Revd. Valentine Haywood, in 1721 and turned to writing to support herself. See Whicher, p. 3. She was a prolific and versatile hack, doing translations and writing plays and fiction. According to Whicher's reckoning, during the decade 1720–30 she wrote, besides plays and translations, thirty-eight works of her own.

[1] Whicher, p. 92.

[2] Whicher, p. 106. Less popular was a similar attempt of Mrs. Haywood's, *The Secret History of the Present Intrigues of the Court of Caramania* (1727). Other secret histories and memoirs of the late 1720s and early 1730s were more modest in their attempts to anatomize the interesting moral decay of the upper classes, never trying to achieve the scope of *The New Atalantis* and *Memoirs of a Certain Island*. These limitations are advertised, for example, in a 1728 work: *Some Memoirs of the Amours and Intrigues of a certain Irish Dean, who Liv'd and Flourish'd in the Kingdom of Ireland, not many Hundred Years since. Interspers'd with the Gallantries of two Berkshire Ladies.* (Mrs. Haywood may have written this. See McBurney, *Checklist*, p. 78.) Restricted to several special targets are such works as *A View of the Beau Monde: or, Memoirs Of the Celebrated Coquetilla. A Real History. In which is interspersed The Amours of several Persons of Quality and Distinction* (1731); *The Fair Concubine: or, the Secret History of the Beautiful Vanella* (1732); *Love à la Mode: or, the Amours of Florella and Phillis. Being the Memoirs of two celebrated Ladies under those Names: In which the whole Circle of Modern Gallantry is display'd* (1732); *Memoirs of Love and Gallantry; or, the Various Foibles of the Fair, Display'd in A Real History of Several Persons of Distinction . . .* (1732); *The Secret History of Mama Oella, Princess Royal of Peru. A New Court Novel* (1733); *The Secret History of Meadilla* (1733); and *Modern Amours: or, a Secret History of the Adventures Of some Persons of the First Rank. Faithfully related From the*

Upon close comparison, her imitation of the *New Atalantis* proves to be quite exact. An elaborate allegorical framework is employed: Cupid narrates the recent events in the island near Utopia where all the inhabitants are heretics to love and worship the goddess Pecunia, whose shrine is an enchanted well (presumably the South Sea Bubble), and we are given breathless snippets of lubricious scandal about the various gilded characters who pass before us. Sometimes, when Cupid decides that the offence against his godhead is especially rank, he relates scandals of novella length. The same atmosphere of aristocratic corruption is deliberately evoked as we hear of orgies in sumptuous palaces, secret lesbian cabals, insatiable adulteresses, and indefatigably lecherous noblemen. Placed in the middle of all this iniquity is the persecuted and innocent maiden that we have already met in the *New Atalantis*.

Mrs. Manley's political purposes were, we remember, well served by this ideology of persecuted innocence; for the Whigs could be plausibly associated, given the polemical conventions of Tory propaganda, with the amoral masculine world of ruthless economic individualism and irreligious *Realpolitik* which is the negative moral pole of the ideology. Mrs. Haywood lacked this political commitment, and the times themselves had become under increasing Whig control less openly contentious. But she inherited the Tory rhetoric, the 'reactionary' condemnation of the present, and the support which it provided for the moral antitheses.

As a result of this rather automatic indignation, her invective is less coherent than Mrs. Manley's, her Cupid more given to dashes, exclamation points, and catalogues than to the more correct and pompous quasi-philosophical reflections of Astrea, Virtue, and Lady Intelligence. Without specific political antagonists such as Mrs. Manley had in the Whig Junto and the Marlboroughs, Mrs. Haywood simply denounces the 'world' which worships money and neglects those authentic inner virtues summed up in words such as love and virtue.

Author's own Knowledge of each Transaction. With a Key prefixed (1733). Such lesser examples of the genre which Mrs. Manley and Mrs. Haywood practised are testimony to their success and influence.

Cupid begins, for instance, by describing the sorry state of his cult in the island adjacent to Utopia:

'Tis true, the Demon has usurped my Name! —my Face! my Voice! —they still revere and call on Cupid, —Cupid they still adore—But not a Cupid accompany'd with Innocence, Virtue, Constancy; but a Cupid, ushered in by wild Desires, Impatiencies, Perplexities, and whose ghastly Train are filled with Shame, Disgrace, Remorse, and late Repentance and Despair! Yet this is the Deity to whom they sacrifice—this is the God they invoke, and with Pecunia drives from their perverted Souls all Sentiments of Honour, Virtue, Truth, or Gratitude. —A blind Gratification of unlicensed Wishes is all they aim at. (i. 4–5)[1]

Lust and avarice have replaced love almost completely, and after relating a few instances of this transformation, Cupid grows even warmer in his denunciations:

What will not these wretched Islanders do for Interest! What Sense have they of present Shame, or future Punishments! —Does not one of the first of their Nobility, neglecting the Embraces of his almost Virgin-Bride, live in Pollution with his own Sister? —Has not another prostituted his Daughter?

Adultery and Incest are grown common Crimes, and scarce wear any other Name than that of venial Transgressions. —And well indeed may these appear less monstrous, when there's a reigning Sin yet more unnatural, more horrid, than Hell, or any Fiend but Man, has power to invent. Both Sexes, as not content to mingle with each other in unlawful Blendings, turn to their own, perverting Nature, and defiling their own Specie; and Man with Man, Woman with Woman sins! (i. 155–6)

The ranting style is familiar from the *New Atalantis*, but it has grown even looser and more disjointed. The attack has been widened even further, or better, generalized so that it becomes more purely a means towards achieving the functions of the narrative as such, rather than a polemical instrument. Lacking a political point of view, the gossip Mrs. Haywood repeated or invented or heightened tends to be sexual scandal for its own sake, gratuitously sensational. The mythological simplicities become even simpler, the characters and situations even less varied, more broadly drawn

[1] All references are to the first edition of volume i (1725) and the first edition of volume ii (1726).

and restricted to stock gestures. Her vicious aristocrats, for example, are simply avaricious and lustful without any of the conspiratorial political motives that Mrs. Manley assigned to them. The stripping away of splendid surfaces to reveal vicious interiors is more plainly an expression of that envious hatred which we expect from middle-class exposés of aristocratic corruption. The picture given of the Duke of Bolton is a good example of the procedure:

See where conspicuous by his Port and Grandeur, the Prince Del Ponto stands: —Observe his Air, his Mien, his Shape, you will find few who equal him in the Graces of his Person. —Nature has been as liberal of her Gifts as Fortune, both have done their utmost to make him appear great and lovely; —yet if you regard him heedfully, you will read something in his Eyes which discovers he has a Soul far unworthy of the Case in which it is inshrin'd. —The meanest of the Plebian Crowd who court his Favour, or implore his Bounty, has not a Disposition more sordid and avaracious; there is none so vile, whom for Interest, he will not basely fawn on; nor any so much below him, whom to make instrumental to his Gains, he will not treat as his Superiors. —He married a Lady of Birth equal to his own, but denies that unhappy Princess every thing befitting her Quality, and on her refusing to come into some Measures to which her Spirit render'd her averse, obliges her to live in a lonely Country-House, a great distance from all her Friends and Relations, scarce allowing her an Equipage fit for the Wife of a private Gentleman. —But notwithstanding his Neglect of her he ought to love, he is not insensible of Beauty—he is accounted one of the most amorous of the Nobility; and 'tis certain, to gratify his Inclinations that way, will make no Scruple of sacrificing everything but Money. —The Wives and Daughters of his nearest Friends, or even Kindred, are not secure from his Sollicitations; and numberless are the Families, whose Honour has been stain'd by his seducing Arts. (i. 149–50)

Mrs. Manley's villains are built along the same lines and possess the same vices, but they are more formidable, equally detestable but more complex figures. Instead of the convincing involvement in the cut-and-thrust power struggle which Mrs. Manley can grant her villains, Mrs. Haywood is restricted to a mechanical division of glittering surface from vicious interior. Her villains are attractive, of course, but she insists that this glitter is an absolutely superficial coating. To the sensibility and moral perception which Mrs. Haywood implicitly assures her readers they possess ('yet if you regard him heedfully, you will read something in his Eyes . . . a Soul far unworthy of the Case in which it is inshrin'd'), this is thin varnish indeed. The Prince is made as amoral and unscrupulous as any of Mrs. Manley's targets, but he has the soul of a shop-keeper rather than of a Machiavellian statesman. Mrs. Manley's villains are imperiously irresistible; Mrs. Haywood's tend, like the Prince Del Ponto, towards a bourgeois craftiness and meanness. His shameful behaviour towards his wife seems hardly worthy of a satanic seducer and betrays its origin in petty gossip.

All of this is not really a scaling down of the aristocratic seducer, but a sharpening of the moral contrast between him and his victim. The lust and avarice with which he is endowed are absolute values; the rhetoric insists that, like his victim's innocence, they are without parallel and almost beyond adequate expression: 'The meanest of the Plebian Crowd . . . has not a Disposition more sordid and avaracious . . . he is accounted one of the most amorous of the Nobility; and 'tis certain, to gratify his Inclinations that way, will make no Scruple of sacrificing everything but Money.'

Villains like the Prince Del Ponto suggest in their completeness more than they actually achieve. The reader's imagination is meant to be staggered by the extent of his successful depredations: 'numberless are the Families, whose Honour has been stain'd by his seducing Arts'. Mrs. Haywood's rhetoric suggests what her stories, in effect, document: the campaign which mobilized aristocratic libertinism conducts against embattled female virtue—'he is accounted one of the most amorous of the Nobility'.

It is this conspiracy which replaces the Whig machinations of the *New Atalantis*, where the plot against innocence was partly a means towards a political end. But Mrs. Haywood was imitating that feature of Mrs. Manley's scandal chronicle which had survived the temporary needs of faction. The supporting Tory rhetoric could be appropriated by being made less specific; the loss in coherence was a gain in emotional and ideological (in the narrative sense I have given it rather than the political sense) intensity.

Mrs. Haywood's book shows us, in effect, just how the *New Atalantis* was read; for *Memoirs of a Certain Island* shows us a commercial strategy at work enlarging just those areas of Mrs. Manley's work that continued to affect readers fifteen years after the scandalous events it claimed to describe.

That process of enlargement is clearest, I think, in the more precise innocence and moral sensitivity Mrs. Haywood insists upon for her persecuted heroines, and by implication, of course, for the readers who participate vicariously in their trials. In the *New Atalantis*, Astrea and Virtue place the reader firmly on the side of the angels. There is not, we learn, a great deal of virtue extant in Atalantis; but the various pathetic heroines, a few isolated male paragons, and those Tory statesmen who are saving their country constitute an embattled élite. In *Memoirs of a Certain Island*, membership in this élite is as much a matter of perception as of virtue, faith as well as good works. Membership in this virtuous élite is determined by an understanding of the mysteries and paradoxes of love, a perception which matters in the *New Atalantis* but which is made the only condition for membership here. The choice of Cupid as the narrator is the first indication of the spiritual specialization. Love, for Mrs. Haywood's audience, equals Virtue and Justice, and the gay damned who flit about her sinful city sin against love. Cupid makes this point quite specifically after listening to a conversation between some ladies:

This little Conversation, said the Deity, may give you a Taste of the Disposition of both Sexes in this Island—most Women are fond of circumventing each other in their Amours, and most Men are more taken with Novelty than any other Charm. Flavia has given a thousand Instances of her Passion for this ingrateful Lover, yet he prefers a new Face to all the Endearments she can bestow, and this Lady can easily absolve herself for breach of that Trust reposed in her, to purchase the vain glory of a heart which perhaps may not be three days at her Devotion. Thus do they spend their days in an eternal Round of Hurry and Confusion. —Pursuit, which to a Soul truly inspired by me, is full of Fears, Perplexities, and Care, is with them the only Pleasure; and Enjoyment, the beginning of a perfect Lover's Happiness, puts an end to the Felicity of these imaginary ones. This is a Humour so near universal, that the few who are of a contrary one, are laugh'd at as Affecters of a Romantick Singularity, and rarely meet with any other return than scorn from the objects of their Constancy. Thus am I affronted even by those who plead my Power as the only excuse they can make for the Foibles they are guilty of. (i. 202)

This is a somewhat tamer place than the world of predatory ambition and ruthless promiscuity that Mrs. Manley invokes. Although it can generate spectacular violence, this is a world of amorous trifling and inconstancy whose function in the narrative is to establish with almost pedantic precision the exact nature of the heroine's virtue. The reader is invited to reject this world (after having its pleasures described in detail) and to identify with heroines who stand out in this vain hubbub, who refuse to modify the exact inner ritual which love demands, a more subtle and exacting technique than the simple chastity demanded of the virtuous in the *New Atalantis*. Love is beyond the psychological excitement and physiological limitations described in the paragraph above. In fact, in Mrs. Haywood's rhetoric it becomes an ineffable concept, beyond normal understanding and the superficial technicalities of ordinary virtue.

This spiritualization can be observed, for example, in the complicated account which Mrs. Haywood gives of Miranda. She is the victim of Romanus, who constructs a plot as elaborate as it is vile. He pretends to have a Platonic interest in her:

. . . he would often assure her, that he consider'd her not as a Woman —that in entertaining her, he did not so much as think of the Difference of Sexes, but that he could not help imagining there was something of a Sympathy in their Souls, which engag'd his tenderest Sentiments. —By this way of proceeding he entirely won her to admit his Visits, and to entertain her as often as he had leisure; —his Conversation is too engaging, and has, indeed, the Appearance of too many Advantages not to be joyfully accepted by those who apprehend not the Dangers of it. —Miranda thought herself happy, in having a Friend so qualify'd, —the little Foibles and Impertinencies of her own Sex took off the pleasure she might else have found in the Society. —She had often wish'd there were such a thing as a Male Friend without Design, and was overjoy'd to have met with one whom she believ'd so perfectly disinterested and at the same time adorn'd with such a Strength of Judgment. (i. 24)

Having gained Miranda's confidence so carefully, he methodically isolates her from all her former friends and her relations. When he does drop the pretence and declares his love she has nowhere to turn. But in place of the violent possession and automatic passionate ignition which Mrs. Manley's trapped heroines have to experience, Mrs. Haywood resorts to her favourite rhetorical and psychological tricks. Words, we are told, are inadequate to describe the paradoxical state of Miranda. When Romanus writes a confession of love and pretends to swoon as he shows it to her, the best that can be done to render her special state of love and distress is to speak of an internal psychomachia that is raging.

But in what Words shall I make you sensible what 'twas Miranda felt in this Surprize? a thousand Passions crowded at once into her Soul; confounded, and asham'd at what she read, she wou'd have spoke, and perhaps, in the first rush of Indignation, have banish'd the Writer from her sight. —but then, to behold him thus dejected, thus overcome with grief, —thus struggling, as she thought, with the fierce Pangs of desperate, dying Love; repell'd the Dictates of severer Honour, and turn'd her all to Pity and Forgiveness. (i. 27–8)

She surrenders subsequently not so much to a rape as to a welter of extenuating circumstances produced by her own deeply felt virtue. It is not her passion that has been exploited, the narrative insists, but her infinite tenderness and moral sensitivity. Romanus's weapons are not violent ones but fiendish strategies which capitalize on this virtue. Her final capitulation, like that of Rosella, preserves her essential innocence:

In this surprize therefore, when all her Thoughts were hurry'd and disorder'd—when her whole Soul dissolv'd in soft Commiseration of his Woes, could inspire Words of Consolation only—he took advantage to undo her, and seize that Joy at once which, 'twas highly probable, should he have given her time for Reflection, would never have been his. —With all the Arts of fond seducing Passion—with all the Pomp of ruinous Desire—Impatiencies—Perplexities—melting Languishments—Sighs—Tears—Distractions—feigned Anguish—real Rapture,

did he attack her on the defenceless part; and while he swore to die
rather than attempt an injury to her Honour, undermined it, and every
moment gaining ground, at last triumph'd o'er all, and revell'd to the
heights of guilty Transport. —'Twas absence of Mind—'twas Surprize
—'twas Inadvertency—'twas Nature, and Excess of Softness—not base
Desires, or polluted Wishes, ruin'd this fair Unfortunate! —Guilty in
Fact, but innocent in *Thought*! —She yielded, unknowing that she did
so. (i. 30–1)

The last is a crucial if delicate distinction. Some of Mrs.
Manley's heroines yield just as reluctantly; but all of them are
endowed with a capacity for carnal joys, all give in to some extent
to the sexual pleasures possible once the horrors of being ruined
are past. Mrs. Haywood's frantic style tries to convey the same
lubricious pleasures that Mrs. Manley specialized in, but the moral
justification is more consistently and thoroughly applied. Her
heroines, such as Miranda, preserve their innocence so that we will
not forget that the seduction we are witnessing is the tragic conflict
which female virtue is forever doomed to engage in with irresistible
masculine evil. The mythology thus persistently evoked acts as a
compensation for the erotic fantasy, a displacement, as it were, of
the central task of the narrative to provide vicarious sexual pleasure.
It is Richardson's achievement, by the way, to rescue this mythology from its degraded position as moralistic covering for erotic
fantasy (or at least to make the cover thicker).

But innocence does not always exclude sorrow and guilt. Those
emotions are definite signs of beatitude in Mrs. Haywood's world
of popular tragedy. Virtue must by definition suffer terribly, and
Mrs. Haywood reaches pathetic heights (bathetic depths if you
will) regularly. The persecuted maiden at her most distressful
receives as much attention as she does when she is in the process
of being violated. Mrs. Manley tended to drop her heroines once
they had been ruined. They were dismissed after a brief pathetic
scene. Mrs. Haywood enlarges this area of the story, making many
of her heroines into variants on the Griselda myth, variants since
there is no one to reward them at the end of it all for their
constancy.

The closest to Griselda is a lady who marries the son of the Duke of Marbien when her father commands her. The Duke opposes the match and abducts his son during the wedding night. Cupid attempts to describe the lady's agitation at this point:

> . . . think what it must be to lose at once all that the Soul holds dear— to know one's self clear, even in Thought, of Sin, yet to be upbraided as the most guilty Criminal; to have the name of Wife, yet be depriv'd of all can make that Title pleasing. —Form, if it be possible, an Idea of such a State, and judge what she endur'd. (i. 211)

The Duke weans his son from such a degrading alliance by giving him 'several of the most beautiful Courtezans the Island afforded' (i. 211). The opposition between the aristocratic debauchery to which the Duke introduces and converts his son and the fidelity and constancy which she comes to represent is what takes up the rest of the story. The letter which her husband writes to her after his father has died and he has become the Duke emphasizes the social implications of this opposition:

> I could wish there were a Possibility of Happiness with you; but when I consider the prodigious Disparity between us, it cannot be. —I would have you, therefore, be as easy as you can in this Separation; and to make you so, as far as is consistent with my Quality, or Peace of Mind, I shall add considerably to your Allowance; and if I do not raise it to an Income which may support you as the Dutchess de Marbien, it shall, however, be more than the Daughter of a Chevalier could expect. (i. 217–18)

We are being asked to reject, on that immediate emotional level which participation in such a story requires, the superficial, artificial distinctions current in the world for the deep and authentic worthiness of the heart. The utter defencelessness of the heroine, a result of her social position as well as her sex, is set deliberately against the consummate craftiness and boundless egoism possible for her husband, which are here due to his social position as well as his sex. He spends some years, we are told, 'roving round the World in search of Pleasures', but comes home at last and admits her as his wife. This is, however, only to accommodate himself, for he has exhausted the pleasures the world can give and seeks some-one to tend him. She submits and her life 'is one contin'd Scene of Affliction' (i. 220–1).

The story of the Duchess of Marbien is thus an extended exer-cise in the pathetic. The only eroticism that is involved comes incidentally when we hear in passing of the Duke's debauches. This relative purity is somewhat untypical of Mrs. Haywood's use of the pathetic, for she usually mixes in a good deal of erotic sug-gestion. The long-suffering maiden more often confronts her seducer with all the signs of her ravishment in full view. Such is the case with Bellyna, who is courted by Ricardo but resists his improper advances. She awakens one night to find herself possessed by him. The usual complications ensue: pregnant, she follows him to his country only to find that he is to be married, a financially proper match which his father had arranged long ago.

The confrontation scene reveals Bellyna as an exceptionally articulate heroine, capable of cutting off the derisive libertinism with which Ricardo defends himself and of striking the appropriate heroic-pathetic attitudes with an energy and intensity which are, we are told, beyond expression: 'It would be altogether impossible to represent what she endur'd from that crowd of mingled Passions which now all at once invaded her Soul. —Never was Rage, never was Despair, never was Grief, accompanied by the most poinant [sic] Remorse and Self-condemnation, more violent than hers' (ii. 119–20). Bellyna has arrived at this ineffable affliction after de-scribing the wrong done to her as an offence against nature and heaven, an injustice so monstrous that she could never have de-served it. The magnitude of her suffering and the extravagant rhetoric which matches it establish her as a martyr.

. . . he only smil'd . . . and with the most cutting carelessness—I remember but little, Madam, (said he) of any thing that pass'd between us—'Tis possible that among other Amusements in a foreign Country, I might take my Diversion with you, but am very certain I never had any serious Thoughts of you. —He was about to add something more of Derision, when unable to contain the struggling Rage too painfully pent up, she interrupted him by crying out, —Villain! can you then deny that you sollicited me on honourable Terms, and that the Shame, the Misery which now I labour under, is owing but to Artifice, and what indeed may justly be called a Rape? —Did you not call all Heaven to witness that you were my Husband; that you would perform all the tender Offices of that Name; and that the Ceremony of the Church should authorize these Joys you then protested were in my power to give? —But had I been less virtuous, you less a Hypocrite, were you in-debted to my Love alone, is this a Retaliation for never-ending Infamy; for abandoning the whole World; for pursuing you thro' Land and Sea; for depending on your Honour for the preservation not only of myself, but also the dear Unborn, who owes its Being to you? (ii. 119)

The reader is encouraged, of course, to breathe a passionate 'no' to all these urgent questions. But the fervour of the moment is increased by the knowledge that within this fictional world of suffering virtue these are purely rhetorical questions. This sort of affliction is exactly what virtue is requited with every time; it is the tragic nature of things.

To be sure, this tragedy is not absolute. Cupid, in this case, holds out hope as he looks into the future and sees the injured Bellyna reconciled to her friends and happy once more, while Ricardo, 'the Slave of Lust, shall linger out his Days in Diseases and Remorse, and full of Regret, but incapable of Penitence, grow hateful to the Gods, and avoided by all good Men' (ii. 125). This poetic justice is an occasional feature, for popular tragedy like this easily becomes melodrama. The pleasures of identification with a pathetic wronged innocent are naturally complemented by the righteous punishment we are allowed to distribute to her corrupter.

An example of the almost sadistic righteous pleasure this can lead to is provided by the story of Bertoldus, a fiendish rake-hell who rapes whatever woman he desires and escapes punishment because of his great wealth. He betrays his friend Anselmo by raping his fiancée, Cipriana. The two of them plot revenge and substitute a diseased whore for Cipriana. Bertoldus is infected and the two of them watch, as we are invited to, with great satisfaction as

Ulcers devour his Flesh, Rottenness consumes his Bones.—A dread-ful Martyr to Lust, he curses now the Pleasures he once courted with so much eagerness. —Yet ignorant from what polluted Source he drew the Contagion, and little suspecting the Cheat put on him by Cipriana and Anselmo, the latter has the satisfaction to hear his Groans, and see his Pains. —Long he cannot live to endure them; and when he descends to dwell to all Eternity among those Fiends who have been his abettors here, must learn to bear severer Tortures from the Vengeance of the offended Gods, than on Earth has been inflicted on him by that of Anselmo. (ii. 140)

Such a gruesome vision of the restoring of the moral balance is entirely appropriate to the mythology of persecuted innocence which Mrs. Haywood is exploiting. The heroics which this mythology dramatizes are of such an improbable purity and ethereal intensity that they can only be compromised and made unconvincing by earthly success, that is, by the normal mediocrity of everyday life with its mixture of good and evil. The reward for virtue such as this must either come in another and purer world or be arranged here on earth by events so extraordinary that they must be of divine origin. The demands and narrative 'logic' of the myth preclude the search for naturalistic details, causes, and resolutions which we demand of the novel and find in some of Defoe.

In *Memoirs of a Certain Island*, then, the world of the *New Atalantis* has been evoked more completely, and the scandal chronicle has been made a more efficient fantasy machine, or at least more transparent in its intentions. The moral antitheses have been sharpened, the ideology of persecuted innocence separated from the mass of scandalous imputation, fully visible as a compelling social myth. It is a myth which expresses obliquely not only the social realities of women's position in eighteenth-century society but the larger ideological realities of the age. For the heroine in her moments of saintly distress is nothing less than an embodiment of that cluster of values and associations which I have called the 'religious' view of experience. She acquires this meaning partly through her participation in a female archetype which is made up of the 'religious' values of submission, passivity, and self-effacement before the ideal,[1] and partly by the nature of her antagonist, the

---

[1] The 'ideal' in this case, what Kenneth Burke would call a 'God-term', is love, that is, the immutable fidelity to those quasi-spiritual promptings of the heart which the virtuous maiden is capable of.

libertin-seducer who embodies that amoral ethos of total possibility which I have called 'secular'.

The heroic maiden and her totally corrupt aristocratic seducer are presented with a broadness which we find at least unconvincing if not ludicrously unreal. But it is precisely this broadness of conception which allows the scandal chronicles of Mrs. Manley and Mrs. Haywood to ignite in their predominantly female audience that series of emotional meanings and quasi-religious associations which makes their characters and situations into a compelling social myth.

V

MRS. HAYWOOD AND THE NOVELLA—
THE EROTIC AND THE PATHETIC

WE have been concerned thus far with works which advertised themselves as any number of things—biography, travelogue, sensational journalism, moral and political exposé—but never as fiction, never as novels or some other equivalent term. All of these works, however, employed narrative techniques and deployed ideological simplifications which make them a significant part of the history of prose fiction in the eighteenth century.

But too much has doubtless been made by students of the novel of the importance of this pseudo-verification for *all* readers of eighteenth-century popular fiction. The degree of belief accorded by readers to the 'documentation' attached to even the most improbable work is an imponderable. The most that can be said is that this documentation may have been more important for one class of reader than for another. It seems likely, for example, that the ideal reader (that is, the social and intellectual level at which a work was clearly aimed) of, say, Captain Smith's *Lives of the Highwaymen* was conceived of by bookseller and author as someone who needed the support of literal truth, whereas the ideal reader of one of Mrs. Haywood's novels such as *Love in Excess* (1719) could be expected to possess a certain imaginative expertise, a sophistication of a sort which required emotional intensity rather than documentary paraphernalia in order to accept and participate in the narrative.

The facts are that the great majority of books which make up what I have called the popular narrative market during the pre-Richardson years of the eighteenth century made little pretence of the actual truth which we tend to think their eighteenth-century audience required. A rigorous insistence upon literal truth was a fairly limited commercial strategy in this market, for the field was dominated by narratives which were a recognizable continuation of the amatory themes and situations which had been a favourite and patently artificial subject since the Greek romances.

What this body of popular amatory narrative may be said to offer to its public as its main attraction is not the 'literal' truth and expansive wonder of the travel narrative, nor the daring biographical fullness (tragic or comic) and eschatological drama of criminal and pirate biography, nor the luscious moral indignation and social aggression of the scandal chronicles, but an emotional (both erotic and pathetic) intensity inherent in the myth of persecuted innocence. I shall attempt in the following discussion not only to gauge this intensity (for its hypothetical eighteenth-century readers, not for ourselves) and dismantle the apparatus which induced it, but to continue the schematization of the myth of female innocence destroyed by a world of male corruption. As in the preceding chapter, my aim is to observe this mythology as it acquires wider and wider currency and even complexity, as the persecuted maiden becomes more spiritualized a figure and the values which she embodies more overtly religious.

The amatory tales and novels which make up the explicitly novelistic pre-*Pamela* eighteenth-century milieu are, then, a compost heap out of which that violet must, in a sense, have sprung. But it is a forbidding if fertilizing pile, full of the monstrous and the ludicrous. There seems, at first sight, literally nothing in this justly neglected heap that can be legitimately exhumed for modern readers or acclaimed as a lost minor masterpiece.

Recently, however, modern scholarship has unearthed several worthy exceptions.[1] The best of these seems to me to be *Lindamira*

---

[1] Robert A. Day has singled out *The Perfidious P—* (1709) as 'the best English epistolary novel before *Clarissa*' from the point of view of technique. See *Told in Letters*, p. 178. Day has also edited Mrs. Mary Davys's *Familiar Letters Betwixt a Gentleman and a Lady* (1725) for the *Augustan Reprint Society*, no. 54 (Los Angeles, 1955). Mrs. Davys's sprightly and intelligent *The Accomplished Rake or Modern Fine Gentleman* (1727) has been reprinted by W. H. McBurney in his anthology, *Four Before Richardson*, where he also reprints an amusing story of a picara called *The Jamaica Lady or The Life of Bavia* (1720). The other two pieces reprinted are, as McBurney admits, of historical interest only:

(1702),[1] a work which Benjamin Boyce has singled out as 'a remark-able demonstration of how something of situation, motivation, and sentiment could be abstracted from the now rather *démodé* French heroic romance and adapted to English middle-class life'.[2] Boyce points out that the adaptation which takes place is not simply a reduction in size and subject but an attractive modification of the worst aspects of the heroic romance: 'the improbable incidents, the unrelaxed *préciosité* of the style, and the exhaustingly grand dimensions of everything'.[3]

This is fair enough. *Lindamira* is a conventional if clearly ren-dered amatory novella. The scene is nicely localized and we are aware of town and country as real places rather than artificial back-drops. We are not bothered, as the preface promises, by 'the feigned adventures of a fabulous knight-errantry', but entertained in convincing fashion by 'domestic intrigues, managed according to the humours of the town and the natural temper of the inhabi-tants of this our island'.[4] The style is clear, agreeably unpreten-tious, and free of the heroic fustian we have observed in the scandal chronicles. Lindamira herself manages to be virtuous without be-ing unbearably priggish and bears up under amorous affliction without resorting to the extravagant and meretricious rhetoric of the despairing maiden. Best of all, perhaps, her progress towards a happy marriage is enlivened by her combats with several genuinely comic adversaries. Her virtue and good sense are pitted against the familiar 'humorous' stereotypes, as she is besieged by several ridiculous suitors.

This comedy is a nice balance for the main plot—the various obstacles which keep Lindamira from marrying the man she loves, Cleomidon. Like his beloved, he is remarkable for his moderation; his good sense and decent reticence separate him at once from the equally gifted but emotionally compulsive heroes of the amatory

---

Mrs. Haywood's *Philidore and Placentia or L'Amour trop Delicat* (1727), and *Luck at Last or The Happy Unfortunate* (1723) by Arthur Blackamore. The most widely read of the exhumed little books is Benjamin Boyce's edition of *Lindamira* (1702).

[1] See *The Adventures of Lindamira, A Lady of Quality* (Minneapolis, Minne-sota, 1949). All further references are to this edition.

[2] Boyce, pp. v–vi.   [3] Boyce, p. vii.   [4] *Lindamira*, p. 3.

novella I will discuss later. Up to this point, Lindamira has also made it quite clear that she is something of a rationalist who despises the cant phrases of love and its power. An earlier lover's protestations have provoked only amused scorn: '...he was very loquacious, yet he often complained he wanted rhetoric to express his sentiments, which he did in such abominable far-fetched metaphors, with incoherent fragments out of plays, novels, and romances, that I thought he had been really distracted.'[1]

Cleomidon and Lindamira are kept from marrying by economic obstacles. He has only a small income himself, but excellent prospects in the form of an uncle, Alcandar, who will settle his estate on him if he marries the rich but otherwise undesirable Cleodora. When Lindamira refuses to deprive Cleomidon of this opportunity, he marries Cleodora in despair. She despairs in turn, and they both suffer quietly for several years.

Release comes when Cleodora dies after childbirth. After overcoming a last obstacle in the form of Cleomidon's scheming aunt, the lovers finally marry. Lindamira concludes with balanced and restrained joy, the roundness of her phrases matching the symmetrical and perfectly just union now achieved:

And now, my dear friend, I am come to the period of all my misfortunes; and my constancy is rewarded with the best of husbands, whose affection to me makes me infinitely happy. Our sufferings has [*sic*] been mutual, and our resentments were equal; and we have but too much experienced what is in the power of malice to do; that no jealousy or suspicion is able to dissolve that union that is betwixt us.[2]

The 'power of love' has triumphed over the power of malice; unselfish true love (despising money but getting it in the end anyway) has won out over avarice and self-seeking. The narrative has justified the preface's promise: 'To expose Vice, and disappoint Vanity; to reward Vertue and crown Constancy with Success, is no disserviceable Aim. All Vertuous Readers must needs be pleas'd to see the Vertuous and Constant Lindamira carry'd with

---

[1] Ibid., p. 12.   [2] Ibid., p. 165.

Success thro' a Sea of Misfortunes, and at last Married up to her Wishes.'[1]

It is quite correct for Professor Boyce to see *Lindamira* as a scaling down of the themes and situations of the heroic romance for a middle-class eighteenth-century English audience, and to see that in making his heroine 'real, English, and her virtue her own', the author anticipated the heroines of Richardson and Fielding.[2] But the rarity of performances such as *Lindamira* must make us wonder why this adaptation of the heroic romance was not done more often. Why, instead of soberly virtuous and judicious heroines like Lindamira, was the public which read such novels offered extravagantly virtuous or compulsively and uncontrollably passionate leading ladies? Why were the virtuous but untitled *dramatis personae* and localized domestic setting of *Lindamira* not preferred to the exotic locale and aristocratic characters so common in other amatory narratives? Why, finally, was the engaging mixture of comedy and amorous intrigue exhibited in *Lindamira* so rarely offered for sale?

The answers lie, I think, in the desires and capacities of the novel-reading audience as estimated by the authors and booksellers who combined to produce popular narratives of this sort. The simulated veracity of the other pseudo-fictional narratives on the market was not the key value here. The amatory novella which came more and more to replace the heroic romance was indeed a modification of the themes, situations, and style of the romance; but on the popular level with which we are concerned, it is more correct to call that modification a simplification or vulgarization rather than a realistic improvement.

Lindamira, Boyce points out, avoided the excesses of the romance and substituted a modest realism supported by a relatively unaffected and straightforward style. The great majority of the

---

[1] *Lindamira*, p. 3.

[2] Boyce, p. x. There is an interpolated story in *Lindamira*, 'The Adventures of Doralisa and the Pleasant Young Ovid', in which Doralisa, Lindamira's cousin, tells her of her amours in France recently. Boyce says that the origin of this story seems to have been an episode from *Artamène ou le Grand Cyrus*. He points out that the author of *Lindamira* can be seen here integrating moral precept and action and cutting down (by half) the length.

amorous novellas written in English before 1740 merely condensed the excesses of the heroic romance, substituted a debased and inflated but simplified heroic rant for the involved *préciosité* of the romances, and used that style to deliver stories of some external complication but of extreme moral and emotional simplicity.

The fable of virtue and constancy rewarded is promised and delivered in *Lindamira*, decently and reasonably dressed but present, as the above summary makes clear, in unmistakable terms. It may be that these ideological simplicities, only occasionally and unobtrusively visible in *Lindamira*, had as much to do with its modest success as the wit and realism we admire in it. That is debatable. What is certain is that these simplicities, further simplified and rendered in bright and lascivious colours, are the main feature of the really popular amatory novella. Furthermore, it is this lurid paradigm, with its rich opportunities for pathetic and erotic involvement, that is of interest in the study of the pre-Richardson eighteenth-century novel; for it is within this popular tradition that the heroines of Richardson and Fielding are to make their tragic and comic points.

We have, of course, already seen the ideology of persecuted female virtue in the scandal chronicles of Mrs. Manley and Mrs. Haywood. The narrative sections of these are scandalous anecdotes swollen up frequently to novella length and complication. Nature of the corrupted sort they claim to describe, say Mrs. Manley and Mrs. Haywood in effect, imitates art, and scandal neatly resolves itself into the pattern of the amatory novella. In following that pattern Mrs. Manley and Mrs. Haywood were aligning themselves with a technique and approach to narrative which claimed to reject the unreal absurdities and impossibilities of the heroic romance for characters and situations sensibly closer to probability and local reality.

It was, moreover, frequently acknowledged that the gradual demise of the heroic romance and the accompanying rise of the novella as a respectable narrative form were healthy signs. There is in the miscellaneous and unsystematic comments about fiction during the late seventeenth and early eighteenth centuries a consistent objection to the improbable and the marvellous, and a justification of fiction when it is concerned with matters which are morally relevant to real life.[1]

The critical *locus classicus* in English for this shift in taste is Congreve's well-known preface to his novella, *Incognita* (1692), in which he distinguishes briefly but carefully between the 'romance' and the 'novel' (i.e. the novella) in terms of their verisimilitude and probability. He contrasts 'the constant loves and invincible courages of hero's, heroins, kings and queens' to the 'intrigues in practice' of novels, which are made up of 'accidents and odd events, but not such as are wholly unusual or unpresidented, such which not being so distant from our belief bring also the pleasure nearer us'.[2]

Congreve recognizes the power of the extravagant romance to

---

[1] J. B. Heidler, in a study hampered by the scarcity of texts, found in his search for criticism of fiction that translations of the French heroic romances which began to appear about the middle of the seventeenth century consistently began by responding 'to the charge of unreality', and that their prefaces 'deal mostly with the theme of realistic portrayal'. He notes as well that novelists like Mrs. Behn were careful to claim literal truth for their works. See 'The History, from 1700–1800, of English Criticism of Prose Fiction', *University of Illinois Studies in Language and Literature*, xiii (1928), 17, 19–20. To be sure, a comment like Shaftesbury's—'. . . may I not be allowed to ask, "whether [he is quoting his own 'Advice to an Author'] there remains not still among us noble Britons something of that original barbarous and Gothic relish not wholly purged away, when, even at this hour, romances and gallantries of like sort, together with works as monstrous of other kind, are current and in vogue, even with the people who constitute our reputed polite world?" ' (*Characteristics*, ii. 314, ed. J. M. Robertson, Bobbs-Merrill paperback edition, 1964)—indicates that critical commendation of 'realism' as a narrative ideal was sometimes a protest against a contemporary taste for the strange and the marvellous. Indeed, in another part of the *Characteristics* (ii. 11), Shaftesbury sees the 'intensity' of the love novella as more perniciously unreal than the worst of the romances: 'But in a country where no she-saints were worshipped by any authority from religion, 'twas as impertinent and senseless as it was profane to deify the sex, raise them to a capacity above what Nature had allowed, and treat them with a respect which in the natural way of love they themselves were the aptest to complain of.' Shaftesbury here complains of those very qualities which I insist, later on in this chapter and at length in the next, had a great deal to do with the successful formula of the love novella.

[2] 'The Preface to the Reader', in *Shorter Novels: Seventeenth Century*, Everyman's Library (London, 1962), p. 241. All other quotations are from this page.

move the reader, 'to be pleased and transported, concern'd and afflicted at the several passages which he has read, viz. these knights success to their damosels misfortunes and such like', but finds himself objecting to this emotional involvement on rational grounds. The reader, he reasons, must inevitably see himself as foolish and his emotional participation as irrelevant 'when he is forced to be very well convinced that 'tis all a lye'. The moderate verisimilitude of the novel, Congreve implies, legitimizes participation by removing a good deal of this rational embarrassment over wasting moral concern and emotional involvement on the palpably fantastic. Congreve shrewdly sees that the effects of both narrative conventions on the reader are essentially the same. He is saying that the novel is to be preferred because its effects make better sense morally and rationally; the reader's participation in a novel is not a gratuitous emotional experience but a valid and useful exercise of his moral-emotional capacities.

The appeal is clearly to that common sense and moderation which has appeared to later centuries as the distinctive trait of the age. Congreve is in his elegant way coming to terms with what we are accustomed to call the middle-class objection to fiction as an untruth, a false and therefore worthless story. And it is all rather familiar ground. Congreve's preface has been cited frequently by modern historians of the novel as an advance in technical awareness, and the novella form which he defends greeted as a happy release from the long romance.[1]

But Congreve's sweetly reasonable defence of the uses of fiction is not the whole story of the gradual shift in fiction from the distant and the improbable to the local and the possible. The formal changes which prose narrative undergoes look impeccably reasonable from this distance, but on the popular level with which we are concerned those formal changes are also a response to a new kind of audience, one unprepared to cope with the sheer bulk and complication of the heroic romance but too 'sophisticated' to be satisfied

---

[1] See, for example, Heidler, *History of English Criticism of Prose Fiction*, p. 20; Walter Allen, *The English Novel* (London, 1954), p. 33; E. A. Baker, *The History of the English Novel*, iii. 103, quotes it at length and calls it an 'oft-quoted preface'.

with chap-books and not so pious as to be content with Bunyan and other popular religious narratives.[1]

The amatory novella owes its success as a popular form during the pre-Richardson years of the eighteenth century precisely to its capacity for vulgarization. Its relative brevity and simplicity are qualities which can be exploited to serve the needs of this new audience, a group eager for the basic pleasures of fiction—identification, projection, vicarious participation, and ideological alignment—and relatively insensitive to the more subtle and specifically 'literary' satisfactions provided by the complementary features of style and structure. This is an audience which is unconcerned or unaware of the greater moral and intellectual validity which is the rationale of the novella's moderate realism. At this level of audience capacity and concern, the participation and involvement of which Congreve speaks are the only operative values; the prose becomes a means to those ends with little validity or structure of its own, being, at best, a vulgarized version of some of the more obvious effects of cadenced prose.[2] The moderate realism of the novella is merely claimed rather than actually

---

[1] There was a continuing demand for religious works and for religious narratives (of which *Pilgrim's Progress* was the most popular) throughout the century; but, as Watt points out (*Rise of the Novel*, pp. 51–2), the public for religious reading does not seem to have increased in proportion to the growth of the reading public. Moreover, the public for this sort of reading seems to have been separate from that for secular literature.

We know, as well, that there was a steady demand throughout the century for fifteenth- and sixteenth-century prose legends and romances much adapted into modern and popular idiom 'as chap-books for the unliterary middle- and lower-class reading public, which was almost entirely unaware of the antiquity of these books'. See E. R. Wasserman, *Elizabethan Poetry in the Eighteenth Century* (Urbana, Illinois, 1947), p. 253.

[2] There is a natural tendency, that is, for the main characters, in moments of stress and passion, to rise (or lapse) into a heightened and 'eloquent' prose which naturally falls into the blank verse rhythm that English inclines towards. Robert A. Day (*Told in Letters*, pp. 196–9) notes this in Mrs. Behn's novels and in the more intense moments in Mrs. Haywood's novels: 'The modulation of prose rhythms into blank verse was evidently considered to be a genuine sympton of "Ardor", a connection which is logical from the theatrical history of the medium.' William J. Farrell ('The Style and the Action in *Clarissa*', *SEL*, iii (Summer 1963), 365–75) has pointed out that Richardson uses this theatrical declamatory style for those moments when Lovelace reveals his 'true nature' as vile seducer and for those moments when Clarissa 'nears her tragic fate'.

achieved or even striven for. Local setting and familiar manners and costumes are often used, but the real centre of interest is the almost allegorical progress of the fable of persecuted innocence in a grotesquely evil world. The emphasis is not upon creating a reasonable or recognizable world of attainable virtue and good sense such as we find in a rare exception like *Lindamira,* but an exotic world of tumultuous passion and strident virtue where mythological simplicities prevail.

We have only to compare Congreve's preface with Mrs. Manley's essay preceding her *History of Queen Zarah* (1705) to find tacit admission of this popularization.[1] Mrs. Manley is concerned to defend 'little Histories' of the sort she is to present, for they 'have banish'd Romances', which have offended 'Persons of good Sense' by their 'Prodigious Length . . . the Mixture of so many Extra-ordinary Adventures, and the great Number of Acts that appear on the Stage, and the Likeness which is so little managed'.[2] Part of the natural appeal of the short tale (the *History of Queen Zarah,* part i, to which this is the preface, is 119 duodecimo pages), she admits freely, is its brevity, appropriate 'to the Brisk and Impetuous Humour of the English, who have naturally no Taste for long-winded Performances, for they have no sooner begun a Book but they desire to see the end of it'.[3] The long and elaborate romance requires extensive leisure, and demands by its complicated rhetorical surface a sophisticated and undeniably 'cultivated' re-sponse. Mrs. Manley is here describing an altogether different cultural and social situation, where leisure is only a part rather than a way of life. 'Brisk and Impetuous Humour' really describes in the shrewdly ingratiating manner of a literary publicist an audience for the most part merely literate and curious rather than educated and/or sophisticated.

Mrs. Manley pleads in an energetic and coherent way for attention to real psychological detail and authorial objectivity. The romance or any unsuccessful narrative is, according to her,

[1] See above, Chapter IV.
[2] *Secret History of Queen Zarah* (London, 1705), sig. A2ᵛ. All of the following references are to the first edition.
[3] Ibid.

old-fashioned and tedious in its attention to moral generalities rather than specific emotional truth: their authors 'have not an exact Notion of the Turnings and Motions of Humane Understanding; and they know nothing but the gross Passions, from whence they make but general Descriptions'.[1]

The sort of narrative she recommends is able, and this is the source of its superiority, to observe the particular and describe it so that the reader is involved. Her emphasis is on that participation which the plausible provides rather than on the moral and intellectual superiority of the real as such:

> . . . if he [i.e. the hero] be very Vertuous, and fals into a Mischance by Accident, they Pity him, and Commiserate his Misfortune; for Fear, and Pity in Romance as well as Tragedies are the Two Instruments which move the Passion; for we in some Manner put our selves in the Room of those we see in Danger; the Part we take therein, and the fear of falling into the like Misfortunes, causes us to interest our selves more in their Adventures, because that those sort of Accidents may happen to all the World; and it touches so much the more, because they are the Common Effects of Nature.[2]

The heroic romance is attacked for its unwieldy complications and its unreal characterizations, but these faults offend in Mrs. Manley's highly pragmatic view because they hinder that involvement which is the central aim of her fiction:

> A Reader who has any Sense does not take part with these Fabulous Adventures, or at least is but slightly touch'd with them, because they are not natural and therefore cannot be believ'd. Thus all the World will find themselves represented in these Descriptions, which ought to be exact, and mark'd by Tracts which express clearly the Character of the Heroe, to the end we may not be deceiv'd, and may presently know our predominant Quality, which ought to give the Spirit all the Motion and Action of our Lives; 'tis that which inspires the Reader with Curiosity, and a certain impatient Desire to see the End of the Accidents, the reading of which causes an Exquisite Pleasure when they are Nicely handled; the Motion of the Heart gives yet more, but the

---

[1] Sig. A1ᵛ.   [2] Sigs. A5ᵛ–A6ʳ.

Author ought to have an Extraordinary Penetration to distinguish them well, and not to lose himself in this Labyrinth.[1]

This is clearly no manifesto. It is not 'realism' as a valid approach to fiction that Mrs. Manley is interested in, but selling her book, producing a machine which will perform efficiently. She is not championing a new approach to fiction, but a more efficient accommodation of fiction to popular taste and the popular uses of fiction.

During the first two decades of the century, the production of original English amatory fiction was relatively small. There was Mrs. Manley, of course, and her very successful naturalization of the French *chronique scandaleuse* to the political controversies of the day. The novels of the long-dead Mrs. Behn continued to be widely read,[2] but the great majority of amatory fiction consisted of translations, mostly from the French. The works of native practitioners did not really rival translations in popularity until the third decade of the century when the 'novels' of Mrs. Eliza Haywood began to appear. The popularity of her novels of palpitating passion would seem to argue that she managed better than anyone else to carry out the accommodation of fiction to popular taste that Mrs. Manley described in her essay.

It is one of the more appalling and therefore interesting facts of literary history that the three most popular works of fiction before *Pamela* were *Gulliver's Travels*, *Robinson Crusoe*, and Mrs. Haywood's first novel, *Love in Excess; or The Fatal Enquiry* (1719).[3] In the decade that followed she was to establish herself as the most important producer of popular fiction before *Pamela* (Defoe produced anonymous, pseudo-documentaries rather than 'novels' in the eighteenth-century sense).

---

[1] Sigs. A6ᵛ–a1ʳ.

[2] Mrs. Behn's name was frequently linked with those of Mrs. Manley and Mrs. Haywood (sometimes Mrs. Centlivre) as a notable (or notorious) female writer. By 1735 an 'eighth edition' of her novels had been published: *All the Histories and Novels written by the late ingenious Mrs. Behn . . . Together with . . . the Life and Memoirs of Mrs. Behn. By One of the Fair Sex. . . .*

[3] W. H. McBurney, 'Mrs. Penelope Aubin and the Early Eighteenth-Century English Novel,' *HLQ*, xx (May 1957), 250. A 'Seventh Edition' was included in the third edition in 1732 of *Secret Histories, Novels and Poems*.

Her fame (or notoriety) cannot be denied; with Mrs. Behn and
Mrs. Manley she seems to have formed in many people's minds
what a contemporary panegyrist called 'the fair Triumvirate of
Wit'. Her importance, however, has been generally neglected, for
modern critics have naturally found little to admire in her novels.
The only clear statement of their significance that I know of
is W. H. McBurney's assessment of her pre-*Pamela* novels.
McBurney notes that her works, more than those of any English
author, caused the large increase in the publication of fiction which
occurred after 1720 (and we must assume that this increase corre-
sponds to a rise in the numbers of the audience for fiction) and
'contributed largely to the composition and mental attitude of the
fiction-reading public which was soon to acclaim the greater works
of Richardson and Fielding'.[1] This is admirably clear. What
remains to be done is to see just how Mrs. Haywood went
about exploiting the particular opportunities the amatory novella
offered.

The best account of the methods and effects in which Mrs.
Haywood specialized is a verse 'tribute' which first appeared in
the third edition of her collected *Secret Histories, Novels, and
Poems* (1732). This was by James Sterling and reflects vigorously,
says her modern biographer, the 'contemporary estimate' of her
early writings:[2]

> Persuasion waits on all your bright Designs,
> And where you point the Varying Soul Inclines:
> See! Love and Friendship, the fair Theme inspires
> We glow with Zeal, we melt in soft Desires!
> Thro' the dire Labyrint [*sic*] of Ills we share
> The kindred Sorrows of the gen'rous Pair;
> Till, pleas'd, rewarded Vertue we behold,
> Shine from the Furnace pure as tortur'd Gold:

---

[1] 'Formative Influences on the English Novel 1700–1739' (unpublished
doctoral dissertation, Harvard University, 1948), p. 225.

[2] Whicher, *Life and Romances of Mrs. Haywood*, p. 16. Sterling was active
between 1718 and 1755, came to London from Ireland with Matthew Concanen
and set up as a political hack. See *DNB*, liv.

You sit like Heav'n's bright Minister on High,
Command the throbbing Breast and watry Eye,
And, as our captive Spirits ebb and flow,
Smile at the Tempests you have rais'd below:
The Face of Guilt a Flush of Vertue wears,
And sudden burst the involuntary Tears:
Honour's sworn Foe, the Libertine with Shame,
Descends to curse the sordid lawless Flame;
The tender Maid here learns Man's various Wiles,
Rash Youth, hence dread the Wanton's venal Smiles—
Sure 'twas by brutal Force of envious Man,
First Learning's base Monopoly began;
He knew your Genius, and refus'd his Books,
Nor thought your Wit less fatal than your Looks.
Read, proud Usurper, read with conscious Shame,
Pathetic *Behn*, or *Manley's* greater Name;
Forget their Sex, and own when *Haywood* writ,
She clos'd the fair Triumvirate of Wit;
Born to delight as to reform the Age,
She paints Example thro' the shining Page;
Satiric Precept warms the moral Tale,
And Causticks burn where the mild Balsam fails;
A Task reserv'd for her, to whom 'tis given,
To stand the Proxy of vindictive Heav'n!

It is all extravagant enough to make us doubt its sincerity and question its origin. But placed at the opening of Mrs. Haywood's collected works, it is simply a publisher's blurb whose sincerity is irrelevant. Sterling is very careful to single out Eliza as a female worthy, a champion of all innocence (the 'tender Maid' and the 'Rash Youth'), but she is especially the female prophet of an oppressed and maligned sex against an organized male conspiracy.

This image invokes the ideological pattern of male tyranny versus female virtue we have already seen in the scandal chronicles. For the contemporary female reader at whom Mrs. Haywood's novels are aimed, to read such sentiments is to participate in an exhilarating manner in an eighteenth-century feminism, not yet a political movement, of course, but a set of apparently stirring moral and emotional affirmations. Part of the effect of Mrs. Haywood's novels, as her reputation became established, doubtless derived from this public personality of feminist champion.[1]

Mrs. Haywood is thus able to pose with ease as a reformer of the age, her position as a finer female sensibility giving her a unique perspective on the specifically masculine vices of the world she describes, such as avarice and sexual exploitation. To an unsympathetic modern reader, and indeed to some of her more discerning contemporaries, however, her novels seem bent upon delighting rather than reforming the age.[2] As Whicher put it, her books 'seem less successful illustrations of fiction made didactic, than of didacticism dissolved and quite forgot in fictions'.[3] And Mrs. Haywood's explicit moralizing, it is quite true, is perfunctory and unconvincing, an uneasy and superficial summary of the moral meaning of the events, shining examples or horrible warnings.

But Sterling's energetic poetic blurb can help us to see that her real effectiveness as a writer of demonstrably popular fiction lay in her ability to provoke erotic fantasy within the mythology of persecuted female virtue; her real didacticism (since all popular fiction is enormously didactic) is of an implicit and pervasive sort, 'dissolved and quite forgot' and therefore effective. Her 'technique' (perhaps instinct is a better word) is to evoke a female ethos to which her readers' response is a moral-emotional sympathetic vibration rather than a self-conscious and deliberate assent to moral ideas.

What Sterling praises is just this: her ability to involve the reader ('. . . we share / The kindred Sorrows of the gen'rous Pair') so that he forgets himself and participates totally ('Command the throbbing Breast, and watry Eye, / And as our captive Spirits ebb

---

[1] This idea is clear in Sterling's poem, as it is in a poem 'by an Unknown Hand' which appeared as part of the prefatory material to Part II of *Love in Excess:*

> A Stranger Muse, an Unbeliever too,
> That Women's Souls such strength of Vigour knew!
> Nor less an Atheist to Love's Pow'r declar'd,
> Till you a Champion for the Sex appear'd!

[2] In the preface to *Lasselia* (1723), Mrs. Haywood acknowledged this kind of criticism by defending herself from 'that Aspersion which some of my own Sex have been unkind enough to throw upon me, that "I seem to endeavour to divert more than to improve the Minds of my Readers"' (p. vii).

[3] Whicher, *Life and Romances of Mrs. Haywood*, p. 18.

and flow . . .'). Mrs. Haywood is being recommended for her power to compel our emotions and force us, if need be, into a satisfying fantasy world ('Persuasion waits on all your bright Designs, / And where you point the Varying Soul Inclines: / . . . And sudden burst the involuntary Tears / . . .'), a world advertised in fairly explicit terms for its erotic possibilities ('We glow with Zeal, we melt in soft Desires!'). The axioms and monitions which Mrs. Haywood sprinkles about are inadequate and irrelevant after the vicarious experiences she has induced in her ideally co-opera-tive reader; her novels are for that reader a supplement to life rather than a coherent comment on it. Sterling's praise of her moral usefulness is as weak as her own claim to warn the unwary of the dangers of excessive love,[1] but his outline of her methods of moving her readers is essentially accurate.

Given its great success, *Love in Excess* is presumably an example of those methods at their most effective. At first glance, this is a novella, actually three separate novellas which add up at last to a novel of 280 pages of extraordinary complication; amorous intrigue is woven around counter-intrigue in a bewildering fashion. But the intricate ballet is really a very simple mating dance whose principle of organization is the frustrated *pas de deux*. The various male and female stereotypes seen in the scandal chronicles are all here, but modified slightly, made more complex to fit the longer format, so that they perceive obstacles and experience conflict as they attempt to act out their roles in the inevitable fable of love.

We begin with a careful but perfunctory scene setting. Mrs. Haywood establishes in a sentence or two that we are in France during 'the late War between the French and the Confederate Armies' (i. 1).[2] Once this concession to the moderate realism and

---

[1] *Lasselia* has been published, Mrs. Haywood declares in her preface, to 'remind the unthinking Part of the World, how dangerous it is to give way to Passion' (p. vi).

[2] The first two parts of *Love in Excess* were first published separately in 1719, and are paginated separately. The third part was published in 1720 and issued with the other two parts, but paginated separately from each of them. All my references in the text are to this 1720 composite edition, printed for W. Chet-wood and sold by J. Roberts. The Roman numerals refer to the three separately paginated parts.

localization of the novella has been made, we pass quickly into a world of contending abstractions, heroic and absolutely stereo-typed characters. First, the hero, the Count D'Elmont. He has won military glory, but we hear of this only in passing. He is honoured at the court, but we are told this quickly. His military and social status is part of the automatic embroidery his character needs:

> The Fame of the Count's brave Actions arriv'd before him, and he had the satisfaction of being receiv'd by the King and the Court, after a Manner that might gratifie the Ambition of the proudest. The Beauty of his Person, the Gaity of his Air, and the unequal'd Charms of his Conversation, made him the Admiration of both Sexes; and whilst those of his own strove which shou'd gain the largest share in his Friendship; the other, vented fruitless Wishes, and in secret, curs'd that Custom which forbids Women to make a Declaration of their Thoughts. (i. 1–2)

D'Elmont, we will learn later, is a combination of the scintillating hero and the aggressive *libertin*-seducer. He is beloved by all, but

> had never yet seen a Beauty formidable enough to give him an Hours uneasiness (purely for the sake of Love) and would often say, Cupid's Quiver never held an Arrow of force to reach his Heart; those little Delicacies, those trembling aking Transports, which every sight of the beloved Object occasions, and so visibly distinguishes a real Passion from a Counterfeit, he look'd on as the Chimera's of an idle Brain, form'd to inspire Notions of an imaginary Bliss, and make Fools lose themselves in seeking; or if they had a Being, it was only in weak Souls, a kind of a Disease with which he assur'd himself he should never be infected. (i. 51)

A traditional figure, the heretic to love's deity like Chaucer's Troilus, he rejects love in language which resembles the cant phrases of freethinking and religious infidelity in their tough-minded materialism. But since D'Elmont is not simply the villified stereotype of the scandal chronicles, he is not allowed to be the rapacious aggressor. His great charms and his eventual conversion preclude that sort of total viciousness.

He begins his amorous career by plotting against Amena, who is, of course, eager but afraid. When Amena, fearing loose talk, cancels an assignation, he deals with her maid and learns that the only avenue open to him is application to Amena's father as a regular suitor. D'Elmont is intent upon seduction, however, and although the word is never used in the following dialogue with Amena's maid, there is no doubt about its presence. The heavy suggestions of sexual conspiracy evident here are a consistent feature of the book.

I would willingly said he coldly, come into any proper Method for the obtaining the Person of Amena, as well as her Heart; but there are certain Reasons for which I cannot make a discovery of my Designs to her Father, 'till I have first spoken with her. My Lord, reply'd the subtle Anaret (easily guessing at his Meaning) I wish to Heaven there were a possibility of your Meeting; there is nothing I would not risque to forward it. (i. 19)

Amena decides not to see him till he declares an honest and public suit. This reluctance establishes her innocence, but the terms in which it is stated prepare us for the erotic scene to come. She tells him that her father has warned her not to compromise herself, and that she has decided to let her life become the prey of her tenderness for him rather than her virtue: 'Press me then no more I conjure you to such dangerous Interviews, in which I dare neither Trust my Self, nor you . . . the way thro' Honour is open to receive You; Religion, Reason, Modesty, and Obedience forbid the rest' (p. 25).

Soon after, through her maid's connivance with D'Elmont, she is surprised in her garden and we reach in time the first of many sexual near-crescendi. Actually, the details of the scene are relatively precise. In fact, there is a bizarre alternation between scenic details which attempt some solidity and incredibly stylized amatory gestures. D'Elmont approaches the window behind which Amena is sitting, and she 'saw him thro' the Glass . . . and she remain'd in a Languishing and Immoveable posture, leaning her Head against the shutter, 'till he drew near enough to discern she saw him' (i. 25). Their movements are histrionic but clearly rendered.

D'Elmont then climbs up on the garden wall, level with her window. She signals that he must go away and refuses to open the window. Having established this convincing resistance surrounded by recognizable windows and walls, Mrs. Haywood moves confidently past the reality of this hesitation into a fantasy world of magic erotic impulses. The stage lights change to dim violet as D'Elmont

look'd on her as she spake, with Eyes so piercing, so sparkling with Desire accompany'd with so bewitching softness, as might have thaw'd the most frozen reservedness, and on the melting Soul stamp'd Love's Impression. 'Tis certain they were too irresistible to be long withstood, and putting an end to Amena's grave remonstrances, gave him leave to reply to 'em in this manner. Why my Life, my Angel, said he, my everlasting treasure of my Soul, should these Objections now be rais'd? how can you say you have given me your Heart; nay own you think me worthy that inestimable Jewel, yet dare not trust your Person with me a few Hours; What have you to fear from your adoring Slave, I want but to convince you how much I am so, by a thousand yet uninvented Vows. (i. 26)

The scene which follows is extremely well constructed for Mrs. Haywood's purposes. It is carefully divided into two parts. In the first, the fable of defenceless innocence is invoked in appropriately grandiloquent terms, and an army of moral allegories begin to march about. The events of the novel up to now, the extenuating circumstances and internal combustion which every heroine requires, are summarized quickly and related to the central myth. This allegorical rendering is a popular and debased version of those resonant personifications which so affected contemporary readers of eighteenth-century poetry; words like Virtue, Pride, and Honour have an emotional currency in the context of the age as well as in the context provided by Mrs. Haywood's narrative.[1]

[1] These allegorical features of amatory rhetoric are perhaps not quite as much of a hindrance to realism in an eighteenth-century context. Chester Chapin's speculation on the force of allegory in eighteenth-century poetry might also be valid here: 'Personifications become "real" to the eighteenth-century mind when they are felt as dramatizations of the values, affections, or qualities which relate to the activities of man in the empirical world—not when they are projected as figures from a world of vision.' See *Personification in Eighteenth-Century Poetry* (New York, 1955), p. 132.

Most important of all, the first part of the scene has established the ideological meaning of the sexual excitement to come. 'Pure' pornography, after all, is a rare and profitless genre; it is never interesting nor involving to think of automata copulating. The sexual encounter cannot be exciting in popular pornography like Mrs. Haywood's unless the participants acquire personalities, that is, unless the actors acquire a human and therefore moral dimension. The sexual act, like any other act described in fiction, presupposes moral values, and the reader is incapable of seeing the act without evaluating it and relating it to a realm of values. To be really effective, to involve and concern the way popular fiction must if it is to be popular, even Amena's 'heaving Breast' and trembling lips cannot do without the ideology of persecuted female virtue. Fiction such as this asks us to take sides, to stand with compulsive desire and terrified virtue against unscrupulous masculine cunning. The result is a double pleasure: the erotic sensations of the scene and the righteous superiority of being on the side of virtue.

In the second part of this scene we pass on to specific erotic details graphically rendered. Probability is strictly attended to; Amena's *déshabillé* is reasonably accounted for by the circumstances in which she is surprised. The lurid anatomical details convey the required image of flurried and compulsive sex; they are conventionally expressed but physiologically correct.

We notice as well that only Amena's palpitations are described. She vibrates, he controls. But his pleasure, even though he is the aggressor, is irrelevant to Mrs. Haywood's readers. He is, in fact, there to serve rather than to master. Mrs. Haywood knows what to omit.

What now could poor Amena do, surrounded with so many Powers, attack'd by such a charming force without, betray'd by tenderness within: Vertue and Pride, the Guardians of her Honour fled from her Breast, and left her to her Foe, only a modest bashfulness remain'd, which for a time made some defence, but with such weakness as a Lover less impatient than D'Elmont would have little regarded. The heat of the Weather, and her confinement having hindered her from

Dressing that Day, she had only a thin silk Night Gown on, which flying open as he caught her in his Arms, he found her panting Heart beat measures of consent, her heaving Breast swell to be press'd by his, and every Pulse confess a wish to yield; her Spirits all dissolv'd sunk in a Lethargy of Love, her snowy Arms unknowing grasp'd his Neck, her Lips met his half way, and trembled at the touch; in fine, there was but a moment betwixt her and Ruine; when the tread of some body coming. . . . (i. 28–9)

The efficiency of the scene extends to the style itself which, for all its dependence upon amatory clichés, has the logic of a mathematical demonstration. Amena is systematically stripped of her defences, external and internal; the balanced phrases and clauses just about contain the rushing participles which do the actual describing ('surrounded . . . attack'd . . . betray'd . . . panting . . . heaving . . . press'd . . . dissolv'd . . . grasp'd . . . trembled . . .'). The construction matches the erotic tension of guilty and illegal lovers on dangerous ground. This tension is to be maintained through all three parts of the novel, as we pass from one near-climax to another. (Richardson was to do the same thing, of course, especially in *Pamela*.)

Amena is, like the heroines we have seen in the scandal chronicles, a victim of circumstances and her own irresistible inner compulsions. Not so the last member of the conventional triangle in *Love in Excess*, Aloisa. She is the unnatural, the aggressive female, an extreme type of which Mrs. Manley exploited in her various portraits of the Duchess of Marlborough.[1] Where Amena is ingenuous and defenceless, Aloisa is resourceful, cunning, and because of her wealth powerful in a world where money is the only source of power. Amena, significantly, has no money of her own and the portion her father is prepared and able to give her is small. Aloisa, in contrast, has a great deal of money which is entirely at her own disposal.

Aloisa is also in love with the radiant D'Elmont, but because of her independence is able to write anonymous letters to him hinting of her affections. She is not, however, totally shameless. Once

[1] See above, Chapter IV.

again, it is clear that the stark simplicities of the scandal chronicles are infrequently required here in the love novella, where the plot is more complex and leisurely. Aloisa is about to sign her name to one of these letters to D'Elmont when she realizes how fundamental a taboo she would thus violate. Her soliloquy and the accompanying commentary underline her ambiguous position as a villainness. She preserves the moral standards of a heroine, if only from a sense of social propriety and personal pride.

[Aloisa] was about to sign her Name to it, not all the Passion which had inspir'd her with a resolution to scruple nothing that might advance the compassing her Wishes, nor the Vanity which assur'd her of success, were forcible enough to withstand the shock it gave her Pride; No, let me rather die! (said she, starting up, and frighted at her own Designs) then be guilty of a meanness which wou'd render me unworthy of Life, Oh! Heavens to offer Love, and poorly sue for Pity! 'tis insupportable! What bewitch'd me to harbour such a thought as even the vilest of my Sex would blush at? To pieces then (added she tearing the Paper) to pieces, with this shameful witness of my folly, my furious desires may be the destruction of my Peace, but never of my Honour, that shall still attend my Name when Love and Life are fled. (i. 10)

Love such as Aloisa feels is forgiven in this ideology, but her interpretation of honour is meant to be rejected as superficial. Her 'furious desires' do in fact destroy her honour as well as her peace in the reader's eyes. By writing the letters, Aloisa has already violated in spirit the law whose letter she honours in this speech.

She violates it further by denouncing Amena to her father, revealing that Amena has been seen in a compromising position with D'Elmont. She makes herself, in effect, the agent of the censorious and hypocritical world that destroys innocence such as Amena's and denies the possibility of love.

Amena is sent away by her father to a convent and Aloisa marries D'Elmont, but he is motivated only by a desire for the power and wealth she represents: 'Ambition was certainly the reigning Passion in his Soul, and Aloisa's Quality and vast Possessions promising a full Gratification of that, he ne'er so much as wish'd to know, a farther Happiness in Marriage' (i. 51). There is calculation, in

other words, on both sides; both Aloisa and D'Elmont have violated the selfless spontaneity required of real lovers in Mrs. Haywood's rigidly defined moral world.

Part I ends here, but Mrs. Haywood's readers know that such a
marriage must lead to tragedy. Aloisa has made a desperate bargain
and ignored a fate which readers of amatory novellas know is
inexorable. Part II thus begins with pompous axioms on fate;
Aloisa's unjust treatment of Amena and her compromise with love
are bound to be resolved by the machinery of fate: '. . . 'twas
time for Fortune, who long enough had smil'd, now to turn her
Wheel, and punish the presumption that defy'd her Power' (ii. 1).

Having sent Amena away into a convent, Mrs. Haywood requires another maiden to create the necessary triangle. We have
seen in Part I the effects of love on Amena and Aloisa, and now,
of course, it is D'Elmont's turn to suffer. But it is no ordinary and
easily stirred maiden such as Amena who is to move him. Heretics
to love are converted by perfect angelic representatives of love,
and their conversion is a spectacular explosion of grace, i.e. desire.

D'Elmont's angel is Melliora, the daughter of his friend
M. Frankville, who asks D'Elmont from his deathbed to care
for his daughter, to keep 'her artless and unexperienc'd Youth'
from falling 'into those Snares which are daily laid for Innocence' (ii. 3). Melliora, her father emphasizes, is an exquisite
hot-house flower, raised in solitary innocence and purity,
'intirely unacquainted with the Gayeties of a Court, or the
Conversation of the Beau Monde' (ii. 2).

It is a familiar complication, but it has perfect justification.
Melliora's absolute virginity has two functions in the mechanism
of the story: first, her innocence of the world makes her weak
and helpless before D'Elmont, its accomplished representative;
secondly, however, her innocence gives her strength to resist
that world in principle, even though she does not understand its
wiles and is about to be undone by it in fact. This sort of defencelessness allows sexual opportunities to be arranged, but makes violence
the necessary completion of those opportunities. Sexual violence
and pathos thus supplement each other nicely; the pathos can be

safely increased as far as possible and the sexual violence which creates it intensified without any protruding nastiness. The more gross the assault, the more heroic and pathetic the virtue of the assaulted heroine.

Her defencelessness and the pathos of it all are, of course, increased even further by the death of her father. D'Elmont and Melliora fall in love with electric suddenness just as her father is saying his last words, and they are in full heat immediately: 'their Admiration of each others Perfections was mutual, and tho' he had got the start in Love . . . yet the softness of her Soul made up for that little loss of time, and it was hard to say whose Passion was the strongest' (ii. 5). Having lost a father and gained a lover, Melliora steps back, as it were, and strikes a pose. The action stops and Mrs. Haywood very carefully defines Melliora's position as she reminds the reader of the special pathos of the situation:

Indeed there never was any Condition so truly deplorable as that of this unfortunate Lady; she had lost a dear and tender Father, whose Care was ever watchful for her, her Brother was far off, and she had no other Relation in the World to apply her self to for Comfort, or Advice; not even an Acquaintance at Paris, or Friend, but him who but newly was become so, and whom she found it dangerous to make use of, whom she knew it was a crime to Love, yet cou'd not help Loving; the more she Thought, the more she grew Distracted, and the less able to resolve on any Thing; a thousand Times she call'd on Death to give her ease. . . . (ii. 7)

The unexpected and the problematical have no place here; simple suspense is only possible before the inevitable. We know that 'heretics' like D'Elmont will be punished and the only uncertainty is the exact moment. In the scandal chronicles D'Elmont would simply have set about to plan the seduction.[1] Here, a greater moral complexity, or perhaps a more subtle eroticism, prevails. In place of the brutal resolution of the unregenerate seducer, D'Elmont feels 'the power of Beauty, and that Heart which had so long been Impregnable surrender'd in a Moment, the first sight of Melliora

[1] See above, Chapter IV, Mrs. Manley's libel of William Bentinck, first Earl of Portland.

gave him a Discomposure he had never felt before, he sympathiz'd in all her Sorrows, and was ready to joyn his Tears with hers' (ii. 5).

He has always been, in everything but love, a man of honour, and his responsibility to his dead friend holds him back from attempting Melliora. But Love now also refines his moral sensitivity and makes him see how he has sinned against love in the past. We the readers, initiates and believers in love from the start, have foreseen this and now enjoy his justly deserved agonies:

> But his Reflections were now grown far less pleasing than they used to be; real Sighs flew from his Breast uncall'd: And Melliora's Image in dazling Brightness! in terrible Array of killing Charms! fir'd Him with (impossible to be attain'd) Desires; he found by sad Experience what it was to Love, and to Despair. He Admir'd! Ador'd! and wish'd, even to Madness! Yet had too much Honour, too much Gratitude for the Memory of Monsieur Franckville, and too sincere an Awe for the lovely Cause of his Uneasiness, then to form a Thought that cou'd encourage his new Passion. What wou'd he not have given to have been Unmarried? How often did he Curse the Hour in which Alovysa's fondness was Discover'd? and how much more, his own Ambition which prompted him to take Advantage of it? and hurry'd him Precipitalty [*sic*] to a Hymen, where Love, (the noblest Guest) was wanting. It was in these racks of Thought that the unfortunate Amena was remember'd, and he cou'd not forbear acknowledging the Justice of that Doom, which Inflicted on him, these very Torments he had given her. (ii. 9–10)

Plunged into melancholy by all these reflections, D'Elmont takes his household (including Melliora, his 'ward') to his country estate. Mrs. Haywood provides a bit of elegance here, as various young and charming aristocrats pass gracefully before us. Love casuistry is the main topic and elegant amatory badinage is what D'Elmont first tries on Melliora.

One can easily and correctly dismiss these scenes as presenting the familiar attractions of romance: a world of perfect manners and absolute leisure, the aristocratic-pastoral reverie into which the middle-class mind likes to lapse. But the easy unreality of such a setting really has an additional and more essential purpose in Mrs. Haywood's erotic mechanism. The country retreat quickly becomes a strictly delimited area where we will not be disturbed by domestic detail, where we will not be distracted from the progress of the amatory fable. Domestic realism is precluded by an erotic and pathetic 'intensity'. The stylized country retreat is an unreal world where passion can assume without contradiction correspondingly unreal dimensions.

It is here that D'Elmont changes decisively. Amena, about to take monastic vows, writes and confesses distraughtly that she still loves him. D'Elmont's reaction to this letter underlines the changes that have taken place, for we are assured that, 'Had this Letter come a Day sooner, 'tis probable it wou'd have had but little Effect on the Soul of D'Elmont, but his Sentiments of Love were now so wholly chang'd, that what before he wou'd but have Laugh'd at, and perhaps Dispis'd, now fill'd him with Remorse and serious Anguish' (ii. 13). D'Elmont writes back contritely to Amena and acknowledges the transformation love has wrought in him: 'I am no more the Gay, the Roving D'Elmont, and when you come to Paris, perhaps you will find me in a Condition more Lyable to your Pity than Indignation . . . my Crime is my Punishment, I have offended against Love, and against thee, and am, if possible, as Miserable, as Guilty' (ii. 17).

Two things follow in this country setting: first and explicitly, D'Elmont's punishment and frustration (in part iii, exile and expiation) for his crimes against love; second and, of course, implicit, prolonged sexual tension through a series of nearly identical, nearly consummated attempts on Melliora. Counter-point is provided by various characters who act out the heavy roles, the opposite male and female roles to D'Elmont and Melliora. Aloisa remains through part ii as the representative of unnatural femininity, aggressive and cunning to secure the love she is possessed by. The possession is good, the scheming definitely bad. D'Elmont can no longer act out the *libertin*-seducer; he has been converted. But he can be tempted, possessed, as it were, by evil spirits for a time. He struggles bravely with his conscience but gives in to the sinister plan of his friend and neighbour, the Baron D'Espernay (whose plan, it later turns out, is really to seduce Aloisa by turning her against D'Elmont).

Melliora alone remains motionless, free of selfishly aggressive action. She remains, except of course for her love for D'Elmont, exactly what she was before—the perfect maiden, the embodiment of perfect innocence. The almost unbearable 'consuming' desire she has for D'Elmont is a proof of that innocence, for only the truly pure (with whom the reader is invited to identify) can feel to such paralysing depths.

The wheels begin to turn against helpless Melliora when the Baron D'Espernay argues in D'Elmont's old way 'that the most rigid Virtue of 'em all, never yet hated a Man for those faults which Love occasions' (ii. 43). The Count falters and lapses back into a state of sin:

> But O her Father's Memory! My Obligations to him! Her Youth and Innocence are Daggers to my cool Reflections—Would it not be pity Espernay (continu'd he with a deep sigh) even if she shou'd consent to ruin so much sweetness? The Baron cou'd not forbear Laughing at these Words, and the Count who had started these Objections, only with the hope of having them remov'd, easily suffer'd himself to be persuaded to follow his Inclinations; and it was soon Concluded betwixt them, that on the first opportunity, Melliora shou'd fall a Sacrifice to Love. (ii. 42–3)

The rape scene which follows is truly incredible, even for Mrs. Haywood. To the heightened language of female tragedy which derives from such famous 'she' tragedies as Rowe's *Fair Penitent* is added a wealth of specific erotic detail far beyond what the stage could manage. Melliora is asleep in her room and, having just bathed, she is arranged with precise provocativeness:

> . . . her Hair unbraided, hung down upon her shoulders . . . part of it fell upon her Neck and Breast, and with its Lovely Shadyness, being of a Delicate dark Brown, set off to vast Advantage, the matchless whiteness of her skin: Her Gown and the rest of her Garments were white, and all ungirt, and loosely flowing, discover'd a Thousand Beauties, which modish Formalities conceal. (ii. 48)

We are conscious of an erotic tableau of cardboard figures posing extravagantly. Mrs. Haywood switches her lens back to D'Elmont who undergoes a moral conflict played out in histrionic grimaces.

The lusciously erotic must, as we have seen before, be accompanied by the meltingly pathetic, and we watch in 'suspense' as he grapples with his honour: 'the resistless posture he beheld her in, rouz'd all that was Honourable in him, he thought it pity even to wake her, but more to wrong such Innocence, and he was sometimes Prompted to return and leave her as he found her' (ii. 48).

D'Elmont is being made to produce his credentials here as a proper lover for Melliora. This is a required hesitation. *Love in Excess* is, in the end, no tragedy, and since D'Elmont is no villain, these hesitations manifest his essential worthiness. Having hesitated, he can now be provoked by a circumstance for which neither of them is to blame.

Melliora dreams of D'Elmont, and as he stoops to kiss her chastely ('Possibly Designing no more than to steal a Kiss from her, unperceiv'd . . .'), she embraces him in her dream and cries out, 'Embracing him yet closer, —O! too, too Lovely Count— Extatick Ruiner!' What follows is, therefore, no one's fault; both are the victims of love's compelling force. We are off on a brief erotic fantasy, one which remembers to insist on the pathetic as its explicit value, which in practice supplements the erotic with the pathetic and delivers certain sado-masochistic pleasures perhaps basic to any sexual fantasy.[1]

. . . he tore open his Waistcoat, and joyn'd his panting Breast to hers, with such a Tumultuous Eagerness! Seiz'd her with such a Rapidity of Transported hope Crown'd Passion, as immediately wak'd her from an imaginary Felicity, to the Approaches of a Solid one. Where have I been? (said she, just opening her Eyes) where am I?—(And then coming more perfectly to her self) Heaven! What's this?—I am D'Elmont (Cry'd the O'erjoy'd Count) the happy D'Elmont! Melliora's, the Charming Melliora's D'Elmont! O, all ye Saints, (Resum'd the

---

[1] Naturally, I do not claim that every reader obtains or desires those satisfactions. I say only that they are there for the taking. The Marquis de Sade saw the opportunities in the fable of persecuted innocence; and *Justine* is a macabre parody of the story of isolated and suffering virtue, one which relentlessly draws the logical conclusion from suffering virtue: Nature itself teaches us to be vicious. The erotic-sadistic moments with which de Sade illustrates his thesis were, of course, commonplaces of eighteenth-century fiction long before he wrote.

surpriz'd Trembling fair) ye Ministring Angels! Whose Business 'tis to guard the Innocent! Protect, and Shield my Virtue! O! say how came you here, my Lord? Love, said he, Love that does all, that Wonder-Working Power has sent me here to Charm thee, sweet Resister, into yielding. O! Hold, (Cry'd she, finding he was proceeding to Liberties, which her Modesty cou'd not allow of) forbear, I do Conjure you, even by that Love you plead, before my Honour, I'll resign my Life! Therefore, unless you wish to see me Dead, a Victim to your Cruel, fatal Passion, I beg you to desist, and leave me;—I cannot—Must not (answer'd he, growing still more Bold) what, when I have thee thus! Thus naked in my Arms, Trembling, Defenceless, Yielding, Panting with equal Wishes, thy Love Confest, and every Thought, Desire! What cou'dst thou think if I shou'd leave thee? How justly wou'dst thou scorn my easie Tameness; my Dulness, unworthy of the Name of Lover, or even of Man!—Come, come no more Reluctance (Continu'd he, gathering Kisses from her soft Snowy Breast at every Word) Damp not the fires thou hast rais'd with seeming Coiness! I know thou art mine! All mine! And thus I—Yet think (said she Interrupting him, and Strugling in his Arms) think what 'tis that you wou'd do, nor for a Moments Joy, hazard your Peace for Ever. By Heaven, cry'd he: I will this Night be Master of my Wishes, no Matter what to Morrow may bring forth. . . . (ii. 48–9)

An interruption by Melantha, the Baron D'Espernay's sister, frustrates this, the first of several violently erotic scenes in which D'Elmont almost 'ruins' Melliora. Melantha, it should be noted, acts as a contrasting character to Melliora, just as her brother is a scheming libertine to D'Elmont's compulsive lover. A few moments after this scene Melantha, unaware of the rape she has just fore-stalled, proposes an adventure.

The contrast between the sexual amorality and emotional trivi-ality of Melantha and Melliora's allegorical Virtue and Honour is deliberate. We are kept busy rejecting Melantha's foolish promiscuity for the authentic inner desires and virtuous control of Melliora. Mrs. Haywood's novels are, in the functional sense with which we are concerned, carefully constructed. Not only is there a crude but effective balancing of moral and emotional simplicities already noted elsewhere, but the balance established is particularly effective after the fervid scene we have just been through. We, the hypothetical readers, need this new assertion of Melliora's virtue after the sexual thrills of the last scene.

Melantha announces that she has been unable to sleep:

> . . . and retired to a Chamber which they show'd me, but I had no Inclination to sleep, I remember'd my self of five or six *Billet-Doux* I had to answer—a Lover, that growing foolishly troublesome, I have some thoughts of discharging to Morrow—Another that I design to Countenance, to pique a third—a new Suit of Cloaths, and Trimmings for the next Ball—Half a hundred New Songs—and—a thousand other Affairs of the utmost Consequence to a young Lady, came into my Head in a Moment. (ii. 52)

The contrast is obvious, but Mrs. Haywood's popular technique demands bluntness as well as repetition. When Melliora refuses to go down into the garden with Melantha to look for D'Elmont (whom she has seen ride back to the house during the night), the ideological lines are clearly drawn yet once more:

> Was there ever any thing so Young, so Formal as you are! (Rejoyn'd Melantha) but I am Resolv'd to Teaze you out of a Humour so directly opposite to the *Beau-Monde*, and, if you will not Consent to go down with me: I will fetch him up to your Chamber—Hold! Hold, (cry'd Melliora Perceiving she was going) what do you mean, for Heavens sake stay, what will Alovysa think?—I care not (reply'd the other) I have set my Heart on a hours Diversion with him; and will not be Baulk'd, if the repose of the World, much less, that of a Jealous, silly Wife, Depended on it. (ii. 53)

The people who read Mrs. Haywood for the pleasures her fiction is calculated to provide obviously found her fantasy world of elegant salons and chateaux irresistible; but there is, at the same time, a moral centre to the ideology upon which Mrs. Haywood built which despises the ethos of that hypothetical world of fashion and noble leisure as vicious and worthless promiscuity. Melantha belongs, quite self-consciously, to this world, the '*Beau-Monde*' (the foreign term is itself a sign of moral turpitude). Melantha, true to the principles of this world (again, according to the moral ideology which the novel exploits), is the calculating ego, amoral and irresponsible in the heartless pursuit of pleasure. Melliora is, as we have seen, supremely conscious of a complicated network of social and religious responsibilities, and here invokes both those sets of restrictions as she attempts to hold back Melantha.

Melantha seeks the kind of sexual experience that poor Melliora has forced upon her. In this moral world such monstrous aggressive behaviour can lead only to disaster. Melantha will achieve none of her desires and be ridiculed and banished in the end. The knight who searches for the Holy Grail cannot find it by looking; he must earn the entry to it by good works and subsequent grace. So too, in Mrs. Haywood's lurid universe, the heroine can only find love and happiness by resisting, by running away from love, by attempting with heroic determination to suppress it. Having resisted mightily, she will one day be rewarded for ever by a tragic apotheosis, or by the legalizing of that which she has avoided but desired all along.[1]

Melliora agrees to go into the garden with Melantha in order to prevent scandal. The Count manages to get Melliora alone and passion erupts again. This time, however, the emphasis is more 'spiritual', the scene being a series of attempts to express the nature and power of love. First the narrator, then D'Elmont, and then Melliora try in conventional but spirited fashion to describe what they admit at once is indescribable. This is *the* characteristic strategy of Mrs. Haywood's rhetoric and is, in context, an essentially erotic device. The pseudo-sublimities and quasi-religious analogies this rhetoric employs are ways of approaching and suggesting the physiological effects of desire which Mrs. Haywood seeks to describe in her characters and provoke in her readers, but which can

---

[1] We have already seen more than once that the heroine must never admit her passion. An interesting variant on this formula occurs in *The Whimsical Lovers: or, Cupid in Disguise. A Novel. By Mr. Symons* (1725) in which the heroine tests the hero by pretending to be forward. Miranda, the author explains, is well read in novels and romances and resolves 'never to marry, unless there were a Possiblity of being assured she should be regarded with the same Ardour *after* Possession as *before*' (p. 12). She makes an assignation but substitutes a whore and watches the scene. It develops that Gaymont, her suitor, finds himself incapable and impotent: 'Oh! Miranda, Miranda! Fair fallen Angel, cried he, how curst, how truly curst am I to find you thus' (p. 31). Resistance, in other words, is required; the erotic and the sadistic, the novella consistently implies, are inseparable.

never be mentioned explicitly. The language is vague and silly enough, but the novelistic context and the wealth of sexual suggestion make it a means of raising the temperature to, as one of Mrs. Haywood's poetical panegyrists put it, 'more than Eastern Heat'.[1]

Melliora, still we remember heated from the last amorous encounter, sees D'Elmont, and Mrs. Haywood is off again, relentless and indefatigable:

There is nothing more certain than that Love, tho' it fills the mind with a Thousand Charming Ideas, which those untouch'd by that Passion, are not capable of conceiving, yet it entirely takes away the Power of Utterance, and the deeper Impression it had made on the Soul, the less we are able to express it, when willing to indulge and give a loose to Thought; what Language can furnish us with Words sufficient, all are too poor, all wanting both in Sublimity, and Softness, and only Fancy! a Lovers Fancy! Can reach the Exalted soaring of a Lovers meaning! But, if so impossible to be Described, if of so Vast, so Wonderful a Nature as nothing but its self can Comprehend, how much more Impossible must it be entirely to Conceal it! What Strength of Boasted Reason? What Force of Resolution? What modest Fears, or Cunning Artifice can Correct the fierceness of its Fiery Flashes in the Eyes, keep down the Strugling sighs, Command the pulse, and bid the Trembling, Cease? Honour, and Virtue may distance Bodies, but there is no Power in either of those Names to stop the Spring that with a rapid whirl Transports us from our selves, and darts our Souls into the Bosom of the Darling Object: This may seem Strange to many, even of those who call, and perhaps believe that they are Lovers, but the few who have Delicacy enough to feel what I but imperfectly attempt to speak, will acknowledge it for Truth, and Pity the Distress of Melliora. (ii. 55–6)

This is the narrator's prologue to the lovers' own self-analyses which follow, and it has a familiar polemical edge. Words fail to express the exact quality of real love, so Mrs. Haywood refers her readers to their own experience. She has reached the limits of eighteenth-century decency and stops to announce that she can go

---

[1] This phrase is from prefatory material to the second part of *Love in Excess*, a poem 'by an Unknown Hand'.

no further, that her readers must take the sexual fantasy on from here. They are encouraged by Mrs. Haywood's incantatory repetitions on the sublime nature of love, and they are flattered by automatic membership in a spiritual élite which understands these mysteries, an élite which they are assured is very small ('the few who have Delicacy enough to feel') and therefore exclusive.

Melliora raises herself from D'Elmont's insistent embraces and admits that she is overpowered by a force which she can neither understand nor resist any longer. She appeals to D'Elmont's honour, but he, too, insists that he is no longer responsible for his acts. Their attempts to define and describe this possession are much less spiritual than the narrator's; the conventional euphemisms and hyperboles have a consistent sexual reference in them:

Life of my Life (Cry'd he) wound me no more by such untimely Sorrows: I cannot bear thy Tears, by Heaven they sink in to my Soul, and quite unman me, but tell me (Continu'd he Tenderly Kissing her) Cou'dst thou, with all this Love, this Charming—Something more than softness—Cou'dst thou I say, Consent to see me Pale and Dead, Stretch'd at thy Feet, Consum'd with inward Burnings, rather than blest, than rais'd by Love, and Thee, to all a Deity in thy Embraces. . . . No more, no more (said she letting her Head fall gently on his Breast) too easily I guess thy sufferings by my own, But yet, D'Elmont 'tis better to Die in Innocence, than to Live in Guilt. O! why (Resum'd he, sighing as if his Heart wou'd burst) shou'd what we can't avoid, be call'd a Crime? Be Witness for me Heaven! How much I have Struggl'd —But in Vain, the Mounting Flame Blazes the more, the more I wou'd suppress it—My very Soul's on Fire—I cannot bear it—Oh Melliora! Didst thou but know the Thousandth part, of what this Moment I endure, the strong Convulsions of my Warring Thoughts, thy Heart Steel'd as it is, and Frost'd round with Virtue, wou'd burst its Icy shield and melt in Tears of Blood to pity me. Unkind and Cruel! (answer'd she) do I not partake them then? —Do I not bear, at least, an equal share in all your Agonies? —Hast thou no Charms—Or have not I a Heart? —A most Susceptible, and Tender Heart? —Yes, you may feel it Throb, it beats against my Breast, like an Imprison'd Bird, and fain wou'd burst its Cage! to fly to you, the aim of all its Wishes! —Oh D'Elmont! —With these Words she sunk wholly into his Arms unable to speak more: Nor was he less Dissolv'd in Rapture, both their

Souls seem'd to take Wing together, and left their Bodies Motionless as unworthy to bear a part in their more elevated Bliss. (ii. 58–60)

The rhetoric impresses us only by its incoherence and we wonder how even Mrs. Haywood's readers endured such garrulous lovers. But in the context provided by the larger situation of isolated and defenceless innocence and the more immediate circumstances of the scene, these are almost gasps and grunts, or, more delicately, an operatic love duet where it is not the unintelligible or garbled language being sung but the surging high notes that move the audience. The dashes, exclamation points, and ersatz cadences of the swelling prose are the real content of the scene and drive the reader along to the near-climax with which it ends. We are conscious not of logical progression but of a series of sighs and groans, a repetition of evocative words and phrases—burnings, blazings, mountings, burstings, throbbings, beatings, hearts, tears, breasts, etc. The language, in other words, is conventional enough to act as a kind of erotic shorthand; the typography of dashes and exclamation points co-operates with this automatic and mindless erotic suggestion to build up the sexual 'intensity' Mrs. Haywood is after.

Mrs. Haywood needed a conventional language such as this; certain things could not be said. Sexual organs and specific sexual acts could not be described, only darkly intimated. The effect of these compulsory euphemisms and circumlocutions was to add a dimension of compelling horror to sex. The sex act itself became, in effect, mysterious and monstrous under the cover of the required luxuriant verbiage. We wonder just what sort of picture Mrs. Haywood's readers drew for themselves when they were told that Melantha interrupted the lovers again just as D'Elmont 'was preparing to take from the resistless Melliora the last, and only remaining proof that she was all his own' (i. 60).

Meanwhile, behind the main scene of elemental passion and sexual tension there is a tangle of intrigue and counter-intrigue. Aloisa is neglected more and more by the love-sick D'Elmont, and she raves furiously to the point of madness. The Baron D'Espernay is on D'Elmont's side in his campaign against Melliora, but only

as an *agent provocateur*. He is really out, we remember, to seduce
Aloisa and offers to give her ocular proof of D'Elmont's infidelity
with Melliora. Melantha has designs on D'Elmont and resolves to
take Melliora's place in the room in which D'Espernay and
D'Elmont have planned to ruin her.

Part ii ends in two confused scenes as this scheming collapses
into the necessary disaster, for love can never be achieved by artifice
in Mrs. Haywood's novels. It must be a spontaneous and totally
fortuitous event. Thus, Melantha is disgraced when Aloisa (by
the Baron's stratagem) bursts in on her and D'Elmont naked in
bed. D'Elmont is doubly shocked to find himself surprised in
adultery and with the wrong woman. In the next scene the Baron
attempts to collect his reward from Aloisa. D'Elmont hears a noise,
rushes in, and in the dark Aloisa is run through the body and the
Baron mortally wounded. Both of them expire. Melliora, aghast,
retires to a monastery. D'Elmont wanders away to seek forgetful-
ness and expiation.

Part iii begins with a very precise allegorical *mise en scène*.
D'Elmont wanders through Italy, remorseful over his unloved
wife's fate and enfeebled by frustrated love. 'Ambition, once his
darling Passion, was now wholly extinguish'd in him' (iii. 2), and
the despair of frustrated love drives him almost to suicide. Love,
Mrs. Haywood expounds, excludes all other interests, and she
defines it once again with pedantic precision at the very outset of
this last part of the novel:

Those who have the Power to apply themselves so seriously to any
other Consideration as to forget him [i.e. 'Love'], tho' but for a Moment,
are but Lovers in Conceit, and have entertain'd Desire but as an agreeable Amusement, which when attended with any Inconvenience, they
may without much difficulty shake off. Such a sort of Passion may be
properly call'd *Liking*, but falls widely short of *Love*. Love is what we
can neither resist, expel, nor even alleviate, if we should never so
vigorously attempt it; and tho' some have boasted, *Thus far will I
yield and no farther*, they have been convinc'd of the vanity of forming
such Resolutions by the impossibility of keeping them. *Liking* is a
flashy Flame, which is to be kept alive only by ease and delight. *Love*,
needs not this fewel to maintain its Fire, it survives in Absence, and

Disappointments, it endures, unchill'd, the wintry Blasts of cold Indifference and Neglect, and continues its Blaze, even in a Storm of Hatred and Ingratitude, and Reason, Pride, or a just sensibility of conscious Worth, in vain Oppose it. *Liking*, plays gayly round, feeds on the Sweets in gross, but is wholly insensible of the Thorns which guard the nicer, and more refin'd Delicacies of Desire, and can consequently give neither Pain, nor Pleasure in any superlative degree. *Love* creates intollerable Torments! unspeakable Joys! raises us to the highest Heaven of Happiness, or sinks us to the lowest Hell of Misery. (iii. 4–5)

This is not gratuitous rhetoric but careful apologetics for the extravagant passions being described. Love is meticulously separated from any recognizable human concern; it is defined in absolutely heroic and therefore unreal terms. Mrs. Haywood is not concerned to reconcile the emotions she describes to life but rather to separate them from it. They possess a purity and intensity which is possible only in a fantasy world. It is necessary that we be reminded of this periodically, that we remember the rules of this very complicated fictional world.

We have heard this sort of theorizing earlier in the novel certainly, but here in part iii it has a strategic structural importance. Mrs. Haywood develops in this part the apotheosis to which the popular amatory tale aspires and which is the ultimate justification for the sexual pleasure it provides. It is therefore crucial that we remember the absolutely compulsive nature of love, that we see the struggles and pangs of D'Elmont and Melliora as quasi-religious convulsions, not sensual wallowings but ecstatic writhings under the flagellations administered by love.

This final part is to continue the erotic pleasures of the other two parts, but it now drives towards the resolution of the fable of persecuted innocence. The two lovers are now free to marry each other; poetic justice has removed their opponents, their ideological opposites, Aloisa, Melantha, and D'Espernay. These latter have attempted to control their fate, to arrange matters for themselves. D'Elmont, too, has been partly an aggressor. Success in love and fulfilment of its joys can come only when he has compensated for this sinful aggression by running away from his desire or, more accurately, by becoming perfectly passive and waiting for love to reward him. In his wanderings he becomes the 'Helpless' (i.e. before love's power) innocent and therefore worthy of that reward in the end.

Italy is the wilderness wherein D'Elmont wanders disconsolately through many temptations. He is solicited by various ladies, chief among them Ciamara, whose advances are violent and explicit. D'Elmont is immovable and tells her of his passion for Melliora. She reacts with the amazement which Lady Booby feels when Joseph Andrews spurns her.[1] Her answer is that of a rational hedonist confronted by a faith that is beyond pleasure and reason:

> Heavens, cry'd she, with an Air full of Resentment, are then my Charms so mean, my Darts so weak, that near, they cannot intercept those, shot at such a distance? and are you that dull, cold Platonist, which can prefer the visionary Pleasures of an *absent* Mistress, to the warm Transports of the substantial *present*: The Count was pretty much surpriz'd at these Words, coming from the Mouth of a Woman of Honour, and began now to perceive what her Aim was, but willing to be more confirm'd, Madam, said he, I dare not hope your Virtue wou'd permit.—Is this a time (Interrupted she, looking on him with Eyes which sparkled with wild Desires, and left no want of further Explanation of her meaning) Is this an Hour to preach of Virtue?— Married, —Betroth'd, —Engag'd by Love or Law, what hinders but this Moment you may be mine, this Moment, well improv'd, might give us Joys to baffle a whole Age of Woe; make us, at once, forget our Troubles past, and by its sweet remembrance, scorn those to come; in speaking these Words, she sunk supinely on D'Elmont's Breast; but tho' he was not so ill-natur'd, and unmannerly as to repel her, this sort of Treatment made him lose all the Esteem, and great part of the Pity he had conceiv'd for her. (iii. 91–2)

Melliora and D'Elmont have switched places, for he is now in danger as she was in part ii. Ciamara grows wild, beholds 'without

---

[1] Part of the comedy of *Joseph Andrews* is undoubtedly due to Fielding's rich sense of parody, and Joseph's rejection of Lady Booby is familiar from the mythology of persecuted innocence. Joseph is facing the insatiable adulteress whom we have met many times so far in the popular novels under discussion. There is need for an examination of Fielding's conscious parody of the traditions of popular fiction.

concern, her Robes fly open, and all the Beauties of her own
expos'd, and naked to his View' (iii. 93), and smothers him in her
embraces, 'wild to gratify her furious Wishes'. Gratification is, of
course, a term of reprobation, a simple carnal instinct in a world
of mysterious, spiritualized eroticism. In his earlier unregenerate
state, D'Elmont would have simply seized the opportunity: but
now that he has loved, he recognizes the categories of female
virtue, and Ciamara appears to him 'a common *Courtizan*'. He
makes his escape, and she takes poison in despair.

This is only one of several testimonies to D'Elmont's spiritual
growth. A bit earlier we have met Melliora's brother, who has come
in search of D'Elmont in order to avenge the attempts made on his
sister's honour. D'Elmont, however, has just saved Frankville's
life the day before. This debt calms him somewhat, and listening
to D'Elmont's story, he

could find very little in his Conduct to accuse: He was himself too
much susceptible of the Power of Love, not to have Compassion for
those that suffer'd by it, and had too great a share of good Sense not to
know that, that Passion is not to be Circumscrib'd; and being not only,
not *Subservient*, but absolutely *Controller* of the *Will*, it would be meer
Madness . . . to say a Person was Blame-worthy for what was unavoidable. (iii. 34)

Frankville is himself in love with Camilla, the step-daughter of
Ciamara, who has arranged a mercenary match for her with one
Cittolini, an avaricious Italian merchant. D'Elmont helps Frankville wrest Camilla from this conspiracy. When he learns that
Melliora has been abducted from her convent, they all leave Rome
to search for her. They lose their way and take refuge in the house
of a person who turns out to be none other than Melliora's abduc-
tor, the Marquess D'Seguillier.

It is all outrageously unreal enough to make us wonder how
anyone could bear it. Once again, the plot must be accommodated
to the mythical simplicities which are the real subject of *Love in
Excess*. D'Elmont has proven himself by surviving temptation and
separation. He has returned with other true believers in love, whose
deliverance anticipates the greater deliverance he and Melliora

are to experience. Mrs. Haywood is gathering momentum and preparing for the love feast which will round off the story. Love now begins to reward its servants, and these coincidences are part of its pleasant magic power.

The Marquess has been a visitor, we learn, to Melliora's convent as the fiancé of her companion there, Charlotta. He has fallen in love with Melliora and abducted her; but he is a complaisant kidnapper who offers no violence and seeks only to convince her to love him by gentle means. Melliora arranges to have Charlotta present in bridal dress, and the Marquess quickly repents his passion and loves her again. Melliora and D'Elmont are about to marry when Fidelio, a page who has come with D'Elmont from Rome, is found dying. This page is discovered to be Violetta, a lady who loved D'Elmont in Rome and followed him in this disguise.

Violetta dies of unrequited love in D'Elmont's arms as he revives her for her dying speech with his tears. With the intensity her situation provides, she describes the bliss into which Melliora is about to enter with D'Elmont:

. . . this is too kind, said she, I now can feel none of those Agonies which render Death the King of Terrors, and thus, thus happy in your Sight, —your Touch —your tender pity, I can but be translated from one Heaven to another, and yet, forgive me Heaven if it be a Sin, I cou'd wish, Methinks, to know no other Paradise than you, to be permitted to Hover round you, to form your Dreams, to sit upon your Lip all Day, to mingle with your Breath, and glide in unfelt Air into your Bosom. . . . Oh D'Elmont receive in this one Sigh my latest Breath —it was indeed her last, she died that Moment, died in his Arms, whom more than Life she priz'd, and sure there are none who have liv'd in the anxietys of Love, who wou'd not envy such a Death! (iii. 154)

After a decent interval all of the couples are married. We end by learning that D'Elmont and Frankville 'are still living, but with a numerous and hopeful Issue, and continue, with their fair Wives great, and lovely, Examples of Conjugal Affection' (iii. 156).

We have had, in effect, a double ending, a tragic apotheosis followed by a glorious conjugal consummation, the two kinds of beatitude recognized within the fable of persecuted innocence. Death and Marriage transport the worthy heroine to suitable heavens. Both bring release from the heroic tribulations of love, but both, of course, are beyond description. The erotic and pathetic tension which keeps our interest can no longer be maintained. Mrs. Haywood must stop here, for love has run its course and the rest (heaven or domesticity, no matter how blissful) is silence.

This double ending is the last reminder of the 'richness' (redundancy from a critical point of view) possible in the complicated amatory narrative such as *Love in Excess*. Mrs. Haywood's astonishing success was due, I would insist, to her ability to manipulate the fable of persecuted innocence to obtain the maximum erotic-pathetic intensity. Having rewarded Melliora with marriage, she fears, perhaps, a let-down, and so Violetta is brought on stage to expire in happy tears. Her death is, in a sense, an orgasm, a suitably violent and spectacular end to the story. It is the orgasm we have been waiting for, the one we have approached so often throughout the story in the many near-consummations. Melliora cannot be allowed to have it, at least in our presence. The scene would not only be unseemly, but, worse, dull. Married love is an ideal towards which all true lovers strive, but it lacks the tension of illicit passion. The heroine would no longer be in danger; sexual experience must be complemented by the fable of persecuted innocence to hold our interest. Mrs. Haywood's ending is, thus, a fine piece of engineering which allows us to have the poetic justice of marriage with the erotic-pathetic climax we deserve. She is, to the end, a magnificent technician in her extraordinarily popular act.

If we go on to read the rest of the novels that Mrs. Haywood produced during the next ten years or so, we may be tempted to dismiss this technical competence as fortuitous incompetence. Like the current manufacturers of popular entertainment, she recognized that variation from the successful pattern is dangerous. The repetition and even redundance which we have plotted in *Love in Excess* are carried over into the rest of her novels; and it becomes apparent as we read that in spite of necessary surface variations, Mrs. Haywood repeated during the next ten years the fable of persecuted innocence, exploiting over and over again the same erotic-pathetic clichés and the same rhetoric of love's power and the tragic and compulsive dramatic universe it implies. Subsequent novels such as *Idalia: or, the Unfortunate Mistress* (1723); *Lasselia: or, the Self-Abandon'd* (1723); *The Injur'd Husband: or, the Mistaken Resentment* (1723); *The Rash Resolve* (1724); *The Surprise: or, Constancy Rewarded* (1724); *The Force of Nature* (1725); *The Unequal Conflict* (1725); and *The Distress'd Orphan* (1726) indicate by their titles the repetition of the erotic-pathetic themes that Mrs. Haywood and her publishers apparently found most profitable.

The heroines of all these novels are the victims of a world which sees them simply as opportunities for lust and avarice, which depersonalizes them, in modern jargon. The love by which they are possessed is represented as tragic, since it most often leads to tragedy or at least to severe hardships. But the love which destroys them is really a way for these heroines to assert personality, a desperate alternative to the depersonalization which the masculine world imposes upon them.

At the same time, however, the myth of persecuted innocence, like all popular myths, is deeply conservative and explicitly careful to avoid the implicit subversive possibilities it contains. The elaborate insistence upon the absolutely compulsive nature of passion, which is the main feature of the many definitions of love, is a way of avoiding an active subversion of the male world, which is for ever safe from revolution. Any female aggression to alter this unjust male world would contradict in its assertiveness and independence the utter helplessness required for heroic status and for the erotic and pathetic pleasures such heroism delivers to the audience. Take away the conditions for tragedy and the pleasures of tragedy are lost.

The world cannot be changed, but it can be escaped and the tragic female condition transcended. The clearest working out of this important possibility in Mrs. Haywood's novels is *The British Recluse: or, the Secret History of Cleomira, Suppos'd Dead. A Novel* (1722). This begins rather cautiously with a dialogue in a

London boarding house where one of the lodgers is an absolute recluse, a lady who keeps so much to herself that none of the others has ever seen her. The lodgers debate the cause of this seclusion, and one of the males present objects with unyielding rationality to the suggestion advanced by one of the ladies that unrequited love or grief at the death of a loved one might be the cause.

All kinds of Passion, every Body knows, wear off with Time; and Love, of all others, as 'tis the gentlest, and is subsisted only by Delight, of course must dye, when Delight is at an End. How then, can it be possible that a Woman, who has for a whole Twelvemonth liv'd in a Retirement, where she neither has seen any Body, nor been seen, if it were so that Love was the Occasion, shou'd not by this be weary both of the Cause and the Effect? No, no, (continu'd he laughing) I rather think, my Landlady, to divert her self, and amuse us, has form'd this Story of a beautiful young Creature, whom, if the Truth were known, I dare swear is some wither'd Hag, past the Use of Pleasures, and keeps her self in private, lest her Countenance should terrify.[1]

The heresy is familiar and Mrs. Haywood never tires of denouncing it. It is the male point of view, a rational, hedonistic, and carnal misunderstanding of love. Love, we have learned elsewhere, is totally irrational, a compulsive and anguishing mixture of pain and pleasure, and, above all, too spiritual to be exhausted by the physiological limitations of 'delight'.

One of the ladies present, Belinda, is fascinated by the recluse and has the landlady introduce her. They prove to be kindred spirits; both of them have been violated by faithless and perfidious lovers. Ruin provides a perspective on earthly concerns which they find they share: 'they agreed so perfectly in their Sentiments concerning the Instability of all humane Happiness—the little Confidence there was to be put in the Protestations of Friendship—and that the only way to attain true Content, was in an absolute Retirement from the World, and a Disregard of every thing in it'.[2] They resolve, after relating their tragic stories to each other (they have

---

[1] *The British Recluse*, pp. 3–4. All citations are from the 'Second Edition' of 1722.

[2] p. 11.

both been ruined by the same man), to abandon the world and live in a country house,

. . . where they still live in a perfect Tranquillity, happy in the real Friendship of each other, despising the uncertain *Pleasures*, and free from all the *Hurries* and *Disquiets* which attend the Gaities of the Town. And where a solitary Life is the effect of Choice, it certainly yields more solid Comfort, than all the publick Diversions which those who are the greatest Pursuers of them can find.[1]

The situation and the commonplaces of retirement which fill it in serve as a decorous framework to the erotic-pathetic satisfactions which are the main concern of the book. The ending has, however, perfect justification; for the monastic calm and religious insights which our heroines achieve are quite consistent with that religious decoration which is a traditional part of amatory rhetoric and which Mrs. Haywood always makes the most of. Mrs. Haywood here contrives to use the generalized spirituality *cum* eroticism of love as a bridge towards a more orthodox and specific spirituality. The religious associations which the persecuted maiden tends naturally to attract to herself are here made explicit. Only love can provide such a perspective on earthly things, for love, like Christian withdrawal, requires that its devotees stand deliberately outside the world of selfish lust and avarice. Moreover, the intensity of love is such that nothing else—certainly not the crowded urban leisure which normal eighteenth-century piety associates with worldly vanity and folly—can now satisfy our heroines. They retire to what is to become a standard *terminus ad quem* for the eighteenth-century novel, the country retreat from which the conventional palinode can be issued denouncing the vain (but entertaining) adventures we have witnessed in the world.

Now this sort of resolution is rare in Mrs. Haywood's novels. She usually prefers an attractive catastrophe or a brief announcement of marriage all round. The full spiritual possibilities of the persecuted maiden and the amatory tales she inhabits are brought out by another type of lady novelist, Mrs. Barker, Mrs. Aubin, and Mrs. Rowe, whom I will discuss in the next chapter.

[1] p. 138.

VI

THE NOVEL AS PIOUS POLEMIC

1. MRS. AUBIN AND MRS. BARKER

THE various types of popular narratives do not, of course, possess the rigid purity of outline that my discussion might imply. Many narratives may accurately be described as miscellanies, in the obvious sense that they contain the digressions, poems, songs, and interpolated stories traditional to narrative, but also in the special sense that they often include several of the fictional paradigms I have already discussed. Travel narratives are complemented by love stories, and persecuted maidens are sometimes found on desert islands; pirates and highwaymen abduct and sometimes ravish love-sick innocents, and glittering and depraved aristocrats appear in narratives with little real claim to be scandal chronicles. One approach usually dominates, however, and the other type characters may simply be making brief guest appearances.

Successful combination of several of the paradigms is possible. Some well-known examples are Defoe's combination of whore or rogue biography with the exotic travelogue in *Moll Flanders*, *Captain Singleton*, and *Colonel Jacque*. Obscure enough now but successful when it was first published in 1726, William Chetwood's *The Voyages and Adventures of Captain Robert Boyle* manages to bring together with great skill quite a number of these fictional stereotypes and paradigms.[1]

Chetwood's book is an interesting and capable narrative, close to some of the best of Defoe in its observation of physical and psychological detail and in its well-conceived central character. Robert Boyle is a combination of Colonel Jacque and Captain Singleton,

---

[1] All citations are from the first edition of 1726. McBurney (*Checklist*, p. 69) lists a third edition published in 1735 and notes that the work has been ascribed to Defoe and to Benjamin Victor. For Chetwood, see above, Chapter III.

and his story is the customary irregular rise of merit and cunning from orphan in London, to country gentleman in Somerset. From my point of view, the story is especially interesting because it conflates several patterns.

Young Boyle finds refuge, after being orphaned, as an apprentice to a watchmaker, and catches his master's wife in adultery. Since he is not the brutal picaro of popular tradition, he plays no trick on the woman, who has disliked and abused him from the first. Instead, he tells his master, who proceeds to castrate the spark.

'Robin' passes from blameless picaro to folk-tale victim of unscrupulous foster-fathers; the watchmaker's hostile wife has already been his 'wicked step-mother'. His uncle, who is holding an 800-pound legacy for him, tricks him into sailing to Virginia. This fairy-tale motif gives way to the calamities of romance and the ideological simplicities of heathen captivity as his ship is captured by Moorish pirates. He is told that if he turns Mohammedan he will achieve rank and power. He remains non-committal, but his solution is voiced by a young English renegade sailor: 'I ask'd him why he could forget the Saviour of the World to turn Mahometan; he told me that he was only one from the Teeth outward, and he thought it better to trust God with his Soul, than those barbarous Wretches with his Body' (p. 27). This is essentially what Boyle does, even though he does not actually turn Mohammedan. He impresses us by being as resourceful and sensible as this sailor, but he cannot be allowed to compromise his heroism by being so articulate, just as earlier the brutal revenge on his unjust mistress was left to someone else.

Boyle survives and is made the slave of another renegade, the Irish–Mohammedan captain of the pirates who captured him. As slave he becomes still another stock figure of popular narrative, the resourceful European artisan-technician, of which Crusoe is the most well-known example.[1] He promises his master that he will build a European garden for him: 'As soon as he was gone I went

---

[1] In Captain Singleton's march across Africa, a crucial role is played by a man Singleton calls 'the Artist', a cutler who makes tools for survival and ornaments out of the gold they find which they trade to great advantage with the natives.

to Work (for Gardening was what I always took delight in, both Theoric and Practice)' (p. 28). His garden and its fountain (a tricky engineering job) amaze the native workmen. This technological conquest is one of the incidental delights of the travel narrative.

At this point he is suddenly and mysteriously locked up by his master. This allows him to see from his cell his master's harem, and he falls in love at first sight with one of the ladies, a newly captured European. He is metamorphosed into a lover, changed abruptly by the compulsive power of love, which does not recognize the inappropriateness of the circumstances. We have gone from Defoe's clear world to the turbid universe of Mrs. Haywood as Boyle becomes a combination of afflicted and defenceless innocence and the resourceful hero-traveller.

I never till this Moment had the least Regard to any of the Female Sex, no more than good Manners and Decency requir'd; but I found myself in a Moment full of aching Tenderness for this strange Woman. Though I had no time for Thought till the Ladies were retir'd, I then began to reason with my self, and found Love like Destiny was not to be avoided; and the more I thought, the more I was plung'd in this tormenting, yet pleasing Passion. Yet I thought it was very odd to fall in Love, considering my Circumstance. I had nothing to hope, and all to fear: I was poor, a Prisoner, and a Stranger, far from my native Country, in want even of Necessaries, and, to compleat my Misery, sunk in one Hour an Age in Love. Every new Thought seemed a Thorn to torment me; yet notwithstanding all these Difficulties, a Beam of Hope would now and then shine thro' the thick Clouds of Despair, and encourage me to love on. (p. 31)

It is as if one of Mrs. Haywood's stricken lovers had suddenly been granted the mental clarity and instinct for survival of one of Defoe's successful individualists. Boyle succeeds not only in communicating his love to the lady (Mrs. Villars, an Englishwoman of substance) but in convincing his master to let him have his freedom so that he can make his lovely English captive comply. They escape and after great difficulty at sea are rescued by a French ship, which is, unfortunately, going in the wrong direction, right back to Morocco.

Mrs. Villars is in male disguise, and circumstances force them to have to sleep together. Boyle exercises virtuous restraint for a time but then finds himself weakening. The resulting scene is still another transformation of Boyle, now an ingenious combination of the pious bridegroom consecrating his love to heaven and the amorous impatient lover with his beautiful and illicit paramour. Unlike the female experts in passion, the author exercises a decent reticence about the sexual act, here carefully established as a lawful marital consummation and described cryptically as 'a Sea of Pleasures, too delicate for Words to express' (p. 12).

> Mr. Boyle, said she, I have overcome my self: I cannot see you in this Torture of Body and Mind, and not contribute to your Ease. Here solemnly swear to be my Husband, and do with me what you please: I hope you are a Man of Honour, and that's what I rely upon. Nothing in this World could have transported me so much as those few Words did: I fell upon my Knees, kiss'd her Hands, and did I know not what! Madam, said I, you have made me the happiest Man the World contains; and if I thought my Heart and Tongue did not agree in what I am going to say, I would pull 'em both out this Moment. When I had said this, I fell on my Knees, and made this short Vow. *Thou God that know'st the Heart of Man; I do beseech Thee punish me with Eternity of Torments, if ever I prove false to this Darling of my Soul, who before Thee I take (as the greatest Blessing) to be my lawful Wife. And here I swear* (said she, kneeling) *to take no other to my Bed and Heart; and with this Kiss*, said she, *I seal the sacred Union.* I told her nothing could be more binding, and the Priest could but confirm what we had done already. (p. 111)

If we consider the resemblance of this scene to numerous other pre-marital promises in amatory fiction, we are struck by the elaborateness of this exchange of vows. Coupled with the omission of erotic detail, the 'ceremony' amounts to a deliberate counterstatement of the amatory narrative as we have observed it.

The lovers are shortly separated by treachery, but even though Boyle grieves, he is kept busy surviving and giving us travelogues of Morocco (where he helps the French ambassador prepare a report for the king of France) and Italy, where Boyle goes to help another escaped slave recover his fortune and bride. In Italy he

hears that his 'wife' has died, having thrown herself into the sea
rather than submit to her captor's embraces.

Granted this unlooked-for freedom and driven, we are assured,
by grief, Boyle becomes a full-fledged hero-traveller, a merchant
and conquistador in America, the last of his various personalities.
He sails to the West Indies, skirmishes with Indians, sketches
travelogues of the area, makes profitable raids on the Spanish and
the Portuguese there, and finally returns to England. There he
settles his affairs, emerges a rich man, and buys an estate in
Somersetshire. On his way to settle in, he rescues a child from
gipsies and a lady from a ravisher. These two turn out to be his
wife and the son born of their brief married life:

> Therefore, let the Reader (if possible) guess the Joy of two Lovers
> meeting, after imagining each other no longer in this World. We thought
> it was all a Dream; but at last being convinc'd of the Reality, we sent
> privately for the Parson, and were ty'd by the outward Ceremony of
> the Church, whose Hearts had been divinely united long before; and
> that Night I took once more Possession of what I valu'd above all the
> World could give. (p. 313)

All along, Boyle has had very little time for pious reflections;
his concession to the pious rhetoric of deliverance is as perfunctory
as his interest in erotic details: 'By this we may learn, there is a
ruling Providence that regulates every action of our Lives, when
they tend to Virtue' (p. 318).

Boyle's story, then, is a mixed mode, permitting various types
of significant fantasy and exploiting several key narrative patterns.
The amorous gallantry that the rigidly chaste Boyle is not allowed
is provided by the interpolated story of a Spaniard he meets, Don
Pedro Aquilio. We are meant to delight in this, as we are in perils
overcome and marvels and foreign rarities observed; the world
through which Boyle travels is not so much an enemy bastion as a
huge field of unlimited opportunity. But through this wild mixture
of events and personalities Boyle remains innocent, carefully virtuous as well as acquisitive, his narrative (a first-person one)
paying perfunctory but regular obeisance to Providence and
rejecting quite consciously the erotic possibilities of the situations

he describes. Indeed, the extraordinary 'wedding' scene and Boyle's subsequent fidelity add a new note of heroic chastity to the travel narrative.

In most of this Chetwood may be said to have been following the successful example of Defoe, but he was also responding with his variegated narrative to other elements of the popular narrative market at that time. He may, in fact, have been more specifically influenced by the success of the novels of Mrs. Penelope Aubin.

The pleasures which Chetwood's combination seeks to stimulate are amusement and information; the edification (in my terminology, the ideological satisfactions) provided by the moral tone and strict propriety of the hero are distinct but secondary features. In Mrs. Aubin's novels these values are reversed. The major purpose of her consistent combination of fictional patterns is to provide the ideological satisfactions of innocence preserved and atheism confuted. The 'secular' delight which Chetwood's variety chiefly stimulates is, as we have seen, only one side of the eighteenth-century approach to the fabulous and expansive movement in which the travel narrative specialized.

Mrs. Aubin's novels were presented to her public as an undisguised attempt to seduce them into virtue through the familiar diversions of popular narrative. Actually, as W. H. McBurney has pointed out, she was quite thorough in fashioning her lures for the frivolous but potentially virtuous and tried to combine 'Defoe's subject matter and method with those of Mrs. Eliza Haywood and of continental fiction'.[1] McBurney finds the stock characters of French amatory fiction in her novels but sees the hazards which she places in the paths of her heroines and certain backgrounds and descriptive details as 'purely Defoesque'.[2]

Leaving aside the vexing question this raises of proving literary influences, we can accept this as a fair speculation but translate it into our terminology. Mrs. Aubin's novels, deliberately and consistently, extend the range and significance of the story of persecuted innocence by grafting it to the delightful disasters of travel

---

[1] 'Mrs. Penelope Aubin and the Early Eighteenth-Century English Novel', *HLQ*, xx (May 1957), 253.   [2] Ibid., p. 254.

narrative. This combination is not, as McBurney's literary genealogy implies, an opportunistic and unnatural cross-breeding but a natural and logical union.[1] Innocence, instead of being hounded from country house to city bagnio or brothel, is pursued by lust literally around the world. The artificial and stylized milieu of love and seduction is replaced by the exotic and appalling dangers of the high seas, filled with pirates, lustful Oriental potentates, and ferocious wild animals. There is a loss in erotic 'intensity' but a gain in ideological coherence, for the 'world' through which innocence now moves is the world itself, presented in geographical fullness.[2]

These dangers on which innocence thrives (i.e. asserts itself as innocence in the middle of potentially destructive experience) are, consequently, increased in volume, variety, and authenticity. The hero-traveller, so attractive but ambiguous a figure for the eighteenth century, is concealed under the passive innocent, swept along by events, protected only by God's extraordinary providences and not at all by his (more often her, of course) own ingenuity and resourcefulness. As a result, the pleasures of travel through the exotic and the marvellous and of observing providential deliverance from the huge disasters attendant upon such rare experience are delivered free of disturbing secular implications; the heroes and heroines of Mrs. Aubin's novels are untainted by the daemonic secular spirit to survive and prosper that we have just noticed in Robert Boyle and which we admire so much in Defoe's protagonists.

Of course, Mrs. Aubin's innocents are improbable stereotypes, but this woodenness is entirely appropriate to her polemical appeal: absolute and unremitting evil such as defines the troubled world

---

[1] Mrs. Aubin's combination is not entirely original if we remember Mrs. Behn's famous *Oroonoko: or, The Royal Slave* (1688), set in a rather fanciful Surinam.

[2] To be sure, Mrs. Aubin's geography is at times hilarious. Don Lopez, in *The Noble Slaves*, finds his shipwrecked beloved at last and describes his search thus: 'I no sooner heard of your disaster, but I procured a ship, having visited all the coast of Peru and Canada: missing you there, I determined to go to Japan, it being the nearest coast to which you could be drove. . . . I designed to visit the holy land, and retire to some desert, and to spend my days in fasting . . . but indulgent heaven kindly drove me here' (p. 22, Dublin edition of 1730). 'Here' happens to be an island off the coast of Mexico.

she describes can only be endured and defeated by absolute and unwavering goodness. Mrs. Aubin had not Defoe's gifts, but did not miss them to accomplish her purposes. The guarded individuality, the complex and mature self-knowledge, which Defoe grants some of his great characters, would have been, in this context of didactic efficiency, positively distracting elements.

Mrs. Aubin's first two novels were published in 1721: *The Life of Madam de Beaumont, a French Lady; Who lived in a Cave in Wales above fourteen Years undiscovered, being forced to fly France for her Religion: and of the Cruel Usage she had there*; and *The Strange Adventures of the Count de Vinevil And his Family. Being an Account of what happen'd to them whilst they resided at Constantinople*. Both of these begin with aggressive prefaces bewailing the times as depraved. Mrs. Aubin, later a successful lay preacher,[1] knows how to pitch her appeal and slides carefully into an *O tempora! O mores!* passage with a smoothness which Mrs. Manley's or Mrs. Haywood's automatic indignation was incapable of:

The Story I here present the Public withal, is very extraordinary, but not quite so incredible as these [i.e. the times]. This is an Age of Wonders, and certainly we can doubt of nothing after what we have seen in our Days: yet there is one thing in the Story of Madam de Beaumount very strange; which is, that she, and her Daughter, are very religious, and virtuous, and that there were two honest Clergymen living at one time. In the Lord de Beaumount's Story, there is yet something more surprising; which is, that he loved an absent Wife so well, that he obstinately refused a pretty Lady a Favour. (pp. vi–vii)[2]

There is a tacit admission here that the events to be narrated are not literally true; Mrs. Aubin's novels are signed, and she appears as an authoress rather than an editor, observer, or compiler. She

---

[1] McBurney's article summarizes the little that is known of Mrs. Aubin's life (c. 1685–1731), some of the information coming from an attack that the Abbé Prévost published against her in 1734. She seems to have been the daughter of French émigrés. Since she published nothing until 1721, she may have been married and suddenly, as McBurney speculates, found herself faced with the necessity of earning a living. In 1729 she was to be found preaching in her own oratory in the York Buildings near Charing Cross, where, according to the *Universal Spectator* (16 Aug. 1729), she was beginning to rival Henley as a 'Candidate for the Town's Applause' (cited by McBurney, p. 245).

[2] All citations are from the first edition of 1721.

is claiming a moral truth, a Christian 'realism' in the strict philosophical sense of the word.[1] This point is made even clearer at the end of the preface to *Count de Vinevil*, where Mrs. Aubin asks her readers to believe not so much in the wild series of calamities to be presented as in the perfect rectitude of her good characters:

As for the Truth of what this Narrative contains, since *Robinson Cruso* [sic] has been so well receiv'd, which is more improbable, I know no reason why this should be thought a Fiction. I hope the World is not grown so abandon'd to Vice, as to believe that there is no such Ladies to be found, as would prefer Death to Infamy; or a Man that, for Remorse of Conscience, would quit a plentiful Fortune, retire, and chuse to die in a dismal Cell. . . . Would Men trust in Providence, and act according to Reason and common Justice, they need not to fear any thing; but whilst they defy God and wrong others, they must be Cowards, and their Ends such as they deserve, surprizing and infamous. (pp. 6–7)

Mrs. Aubin is never violent; she does not fulminate, but tells us gently that she hopes to reform by pleasing: 'In this Story [*Madame de Beaumont*] I have aim'd at pleasing, and at the same time encouraging Virtue in my Readers. I wish Men would, like Belinda, confide in Providence, and look upon Death with the same Indifference that she did' (p. viii). She is even more explicit in the *Count de Vinevil*, where she begins by describing her effort as a deliberate attempt to rescue didacticism for literature. Her novel, she makes clear, is a systematic counter-statement against the fashionable novels of palpitating passion. Mrs. Aubin tries to substitute a positively exemplary Christian 'realism' for the erotic cautionary tales of Mrs. Haywood and others.

Since serious things are, in a manner, altogether neglected, by what we call the Gay and Fashionable Part of Mankind, and Religious Treatises grow mouldy on the Booksellers Shelves in the Back Shops. . .

.   .   .   .   .

[1] Sidney J. Black ('Eighteenth-Century "Histories" as a Fictional Mode', *Boston University Studies in English*, i (1955), 38–44) has pointed out that the term novel was avoided in the early part of the century and 'history' or some other equivalent term used in order to claim a truth to human nature and moral reality rather than to assert literal truth.

I present this Book to the Publick, in which you will find a Story, where Divine Providence manifests itself in every Transaction, where Vertue is try'd with Misfortunes, and rewarded with Blessings: In fine, where Men behave themselves like Christians, and Women are really vertuous, and such as we ought to imitate. (pp. 3–6)

The prefatory pitch of the amatory novella claimed to warn the innocent of the dangers of emotional experience: this is what happens to the innocents who naïvely follow their hearts in a heartless world. Mrs. Aubin goes much further than this: see, she tells us, how impervious real innocence is to all that the evil world can do, see how effective virtue and resignation to Providence and death are in overcoming any and all obstacles. We are being asked, to resort again to my terminology, to reject the erotic-pathetic tragedy which dominates the amatory novella for the melodrama of innocence narrowly preserved again and again by the power of faith and Providence. Mrs. Aubin's heroines are not torn asunder by a conflict between inclination and the demands of formal morality. They embody in a thoroughgoing way a purity and innocence which rules out moral ambiguity; they fight only against lust, cunning, and avarice, never against themselves. Read my stories, says Mrs. Aubin to her eighteenth-century readers, for emotional confirmation of that which you affirm rationally; celebrate again and again the victory of faith and virtue against an unbelieving world.

And there is indeed very little cause to accuse Mrs. Aubin of double-dealing and providing erotic bonuses with her ritualistic celebrations of the victory of innocence. Her novels are free of the lubricious facility we have observed in the previous chapter; she cares very little for the precise psychological-physiological symptoms of passion and declines numberless opportunities for erotic-pathetic fantasy.[1]

But perhaps the most important and certainly the most obvious sign of her integrity (or better, since I wish to avoid ethical judge-

---

[1] McBurney makes this point as well: 'Certainly her novels are unusual in their high moral tone. Nowhere is the reader allowed to linger over scenes of vice as in the works of Mrs. Manley, Mrs. Hearne, or even Defoe himself in *The Fortunate Mistress*' ('Aubin' article, p. 260).

ments, her homiletic efficiency) is the alacrity with which her protagonists are married, or, at least, linked by legal and proper desire, right at the very beginning of the chaos of events which makes up the novel. This marriage or commitment to marriage remains throughout the tangle of disasters a guiding and saving simplification, like the protagonists' faith in Providence.

In *Madame de Beaumont*, for example, one of the heroines has been married for many years when the novel opens. When we meet her she has been living in a cave in Wales for fourteen years with her daughter, Belinda, separated from her husband by the standard machinations of the standard greedy world which always separates lovers. She has a familiarly harrowing story: shut up in a convent by relatives who wish to keep her marriage portion, she escapes from there with her lover and marries him. Mrs. Aubin does not stop there, even though from the point of view of Mrs. Haywood she has already gone too far. Madame de Beaumont is faced with specifically religious dangers and asked to play the role of Protestant champion.

When her husband is ordered to the wars, her father-in-law demands that she turn Catholic (we are in France); and when her husband decides to send her to England while he is away she is offered a large settlement to turn Catholic and stay in France. She refuses. Her virtue is requited by a storm which blows her ship aground on the Welsh coast. There she has remained, not unhappy; since, as Mrs. Aubin has emphasized in her preface, 'He that would keep his Integrity, must dwell in a Cell; and Belinda had never been so virtuous, had she not been bred in a Cave, and never seen a Court' (p. vii).

Madame de Beaumont and Belinda are the first of many hermits Mrs. Aubin's readers were to meet in her novels. Here, to be sure, the hermitage is a bower of virtue, richly furnished and cleverly lit by a skylight, a freely chosen retreat from the vile world. Other hermits we shall meet will live less splendidly and in more inaccessible places than Wales, but Mrs. Aubin will always make their retreat a deliberate rejection of the world or a self-imposed penitential exile. Her insistence on this point is, in a sense, a counter-statement to the reluctant pilgrimage and spiritual ambiguity of the most famous fictional hermit of the early eighteenth century. Just as she rejects the heroine's internal struggle between passion and moral convention, she modifies instinctively (or perhaps simply through incompetence) Crusoe's internal struggle between acceptance of the penitential fitness of his situation and his daemonic energy to survive and escape.

Madame de Beaumont has left her hermitage only once, to find her husband in France, where she finds that he has presumed her dead and gone off in his grief to fight for the King of Sweden (a Protestant champion). Forays into the world to obtain justice can only lead to fresh calamity for suffering virtue such as Madame de Beaumont possesses. Not only does she fail to find her husband, but her father-in-law has her thrown into prison. The resulting heroic pose, as evoked for us by Madame de Beaumont's own narration, is the sort of set-piece that Mrs. Aubin resolves her whirling disasters into again and again. There are highly erotic dangers throughout her stories, but they invariably lead to purely devotional set-pieces such as this one. The purpose of all this suffering is to test the virtuous and enable them to practice their fortitude. Madame de Beaumont's description of her reaction to suffering is thus a subdued prelude to the fully orchestrated pathos to be developed later on in the novel: 'Thus, Sir, I experienced that great Truth, That we have nothing more to do, to be happy and secure from all the Miseries of Life, but to resign our Wills to the Divine Being; nor does Providence ever appear more conspicuously than on such Occasions' (p. 45).

She is telling her story to a Welsh gentleman who has stumbled upon their grotto by accident. He is no intruder, for his credentials are impeccable, a male equivalent of the female recluses. This Mr. Lluelling has 'wisely prefer'd a Country Retirement before noisy Courts, and Business' (p. 10). He sees Belinda and proposes marriage immediately. Harbouring no designs, he seeks her properly by asking her mother. Unmarried until now, he has been no heretic to love and devotee of lust but simply virtuous and indifferent to women. His perfect qualifications are completed by his proposal, which shows the requisite awareness of the spiritual implications of love; his rhetoric establishes the connection between marriage and beatitude that is unknown to the world of power and property:

May I be hated by Heaven and you, and may she scorn me, when I cease to love, to honour, and take care of you and her. Madam, till now, I never loved, my Heart has been indifferent to all the Sex; but from the moment I first look'd on that Angel's Face, where so much Innocence and Beauty shines, I have not asked a Blessing in which she was not comprehended; make her mine, and I shall have all I wish on Earth. (p. 43)

They marry, after a few modest hesitations by Belinda. Happiness is achieved, but Mrs. Aubin's homily demands that happiness be earned by patient endurance of hardship and even disaster. So, the secure rural world of secluded virtue is invaded very clearly by the outside world. The ideological collision is obvious to us, but not to the protagonists, when Mr. Lluelling's cousin arrives from London:

. . . a young Gentleman who was his Cousin-German, and had long wish'd his Death, no doubt because he was his Heir, if he died without Issue. This young Man, Mr. Lluelling had always lov'd and bred up as his Son, having bought him Chambers in the Temple, where he, like most Gentlemen of this Age, had forgot the noble Principles, and virtuous Precepts, he brought to Town with him, and acquir'd all the fashionable Vices that give a Man the Title of a fine Gentleman: he was a Contemner of Marriage, cou'd drink, dissemble, and deceive to Perfection; had a very handsome Person, an excellent Wit, and was most happy in expressing his Thoughts elegantly: these Talents he always employ'd in seducing the Fair, or engaging the Affection of his Companions, who doated upon him, because he was cunning and daring, could always lead them on to Pleasures, or bring them nicely off, if frustrated in any vicious Designs. (pp. 56–7)

We should pause to remind ourselves what the amatory novella as practiced by Mrs. Haywood would have done with such a situation. In one of her novellas, Belinda would be married (or the city rake would be), but either union would be the usual joyless and profitable alliance. She would, as a properly virtuous but sensitive heroine, see Glandore for the wolf in resplendent garments that he is, but feel nevertheless an instant compelling sexual attraction to him. She would be torn between duty and passion, and the dialectic of persecuted innocence would make us see the tragic (and exciting) necessity of such a conflict in a corrupt masculine world.

Here, however, the dialectic of popular prose she-tragedy is discarded for the polemical simplifications of the simple battle between good and evil. All of the familiar moral antitheses of the early eighteenth century are present: country versus city, love-marriage versus lust-seduction, simple rural trust versus urban cunning and duplicity, and aristocratic wit and scintillating surface versus plain-spoken and simply eloquent virtue.[1] The conflict which develops is simple. Belinda loves Lluelling and he her. His cousin seeks his death, his estate, and his wife without a shade of remorse or hesitation.

Lluelling volunteers to go to France to find his father-in-law, and since he is, above all, open and trusting, leaves his cousin in charge. When Glandore quickly declares his passion and threatens to force Belinda if she does not comply, her reply is unequivocal:

'By Heaven, I'll never give Consent, and if you force me like a Brute, what Satisfaction will you reap? I shall then hate and scorn you, loath your Embraces, and if I ever escape your hands again, sure Vengeance will o'ertake you; nay, you shall drag me sooner to my Grave, than to your Bed; I will resist to Death, and curse you with my last Breath: but if you spare me, my Prayers and Blessings shall attend you, nay, I will pity and forgive you.' 'I'm deaf to all that you can plead against my Love, he cry'd, yield or I'll force you hence.' 'No, says she, I'll rather die; now, Villain, I will hate you: help and defend me Heaven.' (p. 62)

---

[1] Lluelling's reaction when he returns from France and finds that his cousin has betrayed him draws out these suggestions: 'My God, continued he, where shall we find Faith in Man? Can neither the tyes of Blood, Friendship, Interest, nor Religion, bind Men to be just: but alas! he lived too long in that curs'd Town, where Vice takes place of Virtue, where Men rise by Villany and Fraud, where the lustful Appetite has all Opportunities of being gratify'd; where Oaths and Promises are only Jests, and all Religion but Pretence, and made a Skreen and Cloak for Knavery; a place where Truth and Virtue cannot live. Oh! curse on my Credulity, to trust so rich a Treasure to a Wolf, a lustful Londoner' (pp. 101–2).

This speech and the scene which contains it have a simplicity totally lacking in the lush erotic tangles of the amatory novella. Belinda's heroism lacks both the extravagant rhetoric and the erotic suggestion of Mrs. Haywood's cornered ladies. We will, indeed, pass rapidly from this point of the novel to the end from one near-disaster to another; the basic pattern of persecuted innocence remains the same. But each near-climax is much closer to simple fatal violence than to the violent sensuality which threatens to engulf the wandering innocent of the ordinary novella. Mrs. Aubin's heroines, like Belinda, convince us that they will either die or survive with their genuine honour intact; Mrs. Haywood's heroines exist in a moral and psychological world where honour cannot be achieved, where the only alternatives (until the god of love descends to grant exceptions at the end) are fidelity to duty (with the 'spiritual' poverty that involves) or self-immolation in illicit passion. In either case, only some kind of disreputable and unsatisfactory survival is possible.

Belinda, on the other hand, is supremely confident of her virtue and absolute inner purity. She faces disaster with all the equanimity of the intrepid traveller and makes speeches at destiny with an imperturbable confidence in providential wisdom. Death, she reasons, is as much a deliverance as any other rescue. Here, for example, she encourages two other captured females with whom she has escaped from a band of robbers and potential ravishers (they have 'rescued' her from her husband's treacherous cousin). Her speech combines hope and resignation.

Come my Companions, said she, let us lie down on the cold Earth, and trust that Providence that still preserves those that put their Confidence in it; 'tis better far to perish here, than live in Infamy and Misery: 'tis true, our Bodies are enfeebled by the want of Sustenance, but Sleep will refresh our tired Spirits, and enable us to prosecute our Journey; recommend yourselves to God, his Power is all-sufficient, and when Human Means are wanting, can supply our Wants by Miracles. Here she fell upon her Knees, and cry'd, 'My God, encrease my Faith, pity our Distress, and send us Help; but if thou hast decreed us to die in this Place, support us under the mighty Tryal, and give us Grace to be entirely resigned to thy Will, and send thy Angels to receive our Souls.'

Her Companions remain'd silent, admiring the Constancy of Belinda, who seemed then scarce fifteen. . . . (p. 118)

The rest of *Madame de Beaumont* is simply a series of nearly identical trials for innocence to pass through. Belinda is saved at the point of 'ruin' several times. Effective contrast and the positive ethical norm which Mrs. Aubin never forgets to provide come in the middle of these deliverances when Belinda is taken by some rustic rescuers to the local gentleman, a Mr. Hide. He finds himself stricken by love and delays bringing her back to her house. This is only a gentle stratagem, designed merely to allow him time to declare his passion. He does so, but when she tells him that she is married and pregnant, his reaction is intended as exemplary, a positive contrast to the brutal male aggression Belinda has just passed through:

At these Words a death-like Paleness overspread his Face, a cold Sweat trickled down his Cheeks. 'My God, said he, it is enough; Madam, I will no more importune you, fear nothing from me, Virtue and Honour are as dear to me as you; since you cannot be mine, I ask no more, but that you'll stay and see me die, and not detest my Memory, since Vice has no share in my Soul.' Here he fainted, and was by the Servants carry'd to his Chamber: Belinda wept, her Heart was young and tender, and the Honour he had shown, touch'd her Soul so nearly, that she much lamented his Misfortune, and cou'd not consent with ease to let him die; therefore she strove with Reason to assuage his Grief, and cure his Passion. . . . (pp. 68–9)

Such behaviour, given the other trials which Belinda and all the other ladies in Mrs. Aubin's novels have to undergo, is indeed another of the moral 'wonders' in an age of extraordinary immorality.[1] Mrs. Aubin is once again concerned to assert that such behaviour is possible. Female innocence not only exists but survives because there is male virtue extant to protect it, not just the sustaining masculine principle of Providence but isolated and noteworthy paragons like Lluelling, Mr. Hide, and Madame de Beaumont's husband. There is in the latter's story, we have been told in the preface, something even more singular than the others

---

[1] See above, the preface to *Madame de Beaumont*.

in its rare virtue: 'In the Lord de Beaumount's [*sic*] Story, there is yet something more surprising; which is, that he loved an absent Wife so well, that he obstinately refused a pretty Lady a Favour' (p. vii).

We hear this gentleman's story when he tells it to Lluelling, who brings him back to Wales to be reunited with his wife. He, remember, had gone off to fight for the King of Sweden when he thought his wife was dead. Captured by the Russians, he refuses to marry a beautiful Russian lady who loves him. He is thrown in prison for his obstinacy, having survived temptation of the same sort Mrs. Haywood's reformed and repentant seducer, D'Elmont, passed through in *Love in Excess*.[1] The Marquis de Beaumont risks extreme physical danger or even death to be true to a wife he thinks is dead. D'Elmont merely risks losing his newly acquired sense of purity and fidelity. Again, Mrs. Aubin's emphasis is not upon the erotic possibilities of the situation, but upon the 'wonder' we should feel in the presence of simple moral heroism and the marvellous coincidence which Providence arranges for the deserving. For the Marquis is rescued from his prison by the same Capuchin friar who had helped his wife escape from prison, the friar having come to Russia to find him.

This and other marvellous coincidences and deliverances justify Mrs. Aubin's concluding summary. Unlike Mrs. Haywood's half-hearted attempts to stick on a moral tag, this is a legitimate gloss, a *moralitas* which fits Mrs. Aubin's purpose and, in an eighteenth-century context, describes the moral uplift and ideological coherence which her works provided for the willing reader:

Thus Providence does, with unexpected Accidents, try Men's Faith, frustrate their Designs, and lead them thro a Series of Misfortunes, to manifest its Power in their Deliverance; confounding the Atheist, and convincing the Libertine, that there is a just God, so boundless is his Power, that none ought to despair that believe in him. You see he can give Food upon the barren Mountain, and prevent the bold Ravisher from accomplishing his wicked Design: the virtuous Belinda was safe in the hands of a Man who was desperately in love with her, and

[1] See above, Chapter V.

whose desperate Circumstance made him dare to do almost any thing; but Virtue was her Armour, and Providence her Defender: these Tryals did but improve her Vertues, and encrease her Faith. (p. 142)

Obviously, we might object, very few atheists and libertines were routed by Mrs. Aubin's novels; just as very few heiresses were prevented from eloping by Mrs. Haywood's novellas.[1] Both of them are preaching to the converted, and Mrs. Aubin, especially, is providing the anticipated discovery of pattern and significance in a welter of incredible confusion. Each deliverance and outrageous coincidence is an example, on the popular religious level that Mrs. Aubin is working at, of that simultaneous unity of plot and theme which Northrop Frye calls *dianoia*. Mrs. Aubin's willing readers, in Frye's terminology, see each event or incident as 'a manifestation of some underlying unity', for her plots have their effect not simply in terms of suspense and linear progression but as a series of events which 'regroup themselves around another center of attention'.[2] What McBurney calls 'the particular temptation of excessive and unintegrated variety against which eighteenth-century fiction was to struggle until Richardson and Fielding',[3] was in Mrs. Aubin's case an appropriate failure, for the unity which her homiletic purpose seeks thrives on a disorderly succession of calamities through which the providence of God and the virtue of her heroes can shine.

Mrs. Aubin may have realized the specific value of variety, or she may simply have been imitating the attractive exotic miscellany which made the pseudo-authentic travel narrative so popular.

---

[1] In the preface to *The Noble Slaves* (1722), Mrs. Aubin shows herself aware of her story's limitations: 'Methinks now I see the Atheist grin, the Modish Wit laugh out, and the old Letcher and the young Debauchee sneer, and throw by the Book; and all join to decry it: It is all a Fiction, a Cant they cry; Virtue's a Bugbear, Religion's a Cheat, though at the same time they are jealous of their Wives, Mistresses, and Daughters, and ready to fight about Principles and Opinions' (p. vii).

[2] 'Myth, Fiction, and Displacement', in *Fables of Identity* (New York, 1963), p. 24. Mrs. Aubin makes no attempt at suspense and declares in her preface: 'You will find that Chains could not hold them; Want, Sickness, Grief, nor the merciless Seas destroy them; because they trusted in God, and swerved not from their Duty' (p. vii).

[3] McBurney, 'Aubin' article, p. 256.

Whatever her reasons, her novels became more and more clotted with interlocking disasters and coincidences, stretching sometimes right around the world. In the *Count de Vinevil*, for example, we wander about the near East; in *The Noble Slaves* (1722), Mexico, South America, and North Africa; back to Europe and the near East in the *Life and Amorous Adventures of Lucinda* (1722); and in *Charlotta DuPont* (1723) from Europe to the West Indies and South America. In the 1726 *Life and Adventures of the Lady Lucy* we go only as far as Germany, but in the 1728 sequel, *The Adventures of Young Count Albertus*, the hero travels all over Europe, is ship-wrecked in Barbary, and dies as a Christian missionary in China.

Except for this last novel, which ends in another kind of triumph, all of Mrs. Aubin's novels end with a parade. We exult as Christian heroes and heroines march in triumph to their country seats to live safely and virtuously for ever, and we watch approvingly as Mrs. Aubin ends with an aggressively polemical Q.E.D.

Since Religion is no Jest, Death and a future State certain; let us strive to improve the noble Sentiments such Histories as these will inspire in us; avoid the loose Writings which debauch the Mind; and since our Heroes and Heroines have done nothing but what is possible, let us resolve to act like them, make Virtue the Rule of all our Actions, and eternal Happiness our only Aim.[1]

In the person of Mrs. Aubin, we can see the lady novelist acquiring a new *persona*, one which is to become more important as the century wears on and to linger through the nineteenth century as a powerful and formative public image: moral censor of the age. To be sure, famous female scribblers such as Mrs. Manley and Mrs. Haywood professed a strident feminism and moral superiority which played a large part, as we have seen, in the ideological mechanisms of their works. But such ladies remained disreputable to the articulate virtuous; their self-righteous feminism was an effective but bogus value which met with scepticism and scorn from those who despised their popular works.

---

[1] *The Noble Slaves* (1722), p. 159.

This public image of the lady novelist and the moral point of view it required had already been exploited in a smaller and less successful way by the unscrupulous but astute Edmund Curll. He had published in 1713 and 1715 two works by Mrs. Jane Barker, *Loves Intrigues; or the History of the Amours of Bosvil and Galesia*, and *Exilius: or, The Banish'd Roman. A New Romance*.[1] There is nothing new or startling about either of these works; the latter is merely a collection of interwoven novellas, of which the title story is merely the longest, and the former is a short cautionary or exemplary tale of the kind popular since the seventeenth century. What is striking about them is that they are both scrupulously moral and free of erotic detail. Moreover, if we trace the ideological changes which take place as Mrs. Barker's career progresses and compare these pre-Mrs. Aubin works with the two works that she published during the 1720s, we will see how important this new counter-tradition of the moral lady novelist was becoming in popular fiction.

Loves Intrigues[2] is the brief story of a 'foolish virgin', Galesia, who is the daughter of an impoverished Loyalist forced to live in the country, 'a very private, or rather obscure Life, just above the Contempt of Poverty' (p. 3). She falls in love quite unsuitably and compulsively with a young kinsman, Bosvil: 'tho' he had nothing extraordinary in Person or Parts, to excite such an Affection; nevertheless, the Moment that his Eyes met mine, my Heart was sensible of an Emotion it had never felt before' (p. 6). Galesia is sent to London to learn its manners and to fall into the classic

---

[1] Little is known of Mrs. Barker. Myra Reynolds notes that a collection of her poems appeared in 1688, *Poetical Recreations: Consisting of Original Poems, Songs, Odes*, with a number of complimentary poems by university scholars, making it appear that Mrs. Barker was the centre of a circle of admiring collegians (*The Learned Lady in England, 1650–1760*, Boston and New York, 1920, p. 161). G. S. Gibbons (*Notes & Queries*, 12th series, xi (1922), 278–9) says that she was a Catholic spinster who spent some time at the Court of St. Germain.

[2] All citations from *Loves Intrigues* are from the first edition published by Curll at Cambridge in 1713. All citations from *Exilius* are from the 1715 first edition, printed by J. Roberts. Another edition was printed in 1715 by Curll, who in 1719 brought out copies of his second edition of *Exilius* (1719) bound up with the second edition of *Loves Intrigues* (1719) as *The Entertaining Novels of Mrs. Jane Barker*. This two-volume edition reached a 'third edition' in 1736.

plight between duty and love. She is sought in marriage by the immensely eligible Mr. Brafort, but 'Almighty Providence order'd it so, that immediately after my Arrival into the Country, he fell sick of a continued Fever, which in the space of ten Days carried him into his Grave, instead of his Nuptial Bed' (p. 11). The rest of the novel is taken up with Bosvil's hesitations and Galesia's love-sufferings because of them. She renounces him at last and takes up healthy country life, but sees Bosvil again a year later and runs distracted with renewed love. Bosvil, however, marries another, and the story ends as Galesia learns that her coyness has probably been the cause of her disappointment.

There is an attractive psychological verisimilitude about Galesia's inability to maintain her detachment as a rural contemplative, and the introspective reflections of the heroine may look forward, as W. H. McBurney has claimed, to the translations of the works of Prévost and Marivaux.[1] But Mrs. Barker never tries to draw the larger moral implications of innocence in a vicious world; she is perhaps too moderate, too competent in a modest way in this novel to resort to the lurid moral simplifications required of popular narrative. Her book is, in fact, scrupulously moral and free of erotic suggestion without the self-righteous polemicizing we have seen in Mrs. Aubin's novels.

Exilius, on the other hand, goes a long way towards achieving the moral simplifications we have come to expect of popular narrative. It presents itself, as well, in a distinctly aggressive moralizing tone as a deliberate anachronism, 'A New Romance', and connects the current low state of romances with a decline in virtue. The rather slight cautionary value put upon *Loves Intrigues* is exchanged for a portentous moral purpose, crucial for those who wish to avoid the general contagion of the age:

Thus it far'd with this Kind of Heroic Love of late; it has been, as it were, rally'd out of Practice, and its Professors laugh'd out of Countenance, while Interest and loose Gallantry have been set up in its Place, and monopolized all its Business and Effects. How far this has been

[1] 'Edmund Curll, Mrs. Jane Barker, and the English Novel', *PQ*, xxxvii (October 1958), 393.

an Inlet to that Deluge of Libertinism which has overflow'd the Age, the many unhappy Marriages, and unkind Separations, may inform us, and at the same Time shew how proper an Ingredient Love is towards the making an happy Marriage; for where Love is not the Cement, as well as Interest the Foundation, the Superstructure of Conjugal Faith seldom stands long; the first Wind that blows at the Change of Honey-Moon, will go near to shake, if not quite overthrow, the Fabrick. . . . To these [i.e. those who do not marry for love] it is not strange that heroic Love appears a Fantom or Chimera; but to those who aim at a happy Marriage, by the Way of Virtue and Honour, need consider but very little, to find that it lyes thro', or borders upon, Heroic Love; so that Romances (which commonly treat of this virtuous Affection) are not to be discarded as wholly Useless. (sig. A4)

What Mrs. Barker calls heroic love is, of course, the scrupulour romantic love-marriage defended by so un-heroic a commentatos as Defoe later on in the century in *Conjugal Lewdness*.[1] She is concerned in *Exilius*, just under the antique panoply of her Roman setting, with drawing out the moral simplifications of the fable of persecuted innocence; but she is not, like the female gallant school of Mrs. Manley and Mrs. Haywood, overtly concerned with the erotic elaboration of its dramatic moments. Heroic love is in her case defined by opposition to tyrannical parental command and, of course, to lustful seducers and fortune-hunters. Mrs. Barker is scrupulously careful that her heroines love 'unsuitably' in the eyes of the morally nearsighted community (i.e. father and family) rather than illicitly or adulterously in contradiction to received morality.

[1] Defoe is quite concerned about the prevalence of 'prudential Matches', and carefully defines marriage as a solemn contract which must be freely entered. He calls his fourth chapter, 'Of the absolute Necessity of a mutual Affection before Matrimony, in order to the Happiness of a married State, and of the Scandal of marrying without it', and defends resistance to parental tyranny in very strong terms indeed: 'As Matrimony should be the Effect of a free and previous Choice in the Persons marrying, so the breaking in by Violence upon the Choice and Affections of the Parties, I take to be the worst kind of Rape; whether the Violence be the Violence of Perswasion or of Authority; I mean, such as that of Paternal Authority, or otherwise; for as to legal Authority, there is nothing of that can interpose in it; the Laws leave it where it ought to be left, and the Laws of Matrimony, in particular, leave it all upon the Choice of the Person, and in the Power of their Will' (*Conjugal Lewdness: or, Matrimonial Whoredom* (London, 1727), pp. 166–7).

The first of her heroines in *Exilius*, for example, is Clelia, importuned by Marcellus, who has been betrothed since childhood to Jemella. Clelia is attracted to Marcellus but piously consults the oracle of Jupiter to see if such a union would be sinful. The oracle answers that 'The Gods will never disapprove / The Sacred Bonds of mutual Love' (p. 8). Such divine sanction means little to the families concerned, and Clelia sees her divided allegiance clearly:

I at the same Time suffer'd much in the Reproaches made me by my Father, Mother, and Brother, for having forgot mine own Honour, and the Honour of my Family, in entertaining a secret Amour, and that too, with one espoused to another; which Reprimands I must needs own were no more than the Crime deserv'd, and very suitable to those strict Rules of Virtue and Honour they always practis'd, and in which they instructed me their dear Disciple and darling Daughter. Now tho' Reason oblig'd me to receive these Reproofs with Moderation and Respect, yet the Tenderness I had for Marcellus made me so far transgress my Duty, as to correspond with him by Letters, Presents, Messages, and the like. . . . (pp. 10–11)

We readers know, of course, that Clelia is giving in to a higher and purer concept of honour in following her heart. Her hesitation and unwillingness to disobey her parents make her, somewhat paradoxically, worthy of achieving that higher concept of love. Marcellus will, after overcoming many horrendous obstacles, achieve his love, and we will be the righteous spectators of virtue and innocence triumphant.

In the telling of this story, we will also hear the similar stories of a number of other couples. In Clelia's case, the conflict between the world and the individual has a certain subtlety about it; there is something to be said for the opposing side. The world is blind rather than evil. But the 'purpose' of a collection of love stories like this (that is, the ideological antithesis which provides the necessary tension) is to enable us to see the tyrannic and monstrous evil into which the conventional arrangements of the world can easily turn. Thus, Marcellus hears the story of Clarinthia, an extravagant version of the fable of persecuted innocence which not only intensifies the evil of the opposing side but names the enemy very precisely, relates it clearly to the paradigm of virtuous and religious innocence versus evil, amoral irreligion.

The story rehearses the usual clichés of cornered innocence, but we notice how carefully the contemporary conflict of 'secular' and 'religious' outlooks is made to support it. Clarinthia's father, Turpius, has attempted to force her to marry his bastard son, Valerius. Her resistance leads to violence, and finally her father himself becomes enamoured of his daughter:

... and when I urg'd the Illegality of this heinous Passion, and that it would cause the Vengeance of the Gods to descend on him, and render him at once miserable and infamous. He made Answer, That the Notion of Deities was a Chimera infused into my Fancy by my Mother, and a customary Education; and that all the World were misled into such Opinions by Priests and Potentates, whose Interest it was to ingage their Inferiors into a Belief of some invisible Powers, thereby to keep them in Subjection. (pp. 28–9)

Clarinthia's perfect scrupulosity is in marked and deliberate contrast to such nihilism. Her father and his servant are on the point of ravishing her when she is rescued by a 'person of Virtue and Courage', who kills them and declares himself her lover. She refuses him, and her anguish is the suffering that will earn her happiness at the end of it all. Again, the central focus is moral, avoiding erotic elaboration for an intensity which is primarily pathetic.

O Clarinthia! Clarinthia! said I to my self, what difficult Paths has Fortune mark'd out for thy Virtue to trace? How can I ever declare to the Senate what detestable Crime caused my Father's Death? Or if I do, perhaps I shall not be believ'd: If I do not, I expose my self, and this noble Stranger, to the Fury of the Laws, and his Honour to everlasting Infamy. I am in a Labyrinth so intricate, that even the Line of Reason is not able to conduct me through its wild Mazes. On every Hand I see nothing but Danger and Distress, such as confound my Resolution and non-plus my Courage. On this Side a rapid Stream of persecuting Laws, on that, a Precipice of perpetual Shame; one to ingulph, the other to dash my Honour in a thousand Pieces. (p. 35)

After another rescue by this stranger, Lysander, she decides that she cannot marry her father's murderer, but that she will never love anyone but him. In the end, it turns out that Turpius (her father) is not dead at all, and she and Lysander marry.

The stories of Clelia and Clarinthia and the rest of Mrs. Barker's heroines are thus relentlessly edifying. These ladies are intended as virtuous beacons who demonstrate the ability of virtue to survive and triumph against overwhelming odds. But they survive, we are told, by the efforts of heroic males who love them purely. They are not delivered by Providence but by the heroic efforts of lovers who are inspired to such feats by their virtue and beauty. The heroine becomes, indeed, precisely what Shaftesbury complained love novellas made of women: a replacement for the 'she-saints' banned by Protestantism, raised 'to a capacity above what Nature had allowed', and treated 'with a respect which in the natural way of love they themselves were the aptest to complain of'.[1]

At one point in *Exilius*, this inspirational and edifying function of the persecuted maiden is made quite explicit. She is, we learn, a divine messenger whose beauty and saintly presence both prove and pre-figure the truths and joys of religion in this life and the next. Her qualities provide emotional affirmation of the religious verities that the world commonly denies.

Exilius, the hero of the title, learns all this when he rescues a kidnapped maiden named Scipiana from a shipwreck. Exilius has been brought up by his father in absolute isolation on an otherwise uninhabited island near Sardinia. He has lately been into the world and won great military glory with the Roman armies in Asia, but he has returned to his hermitage unseduced by the world. When he sees Scipiana, he is forced to recant his protestations of perfect and 'lonely' happiness on his island. On the very spot where the night before he had composed lines in praise of solitude, he soliloquizes:

I here chid my Heart for the Crimes it had committed all its Life against Love and Beauty. I told it that such a Rebel deserv'd to wear less noble Chains than those Fortune had provided for it in the Person

[1] *Characteristics* (Bobbs-Merrill paperback edition, New York, 1964), ii. 11.

of Scipiana. Alas! said I, how ignorant was I last Night of true Happiness, to think it consisted in a dull Neglect, or Stoical Contempt of all Human Pleasures; or to imagine any true Felicity cou'd be had without its true Author, Woman. (p. 100)

The Stoic is a familiar eighteenth-century antagonist, although he is rarely seen in popular narrative, which prefers the more dramatic and dangerous ideological stereotype of the *libertin*. The Stoic and his theoretical rejection of human emotions are usually defeated by ridicule, as in Johnson's *Rasselas*. But there is no room for ridicule in the humourless romance of Mrs. Barker; the ridiculous philosopher, for one thing, cannot be granted a soul-stirring conversion such as this one. Exilius is moved to extemporize some lines in praise of women, who not only make men civilized:

> Nay, more we're taught Religion too by you;
> 'Twas not by Chance that such Perfections grew;
> No, no, it was th' Eternal Pow'rs which thus
> Chose to exhibit their bright Selves to us;
> And, for an Antepast of future Bliss,
> Sent you (their Images) from Paradise. (p. 102)

All of Mrs. Barker's heroines fulfil, implicitly, this exalted function. Exilius is describing the matrix of associations and emotional resonances on which each of her highly moral narratives relies for its ultimate effects. Those associations depend for their effectiveness, of course, upon the moral world outlined by the ideology of beleaguered virtue. The maiden becomes heroic and thereby inspirational by asserting her personality in that brutish, male-dominated world of lust and avarice that I have already described; she responds by her heroism to the conditions of that world, and she is automatically a deliberately controversial and polemical figure.

These implications of female heroism had been realized and exploited with great success in different ways by both Mrs. Haywood and Mrs. Aubin by the time Mrs. Barker came to publish her last two works, *A Patch-Work Screen for the Ladies; or Love and Virtue Recommended* (1723); and its continuation, *The Lining for the Patch-Work Screen* (1726). Mrs. Barker and / or Curll had apparently watched the winds of popular taste and made careful adjustments. As a result, both of these works are deliberate attempts to market a very old product—the framework narrative in which a collection of tales can be told—with the new ideological wrappings of the female moral sensibility. Galesia, the heroine of Mrs. Barker's first effort in 1713, is brought back older and wiser, rehabilitated and refashioned to suit a new stereotype. What Mrs. Barker does is to make her central character-narrator a combination of the female moral censor and the learned and pious semi-recluse lady who is a familiar moral character of the age. The result is that we return constantly in these collections of tales (some very traditional) to a moralizing central character who explains their significance. The moral anatomy of the world implicit in Mrs. Barker's earlier works has become so explicitly the centre of concern here that the heroine has turned 'editor' and commentator, herself aware of the controversy by which she exists. It is this personality, separated from the battery of stage effects and exotic places and dangers offered in *Exilius*, which is now the main attraction. Mrs. Barker's 'development' records the clear emergence of the heroic 'she-saint' from the erotic turbulence of popular female fiction.

In *A Patch-Work Screen*, Galesia loses her way in the country while travelling by stage-coach and meets a lady out a-hunting who invites her to visit her at her country house. She shows Galesia furniture of her own making, 'patchwork' of various materials, complete except for a screen which she invites Galesia to stay and help her finish. When Galesia's trunks arrive, the lady resolves to use the 'Pieces of Romances, Poems, Love-Letters' which they find in them to finish the screen.

This is a pretext not only for telling amorous stories but for introducing the new and revised Galesia. She brings us back to her early history as a foolish maiden, exhibiting the poems she wrote while mourning Bosvil's falseness. The lesson she now professes to have learned eventually from her foolish passion is a lofty one indeed. She describes her subsequent maturation when, under her brother's direction, she began to study biology, 'to understand

Harvey's Circulation of the Blood, and Lower's Motion of the Heart'. Her brother has since died. In her grief she has composed a verse treatise on Anatomy in order to help her forget. Galesia has been transformed, in short, from a foolish virgin of the conventional sort into a learned semi-recluse, able to maintain emotional balance by study and meditation.

The practical results of this transformation are evident from what follows in her narrative. She is now able to see the world for exactly what it is. For example, she is proposed to by a local youth of hitherto wild propensities, but rejects him with an expert knowledge of the methods of seduction. Female innocence, tempered but not compromised by experience and reflection, is now well armed:

> Nevertheless, though I was but an innocent Country Girl, yet I was not so ignorant of the World, but to know or believe, that often those Beau Rakes, have the Cunning and Assurance to make Parents on both sides, Steps to their Childrens Disgrace, if not Ruin: For very often, good Country Ladies, who reflect not on the Vileness of the World, permit their Daughters to give private Audiences, to their Lovers, in some obscure Arbour or distant Drawing room; where the Spark has Opportunity to misbehave himself to the Lady; which, if she resent, there is a ready Conveniency for him to bespatter her with Scandal. (p. 37)

The youth she thus shrewdly rejects is sent to jail and executed a few days later for robbery on the highway.

When her father died (Galesia continues her history), she and her mother found the responsibilities of their estate too much to bear and went to live in London. Here Galesia assumes, with a self-consciousness we have seen only in Mrs. Aubin's characters, the pose of isolated innocence, alone in crowds of the damned. Relating the scandalous behaviour of the town, she tells her companion about it 'to shew you, that in all Places, and at all Times, my Country Innocence render'd me a kind of a *Solitary* in the midst of Throngs and great Congregations' (p. 55).

Her mother chides her for this solitude and urges her to marry. In building the 'patch-work screen', we have already heard several stories of disastrous marriages, but Galesia has grown too wise to enter into similar tragedy. She resists the proposals of Lysander, a young gentleman who has squandered his substance in keeping a citizen's wife as his mistress. Lysander shoots himself when this woman refuses to let him out of her clutches. Galesia trumpets out the moral:

> This was the fatal End which his Lewdness and Folly brought upon him! This was the Conclusion of his guilty Embraces! Thus a filthy Strumpet showed herself in her Colours! And thus was he bullied out of his Estate, Life, and Honour; his Life lost, his Debts unpaid, his Estate devour'd by a lewd Harlot! A very fatal Warning to all unwary Gentlemen. (p. 88)

Galesia stands apart from all this; here and in the 1726 *Lining for the Patch-Work Screen* she acts as chorus, making regularly explicit what the love novella left pervasively implicit. The stories are all familiar enough (there is a version of the Portuguese nun in the *Lining for the Patch-Work Screen* and an unacknowledged paraphrase of Mrs. Behn's *History of the Nun; or, The Fair Vow Breaker*), and indeed even the female symposium (various ladies join Galesia in 'lining' the screen) which provides the frame is an old and frequently used narrative device. What is new is the insistent pious frame of reference; the framework is a deliberate attempt to sell female fiction to a wider audience by making it impeccably respectable.

2. MRS. ELIZABETH ROWE

It is a short and logical step from creating a fictional moral centre like Galesia to having a well-known female paragon write fiction and lend it her personal *cachet*. This is precisely what took place in 1728 when Mrs. Elizabeth Singer Rowe published *Friendship in Death: in Twenty Letters from the Dead to the Living*.[1]

[1] All citations in the text are to the 1733 'third edition', which is divided into three separately paginated parts: *Friendship in Death*, pp. 1–70; *Letters Moral and Entertaining*, part i, pp. 1–138; and parts ii and iii, pp. 1–253. References to *Friendship in Death* are expressed simply in Arabic numerals, while references to *Letters Moral and Entertaining* use Roman numerals to identify the part in question. The entire work is hereafter referred to as *Letters*.

In 1723 Mrs. Aubin had dedicated her novel, *The Life of Charlotta du Pont*, to her 'much honoured Friend, Mrs. Rowe', of whose friendship she declared herself to be very proud.[1] Whether they were actually intimate friends is uncertain, but both ladies certainly agreed about the polemical purpose which fiction could be made to serve. The editor of the 1739 collected edition of Mrs. Aubin's *Histories and Novels* noted this similarity and drew out the image of ideological solidarity which Mrs. Aubin's dedication sought to arouse in her readers:

> The Life of Charlotta du Pont she dedicates to the celebrated Mrs. Rowe, with whom she had an intimacy, as we there see, and may farther reasonably infer from the Tenor of both their Writings, for the promotion of the Cause of Religion and Virtue, and from that Affinity and Kindred of Souls, which will always make the Worthy find out one another, and create Stronger ties of Union and Friendship than those of Blood.[2]

More than any other female writer of the early eighteenth century, Mrs. Elizabeth Singer Rowe was a woman whose life was as well known as her works; both were considered valuable exemplars of piety and propriety until well into the nineteenth century. Most important, she could be held up as a singular exception to the disreputable ladies who dominated the field of female literature. Like the heroines of Mrs. Aubin and Mrs. Barker, she was by definition a controversial and polemical figure.

The possibilities of her exemplary life and literary career are illustrated by a satire which appeared in 1754, *The Feminiad* by John Duncombe.[3] Seventeen years after her death, Mrs. Rowe was well known enough to appear in a heroic capacity in part of Duncombe's poem. Here her saintly presence banishes the literary sins of infamous scribbling ladies, and her exalted death continues to light the way for others.

---

[1] *A Collection of Entertaining Histories and Novels. Design'd to Promote the Cause of Virtue and Honour. Principally founded on Facts, and interspersed with a Variety of beautiful Incidents. By Mrs. Penelope Aubin and now first Collected. In Three Volumes* (London, 1739), iii. iii.

[2] i, sig. A2ʳ.

[3] Duncombe (1729–86) was a miscellaneous writer and clergyman.

The modest Muse a veil with Pity throws
O'er Vice's friends and Virtue's female foes;
Abash'd she views the bold unblushing mien
Of modern Manley, Centlivre, and Behn;
And grieves to see One nobly born disgrace
Her modest sex, and her illustrious race.[1]
Tho' harmony thro' all their numbers flow'd,
And genuine wit its ev'ry grace bestow'd,
Nor genuine wit nor harmony excuse
The dang'rous sallies of a wanton Muse:

. . .

But hark! what Nymph in Frome's embroider'd vale,
With strains seraphic swells the vernal gale?
With what sweet sounds the bord'ring forest rings?
For sportive Echo catches, as she sings,
Each falling accent, studious to prolong
The warbled notes of Rowe's ecstatic song.
Old Avon pleas'd his reedy forehead rears,
And polish'd Orrery delighted hears.
See with what transport she resigns her breath
Snatched by a sudden, but a wish'd for, death!
Releas'd from earth, with smiles she soars on high
Amidst her kindred spirits of the sky,
Where Faith and Love those endless joys bestow,
That warm'd her lays, and fill'd her hopes below.[2]

In a similar fashion, Theophilus Cibber's *Lives of the Poets of Great Britain and Ireland* (1753)[3] includes a substantial account of

---

[1] Robert Halsband identifies this as a reference to Lady Mary Wortley Montagu. See *The Life of Lady Mary Wortley Montagu* (New York, Galaxy paper-back edition, 1960), p. 255.

[2] ll. 139–48, 151–64. Duncombe adds a note to the names of his dissolute trio, 'Manley, Centlivre, and Behn', explaining the nature of their indecencies: 'The first of these wrote the scandalous memoirs call'd Atlantis [*sic*], and the other two are notorious for the indecency of their plays.' Mrs. Rowe, on the other hand, needs no gloss: 'The character of Mrs. Rowe and her writings is too well known to be dwelt on here.' This description of current literary popularity may have been influenced by Duncombe's obvious preferences, but if he thought that his heroine was going unread, he would likely have included a short hit at popular taste. We notice as well that Mrs. Rowe's name is specifically linked with dying well and with joyous and certain existence after death. She appears thus in many references and was something of a culture heroine in this respect.

[3] This collection of brief biographies was only nominally by Cibber, most of the work being done by Robert Shiels and others. The life of Mrs. Rowe

her life and points out the relevance of her works and her personality to contemporary affairs:

The conduct and behaviour of Mrs. Rowe might put some of the present race of females to the blush, who rake the town for infamous adventures to amuse the public.[1] Their works will soon be forgotten, and their memories when dead, will not be deemed exceeding precious; but the works of Mrs. Rowe can never perish, while exalted piety and genuine goodness have any existence in the world. Her memory will be ever honoured, and her name dear to latest posterity.[2]

As prophetic passages, these fail to impress, since Mrs. Rowe has long since passed into the darkest corners and remotest footnotes of literary histories; but as a reflection of eighteenth-century opinion, the sentiments are not at all extravagant.

Mrs. Rowe moved in her youth in pious but elegant dissenting circles, where her friends included the celebrated Bishop Ken and Isaac Watts. After the death of her husband, she retired to Frome in Somerset, but maintained an extensive correspondence, especially with her life-long friend, Frances Thynne, Countess of Hertford and later Duchess of Somerset. She also wrote poetry, and besides a verse retelling of 'The History of Joseph' and various other sacred pieces, produced an 'Elegy' on the death of her husband which Pope so admired that he printed it as an appendix to the 1720 second edition of *Eloisa to Abelard*.

After her death in 1737 her private meditations and prayers were edited by Isaac Watts, and under the title *Devout Exercises of the Heart in Meditation and Soliloquy* remained an enormously popular

included in this compendium was mostly plagiarized from the 'official' biography prefixed to the 1739 edition of her *Miscellaneous Works*. According to the editor of these, Theophilus Rowe, the first twenty-nine pages of this biography were written by Henry Grove, a friend of Mrs. Rowe and her husband. His sudden death, the editor informs us, made it necessary for him to continue it. This life was widely plagiarized right down to the nineteenth century in various biographical compendia. The passage cited here is not in the original Grove–Rowe biography.

[1] This is probably a reference to scandalous memoirs such as that published in 1748 by Teresia Constantia Phillips, *An Apology for the Conduct of Mrs. Teresia Constantia Phillips*; and the notorious *Memoirs of a Lady of Quality* of Lady Vane published in 1751 in Smollett's *Peregrine Pickle*.

[2] London, iv. 340.

work which was reprinted until the middle of the nineteenth century.[1] Her biography was no less a popular commodity than her posthumous works. Her obituary notice in the *Gentleman's Magazine* called her the 'Ornament of her Sex and the Honour of the County of Somerset', and the same issue contained an anonymous verse tribute, 'On the Death of the Celebrated Mrs. Rowe'.[2] Other memorial poems continued to appear in the *Gentleman's Magazine*, and the 1739 edition of her unpublished poems and letters, *Miscellaneous Works*,[3] was prefaced by an impressive gathering of dedicatory poems, most written in her honour while she was alive by, among others, Isaac Watts, Elizabeth Carter, and Thomas Amory.[4] In May 1739 the *Gentleman's Magazine* began a three-part life of 'the excellent Mrs. Rowe, that Ornament of her Sex, on whom we daily receive Encomiums in Verse'.

But Mrs. Rowe was most remembered for *Friendship in Death*, published in 1728 with part i of *Letters Moral and Entertaining*, which were continued with part ii in 1731 and part iii in 1732. It was a work which was widely read and apparently highly regarded.[5]

[1] A 'ninth edition' was published in London in 1777; further editions were published in London in 1784 and 1786, and in 1796 the work was issued as part of 'Cooke's edition of Sacred Classics'. I have found record of its publication as late as 1811 in England and 1831 in America.

[2] vii (March 1737), 188, 183.

[3] These letters reveal Mrs. Rowe as an intelligent and literate woman whose hermitage in Somerset was really only a pleasant country house which was not designed to shelter its main inhabitant from the literature and ideas of the day. In her letters she cites Cervantes, quotes Pascal, shows an intimate knowledge of Milton and Pope, sprinkles her letters with appropriate lines from other English poets such as Prior, Young, and Blackmore, and even describes her reading of Collier, Shaftesbury, and Berkeley. At one point she admits reading Fielding's *The Modern Husband*, which she thought a very good play, 'if nature, wit, and morality can make it so' (ii. 143).

[4] In the *Gentleman's Magazine*, viii (April 1738), 210, appeared 'On the Loss of my eminent and pious Friend, Mrs. Rowe'; and in ix (March 1739), 152, an untitled and anonymous verse tribute was printed, and 'On the Death of Mrs. Rowe' by Elizabeth Carter. Amory, in his *Memoirs of Several Ladies of Great Britain* (London, 1755), summarized her life briefly and testified to the popularity and worthiness of her works: 'The ingenious, who did not know Mrs. Rowe, admired her for her writings; and her acquaintance loved and esteemed her for the many amiable qualities of her heart' (p. 334).

[5] By 1738 a fifth edition was advertised in the February number of the *London Magazine*. I find record of editions published in England in 1740, 1743, 1750, 1753, 1756, 1774, 1776, 1786, 1804, 1811, and 1816. The editions

It seems to have become a standard minor work whose devotional uses were widely recognized, a book likely to be found in small home libraries of essential and edifying books.[1]

Dr. Johnson, for example, recognized that Mrs. Rowe's works were a touchstone for those who aspired to combine devotion with literary pleasure. In a review of *Miscellanies in prose and verse, published by Elizabeth Harrison*, which he wrote for *The Literary Magazine or Universal Review* in 1756, Johnson noted that the authors of the prose essays in this collection were to be praised because they had tried to imitate 'the copiousness and luxuriance of Mrs. Rowe', and to achieve something of 'her purity of sentiments'. Mrs. Rowe, he added, was the writer who had best managed 'to employ the ornaments of romance in the decoration of religion'.[2]

Boswell, years later in 1781, cited Mrs. Rowe's *Letters* in one of the essays he contributed to the *London Magazine*. One grows fondest of children, he writes, when they are about three years old, and one suffers most if they happen to die at that age. There is, he says casually, 'something of a peculiar pleasing fanciful consolation in the letter from a child of two years old in Heaven to its disconsolate surviving mother, in Mrs. Rowe's Letters from the Dead to the Living'.[3]

Johnson's and Boswell's comments are evidence of a solid, albeit minor, reputation. The name of Mrs. Rowe was one which the educated reader could be expected to recognize; her works, espe-

of 1740 and 1743 were printed by Samuel Richardson, who had printed in 1738 volume ii of her *Miscellaneous Works* (see William M. Sale, Jr., *Samuel Richardson: Master Printer* (Ithaca, New York, 1950), p. 200).

[1] An interesting example of Mrs. Rowe's status as a minor pious classic comes in a note in Mrs. Q. D. Leavis's *Fiction and the Reading Public* (London, 1939), p. 147. Mrs. Leavis quotes the *Autobiography* of Eliza Fletcher, born in Yorkshire in 1770 and one of the great ladies of Edinburgh at the turn of the century: ' "My father's library was upon a small scale—the Spectator, Milton's Works, Shakespeare's Plays, Pope's and Dryden's Poems, Hervey's Meditations, Mrs. Rowe's Letters, Shenstone's Poems, Sherlock's Sermons, with some abridgements of history and geography, filled his little bookshelves." '

[2] *Boswell's Life of Johnson*, eds., G. B. Hill and L. F. Powell (Oxford, 1934), i. 312.

[3] *The Hypochondriack: Being the Seventy Essays by the Celebrated Biographer, James Boswell*, ed., Margaret Bailey (Stanford, 1928), ii. 93–4.

cially the *Letters from the Dead to the Living*, were part of normal literary experience. In fact, among the various scribbling ladies who contributed to the mass of prose fiction which precedes the florescence of the novel in Richardson and Fielding, Mrs. Rowe was probably the most highly respected and remembered during the eighteenth century itself.

It is hard to understand why. Her most popular work is a deadening book, written in ecstatic and inflated prose and full of the most explicit and tedious moralizing about the pains of a life of sin and the comforts of living virtuously. Its situations and characters are mechanical and verbose, and strike any modern reader as almost comically unreal. There is none of the erotic sensationalism that we have observed made the love novella so attractive, or any of the bizarre complications and exotic dangers that Mrs. Aubin relied upon to sell her books. Worst of all for us, perhaps, Mrs. Rowe's book reeks of what must be called morbidity about death, which we are reminded on every page is always menacing us and can never for a moment be lost sight of.

Yet eighteenth-century readers were quite willing to overlook these 'faults', and no one felt compelled to condemn its attitudes towards life and death as distortions of reality. To understand and to account for the respect with which a work like Mrs. Rowe's *Letters* was treated, we must examine it for the values which many of her contemporaries found in it.

Those values were primarily devotional and polemical, for the *Letters* was an aggressively didactic work. Mrs. Rowe hopes, she declares in her preface, to convince her readers through her stories of the immortality of the soul, not by rational or discursive means, but by making 'the Mind familiar, with the Thoughts of our Future Existence, and contract, as it were, unawares, an Habitual Persuasion of it, by Writings built on that Foundation, and addressed to the Affections and imagination' (sig. A3^v). The need for such aids to belief is clear, she notes, for the notion of the soul's immortality is an idea 'without which, all Virtue and Religion, with their Temporal and Eternal good Consequences, must fall to the Ground' (sig. A3^r).

Here the polemical edges are noticeable, for one did not in the early eighteenth century speak in the abstract atmosphere of speculative controversy when asserting the immortality of the soul. Neither a universally assumed article of faith nor an imponderable theological theory, it was, as Mrs. Rowe's apocalyptic clause makes clear, a highly emotional question, the answer to which put one on either side of a struggle. Mrs. Rowe, like so many other seriously committed Christians of her day, saw the times as perilous for true believers, who were attacked on every side by the mobilized forces of irreligion and infidelity.

Mrs. Rowe's preface declares an intention that is not simply didactic in the ordinary sense; it is apparent that her interest is not merely to warn the unruly heart or undisciplined emotions that they must listen to the voice of conventional morality. Even more authoritatively than Mrs. Aubin, Mrs. Rowe speaks unashamedly like a propagandist for the cause of virtue and religion. Her book is, in fact, an extremely self-conscious polemic which is armed for ideological battle with what she conceives of as a very palpable and menacing enemy. That enemy cannot be isolated or named very precisely, but he is no less real and all the more dangerous for being so shadowy, so subtly pervasive.

Mrs. Rowe concludes her preface by insisting, again like Mrs. Aubin, that her work is much more than amusement. It is in its end, she claims, totally unlike ordinary amusement, 'for which the World makes by far the largest Demand, and which generally speaking, is nothing but an Art of forgetting that Immortality, the firm Belief, and advantageous Contemplation of which, *this* Amusement would recommend' (sig. A3ᵛ).

It is clear, then, that Mrs. Rowe is out to use the profane instruments of a burgeoning literary genre for sacred purposes, in Dr. Johnson's words, 'to employ the ornaments of romance in the decoration of religion'. Yet 'religion', in this case, means a transfiguration of death by an affirmation of personal immortality, and 'romance' equals the conventional intrigues of the amatory novella. In Mrs. Rowe's fervid little stories death is defeated, but only by those who are capable of love which is true and pure and always conjugal, at least in intent. Her crude and explicit exploitation of the clichés of the popular novellas and scandalous memoirs of the day is nothing less than a sign of the crucial transformation of fiction which takes place during the first four decades of the eighteenth century: the aimless if graceful literature of love which floods into England from France and Spain during the late seventeenth century and through the eighteenth century is subtly changed by the ideological climate, and in English Protestant hands responds to the pressure of the times to become fiction which is essentially a dramatization of the plight of an embattled and self-consciously 'virtuous' individual in a hostile and innately vicious world. It is primarily from this dialectical opposition between religion and infidelity, between the lonely virtue and implicit faith of the hero and the common corruption and cynical disbelief of the rest of the world (a simplification, of course, but fiction is by its nature concerned with ideological paradigms and not with the complexities of history) that the English novel derives the ideological matrix in which Richardson's Clarissa, for example, may be said to achieve a heroism close to sainthood.[1]

Mrs. Rowe evokes a 'scene' in her stories where the values of the antagonists (infidelity in religion and in love) stand in vital antithesis to those of her protagonists (belief in immortality and in conjugal love). It is to this key opposition (an *agon* really) that eighteenth-century readers responded, and the value of Mrs. Rowe is that she expresses the emotional elements of this conflict with crude clarity.

The first part of the *Letters*, *Friendship in Death*, consists of twenty separate novellas, told indirectly in letters from visiting spirits to persons who are still living. Most of the *Letters Moral and Entertaining* are written by the living to the living but deal with the same stock situations.

In *Friendship in Death*, each correspondent makes, as would be expected, a special point of his celestial situation. These are very

---

[1] John A. Dussinger's recent article, 'Conscience and the Pattern of Christian Perfection in *Clarissa*,' *PMLA*, lxxxi (June 1966), 236–45, has emphasized Richardson's attempt to 'represent in his heroine the ultimate refinement of sensibility as the condition of salvation' (237).

serious-minded ghosts and their task is never to frighten but to dispel all doubts about the existence of the spirit world, for each one knows that the person he writes to will be surprised or terrified to find such certain proof of personal immortality. Most earnest eighteenth-century Christians would have taken (or at least wanted to take) a fictional situation like this very much more seriously than we perhaps would; the Cock-Lane Ghost is only one instance of the lingering and almost desperate hope of an age more and more dominated by scientific positivism for palpable proof of the old mysteries.

We note as well that the correspondent always describes the afterlife in pastoral terms, and we read of the usual enamelled vales and bowers of pastoral poetry. Heaven is not seen as a great urban cluster of the just; the celestial city, the New Jerusalem, has been exchanged for polemical purposes for the pastoral seats of glory. The town, which in the conventional fictional situation might be an exciting and certainly interesting place, is now the entire lower world of mortality, which is always seen by these epistolary spirits as a place well worth leaving. Indeed, one of their purposes in writing is to warn the friend or beloved of dangers of various sorts which are endemic to the seats of men. Throughout all of the *Letters*, in fact, this denunciation of the world is the most obtrusive concern of the plots. And so the various harried heroines and sighing heroes retreat to the country.

This rural retreat can be a number of things. It can be a place where real spiritual tranquillity is to be found for the more philosophic of Mrs. Rowe's correspondents. The eighteenth-century version of the holy hermit, the man of the world turned contemplative whom we meet so often in Mrs. Aubin's novels, appears in *Letters Moral and Entertaining* in the presence of Philander, an ex-'Statesman'. He has left his place in the world, he writes to a nameless 'Lord' (a friend who, we gather, is still very much a part of the world) to tell him how he has found new faith in immortality through isolation:

. . . abstract from business or diversion, my mind retires, within itself, where it finds treasures 'till now undiscover'd, capacities form'd

for infinite objects, desires that stretch themselves beyond the limits
of this wide creation, in search of the great original of life and pleasure:
I find new powers exerting their energy, some latent exercises, which
'till now, I have been a stranger to. I have, indeed, heard from the men,
who teach such holy fables, (as I then thought them,) that the soul was
immortal, and capable of celestial joys: But I rather wish'd, than believ'd
these transporting truths, and put them on a level with the poet's rosy
bowers, their myrtle shades, and soft *Elysian* fields; but now I am convinced of their evidence, and triumph in the privileges of my own being.
I rejoice to think that the moment I begun [*sic*] to exist, I enter'd on
an eternal state, and commenc'd a duration, that shall run parallel, to
that of the supreme and self-existent mind. (i. 58–9)

Philander knows that his titled friend will smile at such sentiments, but Philander has scaled, we are told, both amatory and
political heights and has found only boredom and disgust at their
end.

Unlike Philander, Cleora still lives in the town. She is replying
to a series of eight letters in which a friend has advised her to
seclude herself from the world, but she answers that she is reluctant
to leave it because she is still not quite convinced about the certain
existence of the next world and its joys. She feels 'a sort of reluctance to part with everything below, and a dread to enter on those
unknown regions, from whence none return, to tell us what they
find' (i. 106). Retirement, in other words, is tantamount to translation to a sphere of faith and beatitude to which Cleora does not
feel qualified to aspire.

The country retreat is also, as commonly in the amatory novella,
a haven for victims of illicit passion. Sylvia has fled to retirement
in the country because of a guilty passion for a French count, the
husband of a friend she has visited for a time; and it is only in this
retreat that she can 'sometimes read the Bible, in contempt of all
modern refinements'. It is only in the country, she declares, that
she can be free 'from the tumultuous effects of a guilty passion',
only there that the proper perspective can be achieved:

I am now reconcil'd to myself, and find an ineffable satisfaction in
the silent approbation of my own conduct; a satisfaction superior to
all the empty applause of the crowd. I reflect with pleasure on the

happy change. My soul seems now in its proper situation, and conscious of its dignity, looks above this world for its rest and happiness: I am almost in a state of insensibility, with regard to mortal things, and have fixed my views on those infinite delights, which will be the certain rewards of virtue. (i. 21)

Amoret has likewise overcome 'her criminal passion' for Sebastian by retiring to the country. Sebastian, unlike Sylvia's blameless count, is a practiced seducer right out of the lurid novella who has technically 'ruined' Amoret, and the horror of this sinful moment is only banished, she declares, by the total seclusion of 'some unfrequented shade, where the images of vanity and sin may never enter!' (i. 29).

Throughout these reports from the country one sees a constant awareness of the opposing point of view which is ever ready to mock or condemn seclusion and its pretensions to beatitude. The relationship is a dialectical one; the country sustains itself as a moral position by virtue of its unremitting opposition to the values of the social and urban world. This is quite explicit in Celadon's complaint to the treacherous Amasia, 'who had seduced him into criminal love for her'.

Curse on the maxims of the world, and that impropriety of language, that would disguise the basest of crimes, with the names of amusement and gallantry! Let me be singular, let me be unpolite, let me be un-fashionably good, if I can but keep my peace, and justify myself to my own conscience! Let me inviolably observe the rules of truth and justice, be fearless and open to the inspection of God, and may everlasting reproach rest, on all the modish appellations and refinements, that would soften the horror of a base and treacherous action! (i. 54)

The perfidious Amasia is the bride of Celadon's friend, Alta-mont, who has instructed and confirmed him in these very admir-able principles. Celadon's remorse turns into a near-fatal fever and the effects of this are aggravated by Altamont's constant com-passion for him. Here, then, is the common love triangle so dear to Restoration comedy and so much a part, either for comic or tragic purposes, of what we can call 'aristocratic' literature. But Antony renounces Cleopatra in this case; Celadon recovers from his fever and resolves to exile himself to expiate his crimes. The conventional love rivalry has been turned primarily into a denunciation of the system of values which could find something to laugh at or to admire in an adulterous situation.

The intent here, as it is throughout Mrs. Rowe's work, is not to produce plausible character or dramatic situation. In fact, little or no attempt is made to lay the fictional groundwork, as it were, for the presentation of these elements. Mrs. Rowe uses a kind of shorthand which enables her to refer her readers to the familiar conventional fictional situation, and then to beat the moral implications out of it, to make them see the twistings of the love intrigue *sub specie aeternitatis*. You have read this story many times before in the course of being merely amused, she says to her readers, now here is what it really means to you.

This shift in emphasis, this deliberate exploitation of fictional material at hand, is obvious, for example, in the fairly long account of Rosalinda in parts ii and iii of *Letters Moral and Entertaining*. She has run away from her tyrannical and bigoted father after he has attempted to force her into marriage with someone who was both a foreigner and a papist. We hear almost nothing of the events which lead up to the crime, but at length about the moral dilemma which Rosalinda faces in running away: 'I was their only child, carefully instructed in those sacred Truths, which by the assistance of Heaven I will never renounce, but rather give up my title to all the dazzling advantages the world can tempt me with' (ii. 2). She is justified, in other words, because her father has switched his allegiance to the 'world'. She becomes, incognito, an upper servant for a country family and revels in bucolic simplicity:

I have entirely put off the fine lady, and all my court airs; I have almost forgot I am an Earl's daughter, and should start at the name of Lady *Frances*; Instead of that, I am plain *Rosalinda*, without any other appellation, but what the gentle swains now and then give me, of a handsome lass, or a proper damsel; with which I am infinitely better pleased, than when I was an angel, or a goddess, and impiously addressed in the strains of adoration. (ii. 5–6)

Rosalinda stands firm in her choice, even when her correspondent tells her that her father will now leave his entire fortune to a monastery. She draws the moral lines of the situation with unflinching righteousness, and we are intended once again to be aware of a very real struggle between opposing ways of life. 'This was what I expected; and I am sure you will not persuade me to renounce Heaven, and damn myself, for the sordid purchase of eighty thousand pounds; nor would you considerately advise me, to hazard a celestial advancement for a gilded coronet, or prefer the flattery of mistaken mortals to the approbation of Angels' (ii. 15).

It is, of course, the constant awareness of such moral issues in social and usually financial situations which is to make *Clarissa* possible. Marriage, Mrs. Rowe reminds us frequently, is more than a social or financial act; it is *the* decisive moral act of the individual's earthly career. There is a direct relationship between the desire and capacity to love purely (and of course such a love always has marriage as its goal) and salvation. This love is typically to be found outside of the 'world', sometimes, if tragedy intervenes, only beyond the grave. Rosalinda is lucky, finds and marries in the country a suitor who is of noble birth, but, more important, one distinguished by nature 'with an air of grandeur, beyond all the borrowed lustre of titles or equipage' (iii. 132).

The point that real love is only to be found by retiring both from the cities of men and the values of the world is made again in six letters from Laura, a town belle now in the country, where she has been brought by her brother. His interest in the country is, however, of a highly improper sort, for he has retired in order to dally without scandal with his new mistress, a ruined tradesman's daughter whom he has seduced. Laura's brother is a self-declared 'infidel' who has converted her to this way of thinking. But rural solitude destroys false peace of mind.

Death, that ghastly phantom, perpetually intrudes on my solitude, and in some doleful knell from a neighbouring steeple, often calls upon me to ruminate on coffins and funerals, graves and gloomy sepulchres: These dismal subjects put me in the vapours, and make me start at my shadow; nor have I acquired any degree of fortitude by turning freethinker. . . . (iii. 226)

Laura grows gradually accustomed to country solitude, but finds religious faith only with the aid of love, in the person of Philocles, a youthful neighbour. This pious youth responds to Laura's advances not as she expected with 'gallant and modish' raillery but with talk of 'the satisfactions of virtue, the tranquillity of the mind in the rectitude of its passions'. He has received a supernatural premonition of his imminent death, a notion that Laura cannot forbear laughing at. Philocles then admits that her beauty has made him break his vow to avoid the 'distracting passion' of love, and he confesses that his love and the knowledge of his death make her 'infidelity' doubly distressing to him. He promises, to the accompaniment of her mocking raillery, to visit her from the spirit world in order to prove his love and save her from unbelief. He dies soon after and, as good as his word, appears in a pastoral spot to the grieving Laura, who then writes to a friend of her reactions after this meeting.

This momentary view of celestial beauty has obscured all earthly glory: Never will the sun disclose a scene of pleasure to my sight; the vanities which lately amused me, have lost their charms; my thoughts are fixed on superior objects, a divine and immortal ardor inspires my soul, and determines all its motions: With the evidence I now have of a future existence, my notions of happiness are refined and enlarged, my hopes bright and unlimited. (iii. 251)

The love story has been lost in the conversion of Laura, for love is really a means of conversion. 'True love', not the carnal and sordid affairs of the godless, like Laura's brother, is something which can only convince us of the immortality of the soul. Philocles is the apotheosis of the lover who will provide religious certainty through his love; under normal circumstances he (much more often 'she') will not die and reappear in angelic light, but Mrs. Rowe does not want her point lost. She is making the normally implicit crudely explicit. This explicitness is as much a result of her polemical motives as it is of her artistic ineptitude. Love must be redefined, saved from the cynicism of the *libertin*, and made much more than the useful procreative urge that the philosopher calls it.

But love, Mrs. Rowe realizes, can be a dangerous and violent force as well. When love is not possible within the legal framework of marriage, it must be rejected. Illicit love leads, however, not merely to social difficulties but to 'existential' terrors. Such is the lesson to be learned from the story of Amasia, who has allowed herself to be seduced by the rich and married Philario, in spite of the promise she made to her dying mother to have nothing to do with him. Amasia, now remorseful but still mad with love, describes her situation as she raves in a fatal fever:

This truth sits heavy on my soul, and brings my guilt with its full aggravation in view: my mother's dying admonitions, my broken vows terrify me to distraction. My crime was not the effects of ignorance and inadvertency; pitying angels set the penalties of eternal damnation, and the recompense of an immortal crown, in prospect before me; the caverns of death disclos'd their terrors, and the realms of celestial light open'd their glories to my active imagination: I was forewarn'd by the advice of a dying parent of the infamy and ruin to which this soft temptation betray'd me: I had experienc'd the satisfactions of reason and virtue. But for you I ventur'd on present and future perdition, and gave up my title to all the joys of immortality; and now, ye regions of divine delight, you have no attractions for a mind so impure, I would only fly to you, as a retreat from infernal Misery. (i. 5)

Love of this sort is real and certainly tragic, but, says Mrs. Rowe, it must not be thought of as thrillingly romantic (that is, as the erotic-pathetic fantasy which the love novella constantly resolves itself into). She asks us, rather, to view this tragic love in the light of death and eternity. The very turbulence of such passion is not the sign of inner virtue that the novella implicitly makes of it, but merely the result of the moral and psychological insecurity it brings.

If it is legal or platonic, we must remember, love can be the way to secure faith. Herminius, for example, declares that his love for the married Cleora has saved him from the very libertinism which led him to attempt her. Her modesty and piety have converted him thoroughly and made him 'a proselyte to virtue' (i. 42).

Lysander, too, has led a thoroughly dissolute life. He has just

been seduced by his *valet de chambre*, 'Palanty', who had disguised
herself as a man and served him because of desperate love. But
Lysander is now directed into a marriage with a virtuous and
respectable young lady, Cimene. This is the first time Lysander
has loved legally and he is properly overwhelmed by the difference
between lust and sanctified love: 'Till now I never knew the force
of love, nor any of the refined sentiments that noble passion inspired. In what guiltless joys did the hours pass that I spent with
my loved *Cimene*!' (ii. 56–7).

The jealous and pregnant 'Palanty' takes poison and dies;
Lysander grieves but marries Cimene. He is, however, plagued
by remorse for his past excesses and especially for his part in
Palanty's death. But suddenly we discover that Palanty has appeared to him and left a letter in which she warns him to reform,
for 'hell is no poetick fiction, no enthusiastick dream, nor pious
fable of some mercenary priest' (ii. 61). This is the jargon of the
opposing side; here are the cant phrases of infidelity triumphantly
rejected.

Lysander, needless to say, is completely converted by such a
demonstration. Once again, the conventional fictional triangle has
yielded excellent polemical results. The willing reader has experienced the disastrous effects of illegal passion in the fate of Palanty,
whose transvestite trick is potentially a very engaging one, and is
indeed a frequent contrivance of the novella. Mrs. Rowe consistently
deflates the romantic capability of such situations, and here the
chain of events is designed to degrade the illegal and desperate
connection Palanty seeks and to exalt the conventional marriage
Lysander eventually enters. True and legal love of this sort pre-
figures paradise, but to experience illegal lust and the remorse
which must, in Mrs. Rowe's fictional world at least, accompany it
is to learn about hell. This is usually only a psychological or at
least a social equivalent of hell, but Mrs. Rowe insists once again
upon adding a real visitor from the infernal regions to make the
connection explicit.

It is to bring confirmation of eternal fire that Eusebius writes
to his son to urge him to break off an adulterous connection and to

recall the challenge he has just sent to a friend who has given him the same advice. But Eusebius's ghostly warning is really a denunciation of a whole way of life, for death in a duel means only one thing:

> . . . you will mingle with a Society that make very different Judgments of Things, from what pass for Maxims of Honour among Mortals. You will appear with a very ill Grace, and on most impertinent Occasion, among the Spirits of Darkness, to whom you will be an eternal Object of Derision. The boasted Beauty and Charms of your Mistress, will be but a poor Excuse for your Gallantry, tho' you should tell them in *Heroics*, how *the world has been lost for a woman.* (p. 63)

The last phrase, in Mrs. Rowe's italics, is a heavy allusion to an opposing ethos. Mrs. Rowe's book is part of a pervasive eighteenth-century protest against the 'senseless' maxims of aristocratic honour and against the cult of amatory *gloire* implicit in the traditional literature of love. It is a protest whose roots can be called 'modern-rationalistic', or, since there is a strong social mythology at work, 'practical-bourgeois'. The amatory novella generally locates itself in a world of aristocratic splendour and leisure, although avarice and lust lurk immediately under the shining surface. Shocked but delighted, the reader observes a world where love can assume an extravagant intensity denied to it in real life; there, heroes and heroines frequently lose themselves, if not the world, for love. Mrs. Rowe, in her single-minded way, will have none of the ideological equivocation of the novella and shows us nothing but the eternal consequences of such behaviour.

In Mrs. Rowe's relentlessly pious perspective, love of the proper sort functions as a preparation for death rather than as one of the traditional distractions of the flesh. We see throughout the *Letters* that love is the main part of man's natural resources for defeating death and making human life really possible. This point is made specifically and repeatedly in the most famous part of the *Letters*, *Friendship in Death.* There Mrs. Rowe makes the buried analogy between love and paradisal bliss explicit, rescuing it from its status as merely part of the conventionally blasphemous rhetoric of love.

In *Friendship and Death* we read of the harrowing death beds of several dissipated libertines, for sexual licence is a necessary corollary of religious infidelity. The dead Cleander, for example, writes to his brother to describe the death of 'the unhappy Carlos'. Carlos dies raving in the throes of uncertainty about the afterlife, and 'never did mortal give up his life in a manner more cowardly and inconsistent'. Carlos's behaviour towards one of those at his bedside is worth noting:

> The abandon'd *Amoret*, who had followed him in the Disguise of a Page; was seldom permitted to see him; and whenever she approach'd him, he trembled, and fell into the greatest Agonies, closed his Eyes, or turn'd them from her, but spoke nothing to support her in the Distress he had brought on her, nor express'd the least Remorse for having seduced her to leave the noble *Sebastian*, to whom she was engaged by Marriage Vows, and a thousand tender Obligations. (p. 44)

Remorse for such offences is the first step to faith; remorse will lead to real love and real love can only flourish in faith. Mrs. Rowe's logic is circular; the lover is by definition a believer in the immortality of the soul, for the joys of love, we are shown, prefigure the joys of immortality.

Thus Altamont, a 'gentleman who died at Constantinople', describes his death with perfect calm. He simply wandered off 'when the destined hour drew near', lay down on a flowery bank and fell asleep with the voice of his dead beloved, Almeria, echoing softly in his dreams. He awakens painlessly in paradise and is met by Almeria.

> . . . but how Dazling! how divinely Fair! Extasy was in her Eyes, and inexpressible Pleasure in every Smile! her Mien and Aspect more soft and propitious than ever was feign'd by Poets of their Goddess of Beauty and Love: What was airy Fiction *there*, was *here* all transporting Reality. With an inimitable Grace she received me into her aetherial Chariot, which was sparkling Saphire studded with Gold. (p. 7)

Death is no terrible event for lovers such as Altamont but a gentle sigh which unites them with their beloveds. This taming of death is one of the main tasks of Mrs. Rowe's *Letters*; departed spirits continually insist that death is an easy and joyful transition. But once again, the ease and joy of the passage are the result of an emotional association between 'pure love' and the certain joys of the afterlife.

One spirit, Clerimont, is even disappointed when his beloved Sylvia recovers from what appeared to be a fatal illness. Not only, he adds, would death have brought infinite happiness, it would have brought release from the importunities of Cassander. He is a suitor who, as Clerimont reveals, already has a wife, a 'young and beautiful Italian' (p. 41), stolen from her parents and left abandoned and ruined in a nunnery.

These are the materials of the novella and Mrs. Rowe's panegyric on death is carefully contained within the conventional tragic turns of the love tale, what I have called the fable of persecuted innocence. The deed letter writers have often themselves died of tragic or frustrated love. The novella chose to stop there, having made its erotic and pathetic points. But Mrs. Rowe is exploiting the conventional plots to make her point about the immortality of the soul, and her strategy is to make earthly love merely a prelude (although a highly significant and revealing one) to eternal celestial domesticity.

Delia, for example, tells Emilia of her entry into a pastoral paradise where she meets Emilia's brother, whom she had loved in life. 'That tender, innocent Passion I had long conceiv'd for him, kindled at the first Interview, and has taken eternal possession of my Soul' (p. 24). Amintor, who has been killed by pirates, writes to his wife, who has been captured by slave traders and is now living as a concubine in the harem of an 'illustrious bassa'. He has treated her with unusual gentleness so far and has not yet forced his oriental desires upon her. Amintor writes to tell her that all shall be well some day; for when she dies 'we shall meet to part no more; which Circumstance, though you through your Partiality for me may too highly value, believe me, you will find it by much the smallest Blessing of this Place' (p. 29). Thus love provides a transition from one world to the next; it guarantees that we have lived a proper life and it gives us a reason for wanting to leave this world, since the afterlife is best imagined as a glorified and intensified version of the joys of lovers.

Death, finally, is robbed of all its terrors by faith, and this faith, Mrs. Rowe makes clear, rests upon a belief in the power of love. Human affections, she wishes to convince us, can be so powerful that their dissolution must seem unthinkable. Such feelings are not merely pleasant delusions, they are intimations of immortality.

Mrs. Rowe's famous little book, then, is a literary polemic against unbelief, waged on the emotional and human level, for assurance of immortality and salvation is provided ultimately through conjugal love (or the capacity for it), which is elevated to the status of beatitude. Death, the great problem which rationalism and infidelity cannot solve, is defeated by true and pure love, the great human necessity which reason cannot explain or eliminate. In drawing up her polemic, Mrs. Rowe was simply purging the novella of its erotic grossness and by virtue of her shift in perspective on its themes extracting the resonances and associations it naturally contained.

The amatory novella, as we have seen, no matter how scandalous or lubricious, uses spiritual analogies and quasi-blasphemous hyperbole as its characteristic rhetorical strategy. Dissecting the works of Mrs. Manley, Mrs. Haywood, and their lesser contemporaries has shown how important this rhetoric is for creating and maintaining that ideological alignment of reader and heroine which formed the basis of their popularity. The moral polarities upon which the mythology of love rests are well served by this traditional rhetoric; and the true lovers with whom we readers melt and suffer are those initiates, as it were, who perceive the validity of these analogies and are capable of experiencing love at a pitch and intensity which makes them more than figures of speech.

It has already been observed at length, moreover, that lovers are opposed in general by a world of financial and sexual materialism which reduces love to a biological impulse and marriage to a profitable alliance. Specifically, the heroic maiden is confronted by *libertin*-seducers who treat love and marriage-for-love as mere chimeras and reject them in the materialistic jargon of infidelity and irreligion. Concerned as we are with audience effect, we can see how important the associations suggested by the rhetoric of love are: they place the reader on the side of the angels in what many in the eighteenth century apparently saw as an ultimate struggle for the world—the battle between religion and the massed and threatening forces of infidelity and atheism.

But pains have been taken to show how this 'spirituality' of the persecuted maiden and her occasional allies is often simply part of the massive apparatus for making her story a more efficient fantasy machine. In the capable hands of Mrs. Haywood, for example, this spirituality is not only a value with which we identify but a source of energy which impels the heroine through a whole series of erotic and pathetic scenes. She loves compulsively and often tragically, drawn to a married man or a libertine whose morals she may despise rationally. But the logic of the supervising mythology of love makes that self-destructive desire in itself a sign of authentic spirituality, tragic and destructive only because of the corrupt world which surrounds it. It suits the successful amatory narrative's purposes to identify spirituality with this irrational and totally spontaneous erotic impulse which it calls love. Only rarely do we pass from this implicit spirituality-cum-sensuality of compulsive desire to a more orthodox and less fervid spirituality through which the prevailing corrupt world can be defeated or transcended.

The connection between the persecuted maiden's struggle against the vicious world and the clash between religion and amoral secularism is, however, fully exploited in varying ways by the lady novelists we have just discussed. Together they form an important and often deliberate counter-tendency to the tradition established by Mrs. Behn and continued, notably, by Mrs. Manley and Mrs. Haywood.[1] The value of these pious narratives for us is that they provide access to a deliberate working out of the implications which are behind the great popularity of the story of persecuted innocence during the early eighteenth century.

The novel develops in its main direction (that is, as a powerful moral and social force) by learning to embody in a moving and

---

[1] See E. A. Baker, *History of the English Novel*, iii. 121–6.

convincing form the ideological antithesis between the faithless world and the simple and heroic believer. Mrs. Rowe's *Letters*, Mrs. Aubin's novels, and the short stories of Mrs. Barker are nothing less than important symptoms of the gradual accommodation of fiction to the ideological needs of the time.

EPILOGUE

THE RELEVANCE OF THE UNREADABLE

SOME justification is doubtless needed for having summoned these justly neglected spirits to rehearse their popular triumphs. We can, after all, garner little wisdom from the thin righteousness of Mrs. Manley and Mrs. Haywood; and even the strenuously pious efforts of Mrs. Aubin and Mrs. Rowe provoke little more than bemused wonder at the taste of the age. Travellers like Crusoe and the pirates and criminals of popular narrative have a vigour and capacity for survival which we can easily appreciate and relate to the struggles inherent in our own existence, but we grimace and turn the page when the inevitable moralizing begins. The *moralitas* which Defoe's and Captain Smith's wide audiences required strikes us as gratuitous, a pious assertion rather than an integral part of the hero's experience.

We search in vain, as well, for the pleasures of style and structure in popular works such as these. The hysterical romantic fustian of Mrs. Manley, Mrs. Haywood, and other lady novelists is clearly unreadable; the edifying purposes of Mrs. Rowe and Mrs. Aubin improve neither the prose nor the coherence of the popular novella. Defoe's chronicles of travellers and criminals are written in a lucid and attractive demotic, and his rendering of lower-class milieux and middle-class psychology is compellingly real and justly celebrated as a new direction in prose fiction. But Defoe's narratives, are often garrulous and disjointed by modern standards of narrative coherence; his imitators are merely diffuse or incoherent without any of his saving realism.

In fact, the great bulk of eighteenth-century pre-Richardson popular narrative is largely beyond redemption—morally or aesthetically. In a sense, there are few resonant conclusions to be drawn from our discussion of five recurrent narrative patterns, and perhaps nothing totally new or startling about eighteenth-century life and letters has emerged from our analyses. What has become clear, I hope, and what justifies keeping these works in mind in any attempt to visualize historically the early eighteenth century is the exact nature of the sizeable market for popular narrative which existed. The paradigms which have been elaborated are valuable because they allow us to speculate reasonably about the audience which constituted that market, to describe what I have called their ideological features by extracting the ideological strategies of the works they fed upon.

Popular narrative allows us to do this because it is, as we have seen, essentially opportunistic; it sets out to flatter and exploit rather than to challenge or redefine the assumptions of its implied audience. In terms of this immediate function as entertainment machines and fantasy inducers, the narratives we have discussed have demonstrated their efficiency. Criminal and whore biographies, travel narratives of merchants, pirates, or hermits, scandal chronicles, and amatory or pious novellas all delivered certain predictable satisfactions to their audiences. I have simply attempted to describe those satisfactions and to dismantle the apparatus (i.e. the rhetoric, the values behind the rhetoric, and the stock events which provoke the rhetoric) which delivered them. The aim of my analyses has been descriptive rather than evaluative, the final end being to see these works for what they were to the readers for whom they were intended.

In attempting this reconstruction, one key opposition has emerged, one moral meaning to which the ideologies that inform popular narrative return consistently: what I have called the secular-religious antithesis. This is not, it must be insisted, a gratuitous piece of terminology on my part nor a hidden clash revealed by crafty explication, but simply a modernization of the more emotional popular polemical jargon of the age. Given the 'struggle' which orthodox religion and morality saw taking place between itself and the forces of infidelity and irreligion, it was only natural as well as effective for popular narrative to exploit the moral antithesis thus available. Very often, of course, the connection between the actual conflicts which a given narrative treated and this key opposition was extremely tenuous and incidental. But it has been shown that the moral resonances and associations of the secular-religious confrontation were not only made explicit in many specific cases but were invited implicitly by the characteristic rhetoric and structure of the various types of popular narrative. In their own time and place, in other words, the persecuted maiden, the traveller-merchant-hermit, the pirate, and the criminal claimed part of their status as attractive and repeatable type figures by their participation in this frame of reference.[1]

The use of the secular-religious antithesis is of great interest, not primarily as a profound self-portrait of the age, but as the most prominent guide to the uses of fiction for its readers during the early eighteenth century. All of the stock figures which can be abstracted from popular narrative provided vicarious experience not only of exciting worlds of power, sex, and affluence but of a soothing moral universe where the reader felt himself comfortably on the side of virtue. Individual characters, then, were not only dissolved back into the familiar type characters but into the moral personifications of the secular-religious opposition as well.

The incompetence at realistic narration of the sorry hacks and well-meaning ladies who produced this fiction is thus not really an issue, for the narratives they wrote were geared to well-known narrative clichés and to equally familiar moral clichés. Both the repetition of the stock figures and the accommodation of the required moral simplicities made the calculated effects and achievements of popular narrative tend decidedly away from that particularity of scene and authentic individuality of character which we look for in the emerging realistic novel.

Defoe and Richardson cannot be dissociated from these ideological and semi-allegorical effects. In fact, in achieving a new synthesis

---

[1] Popular fiction may be said to obey at its own lower cultural level the tendency that Paul Fussell has observed in the high culture of what he identifies as the Augustan humanist tradition. Augustan imagery, he points out, tends to be 'repetitive and recurrent', because it 'operates generally as polemic rather than as revelation or epiphany. What it bodies forth are public moral arguments, not private apperceptions'. See *The Rhetorical World of Augustan Humanism: Ethics and Imagery from Swift to Burke* (Oxford, 1965), p. 140.

between specific reality and generalized moral significance, they made realism and psychological verisimilitude serve the ideological needs we have found their now-obscure contemporaries attending to. We have not only outlived those needs but developed others of our own, and in looking at eighteenth-century fiction we cannot see the ideological forest for the finely drawn trees. To read the mass of popular narratives from 1700–39 is to stand back and see the forest take shape, to recognize that realism and psychological verisimilitude were new and superior means towards older ideological ends.

INDEX

Fletcher, Angus, 33.
Framework narrative, 121, 237.
Frantz, R. W., 60.
Frye, Northrop, 228.
Fussell, Paul, 264 n.

Gay, John, 49, 73.
Gay, Peter, 17 n.
Gentleman's Magazine, The, 243.
German Atalantis, The (1715), inferior imitation of the *New Atalantis*, 153 n.
Gibbons, G. S., 230 n.
Gildon, Charles, 14.
Girard, René, 63 n.
Glanvill, Joseph, 15.
Goldmann, Lucien, on the 'structure' of the modern novel, 63.
Gothic novel, hero-villains of, compared to pirates, 76 n.
Gove, Philip, 6 n.

Halewood, William H., 14.
Halsband, Robert, 241 n.
Haywood, Eliza, 8, 10, 119–21, 153–67, 168–210; biographical summary of, 153–4 n.; compared with Mrs. Aubin, 219, 223–5, 227–8, with Mrs. Barker, 232, 236; continuator of tradition of Mrs. Behn, 260; as female moralist, 229; as feminist champion, 181–2; most important pre-Richardson novelist, 179; rejects heroic romance implicitly, 173; spiritualizes persecuted maiden, 260; techniques of, 182–3, 213; translator of Madame de Gomez's *La Belle Assemblée*, 20 n.; unreadability of, 262.
Works cited:
Arragonian Queen, The (1724) and *The Masqueraders* (1724), first use of sub-title 'secret history', 154.
British Recluse, The (1722), escape from tragic ending of amatory narrative, 208–10.
Distress'd Orphan, The (1726) and others, exploit erotic-pathetic themes, 208.
Lasselia (1723), 182 n., 183 n.
Love in Excess (1719), 183–207; aggressive female in, 188, 193;

allegorical rhetoric of, 186; compared with female 'she' tragedy, 194–5; country retreat in, 192–3; double ending of, 206–7; euphemisms and sexual intensity in, 200–1; hero (Count D'Elmont) as *libertin*-seducer, 184; heroine (Melliora) as erotic-pathetic object, 190–1; necessary amorous reluctance of heroine, 198; moral ideology of, 186–7, 196–8; presented as fiction, 168; quasi-religious definition of love in, 202–3; simplicity of plot, 205–6; stereotypes of scandal novel complicated in, 183, 191–2; style and erotic tension in, 188, 195–6.
Memoirs of a certain Island Adjacent to the Kingdom of Utopia (1725), 153–67; compared with Mrs. Manley's *New Atalantis*, 155–67; adjusts Tory rhetoric of, 158–9; heroines more innocent and sensitive than those of, 159–66; lacks political focus of, 155; looser style and broader attack than, 156–7; more moralistic than, 162; heroine of, as Griselda figure, 162; poetic justice in, 165–6; published when translations of French *chroniques scandaleuses* appeared, 120 n.; tragic fate of typical heroine in, 164–5.
Philidore and Placentia (1727), 170 n.
Heidler, J. B., 174 n., 175 n.
Heroic romance: adapted by *Lindamira*, 170, 172; attacked in preface to Mrs. Manley's *Queen Zarah*, 178; decline of, as healthy development, 173–4; decline of, discussed by Congreve's preface to *Incognita*, 174–6; replaced by novella, 126; vulgarized by amatory novella, 172–3.
Hertford, Frances Thynne, Countess of, 242.
Highland Rogue, The (1723), 45–6.
Highwayman: as antithesis of revolted apprentice, 56; as brutal criminal, 50; as folk hero, 41–5; as socially